MAN
TO
MAN

By Dr. Charles Silverstein

Man to Man: Gay Couples in America
The Joy of Gay Sex (with Edmund White)
A Family Matter: A Parent's Guide to Homosexuality

MAN
TO
MAN

Gay Couples in America

BY DR. CHARLES SILVERSTEIN

QUILL
NEW YORK
1982

Library of Congress Cataloging in Publication Data

Silverstein, Charles.
    Man to man.

    Originally published: New York : Morrow, 1981.
    Includes index.
    1. Homosexual couples, Male—United States. I. Title.
[HQ76.3.U5S57 1982]   306.7'6'0973   81-15734
ISBN 0-688-00041-X   AACR2
ISBN 0-688-00803-8 (pbk.)

Printed in the United States of America

7 8 9 10

Dedicated to "Josh" and "Andy"

The three of us spent two full days together, re-living moments from the past and talking about the future. They were the best two days I spent during my year of interviewing. I wish everyone could meet and talk with them.

Acknowledgments

I owe much to the many people who assisted me in every phase of this project. By far my greatest appreciation goes to the many gay men who volunteered as subjects. Their candor and trust have been invaluable. In various parts of the country, local gays searched out gay couples to be interviewed so that I could come into the city and begin work almost immediately. My thanks to Todd Leslie, Ray Lake, Steven Bennett, and Chuck Rhodes, as well as a few others whose names cannot be mentioned. Lawrence Gibson assisted me by doing a number of interviews in my place when the burden became overwhelming toward the end. Daniel Neudell spent hundreds of hours transcribing interviews and my notes. William Bory took the first draft and cheerfully translated it into English so that even I could read it. Christopher Cox took the second draft and worked with me, sharpening and shortening the manuscript. Then Artem Lozynsky spent many days with me, reorganizing the text, his reader's eye seeking out ambiguity and suggesting ways to clarify the work, always making it read better. Ian Young and Don Sussman were both helpful suggesting changes in earlier drafts. Only one person will get the credit for whatever is useful and true within the following pages, but many have contributed to them. To all of them I owe my appreciation not only for their time and help, but also for the spirit of friendliness in which the help was given. The remaining errors, of course, are my own.

Contents

Introduction

On a hot summer night in 1970, I went to a dance sponsored by the Gay Activist Alliance (GAA) at the Firehouse. For years my sexuality had been hidden behind a facade of respectability, confined to nighttime masturbation. Everything I knew about homosexuality was derived from fantasies in which desire and fear intermingled. But that Saturday night I was tired of the facade, the small ad in the *Village Voice* that announced the dance sounded friendly, and my mind was made up. It was time I found out what this life was all about.

The Firehouse, literally an old firehouse bought by the GAA and converted into a meeting and recreation hall, was located in the not yet fashionable section of New York City called SoHo. It was an area of eerily deserted streets lined with factories and warehouses, dark except for the occasional light from an artist's loft. As I drove up and parked the car, I saw a long line of young men (there must have been a hundred of them), all laughing, touching (constantly touching), groping one another, kissing. It seemed to be a line of friendliness and joy such as I had only dreamed of in my fantasies. Many were in cutoff jeans and tight T-shirts, proudly displaying the bodies I adored but was afraid to approach. There must have been dozens who titillated me, but the vision was all too overwhelming for a man who had spent so many years avoiding the scene. Another might have rushed to be part of it, but I was frightened; it was all too much, too soon. I felt that the sexual energy of *these* homosexuals was a bit outrageous. "This line is much too long. I'll never get in," I said to myself and went right back to the car and drove home.

But the process of coming out had begun. Soon I started going to meetings at the GAA and became a member of one of their committees. I made new friends. The members of the GAA, many of whom had belonged to the defunct Gay Liberation Front, united around the central issue of civil rights for gays.

The leaders of this movement, which began with the Stonewall riot of 1969, were all in their twenties, all city-bred (many from New York City), and all politically astute. As the first large-scale homosexual organization with bold political interests, the GAA was devoted to political consciousness with strong left-wing leanings. It was a mixture of socialistic belief, personal indignation, and the tactics of confrontation leavened by a wonderful feeling of friendship. To us as members of the GAA, the world was about to turn in our direction, and we would be the first to give it a good spin.

It was a wonderful place in those days. The Firehouse had just opened, and hundreds of gay men and women attended the weekly membership meetings, a tempest of political factions that operated (or pretended to operate) under *Robert's Rules of Order*. Everyone had an opportunity to speak: socialists, psychotics, transvestites, businessmen, the unemployed, and even the rare conservatives. On Saturday nights, the chairs would be moved against the wall, and a thousand or more gays would dance frantically in partial states of dress—since there was no ventilation—until the early hours of the morning. Those who wanted to talk during the dances could relax on the second floor, drinking tea or coffee—I served the coffee—the beer drinkers retreated to the basement.

Out of those early years at the Firehouse came the philosophy of "zapping," a form of demonstration in which we forced both society and the legal establishment to take notice of us. For instance, there was the time that several GAA members went to the City Clerk's office to get a marriage license for two men, bringing with them a wedding cake topped with two men. They were refused a license; nevertheless, they began to cut the cake and serve it to the office staff, who had no idea how to handle the situation. When the police arrived, they too were served pieces of the wedding cake; they didn't know whether to laugh or get angry at the "two lucky guys." But there were other, less pleasant, times when GAA members were beaten by the police or passersby during more serious demonstrations.

We paid the high price of visibility in those early days of the movement, but we truly believed that we were the vanguard of a new society free from the restraints of the past. We all knew, or thought we knew, what homosexuality was about. For one thing, we called ourselves "gay," not "homosexual." We didn't know where the word came from, but "gay" didn't have the clinical overtones of "homosexual," the associations of abnormality and immorality. By calling ourselves "gay," we were rejecting traditional labeling by an oppressive society and defining for ourselves this new-found identity.

We believed that gay love relationships, in all their variety, were to set the standards for new social and cultural changes in this period of transition, and that gay love would eventually lead to sexual freedom. We rejected the apparel of the businessman-as-conformist for long hair, dirty denims, work shirts, mustaches, and beards. Because we knew that money was the basic cause of all forms of discrimination in our society, the huge profits we netted from our dances were squandered, as if our association with such sums tainted our goals with capitalism. But the organization was not without its weaknesses. Officers sometimes stole money, and in one case a treasurer stole over a thousand dollars; he later ran for the presidency—even we were shocked at his gall. Although we rejected sexism, women seldom had a chance to speak in the wonderful bedlam of our meetings. We rejected the idea of treating other people as sexual objects, and yet no better place for cruising could be found, especially for those who wanted friendship as well as sex.

The members of the GAA had a somewhat schizophrenic perception of gay lovers. On one hand, we rejected sexual role playing, as in stereotypic marriage, in favor of sexual egalitarianism. Role playing, sexual or otherwise, was considered a remnant of the oppressive heterosexual culture based upon property rights and competition. On the other hand, most GAA members seemed to believe that a lover was a good thing, and dreamed of falling in love without pausing to realize that the desire to be half of a couple was conformist, regardless of how the roles were defined. Even those members of the organization who were Socialists or Communists failed to see that the tradition of the couple was firmly rooted in capitalism. They were content to argue the variations: Should lovers refuse to commit themselves to relationships for life? Or should they have affairs outside the relationship? Would the relationship be more successful if the lovers lived apart? But all this speculation was an implicit validation of the middle-class tradition of coupling.

Long-lasting relationships were not much in evidence at the Firehouse. Oh, we all heard they existed, but even we questioned whether they were possible in gay life—at least among gay men. We saw lovers find one another at the Firehouse, then saw them drift apart when the first rush of sexual energy was over. We also saw some gays find and remain with lovers (I found mine while serving coffee at the dances), but these were the exceptions. It never occurred to us that we broke up so frequently because we were young, not because we were homosexual.

We simply didn't know very much about homosexuality or gay male lovers in those days. We still don't. What is becoming clear, however, is just how biased all the information about gay love has been—not only from heterosexuals, but from the gay media as well. From books written about gay life by gays one would assume that all gay men live in cities, are well-hung, and work out at a gym; all vacation on Fire Island or in Provincetown or Key West; all indulge in abundant and expert sex; and all have suffered grievously from centuries of heterosexual persecution. This "skin-deep" image is of our own making and is one of the ways in which we have persecuted ourselves.

In the years since those early days of the GAA, I have settled into my own love affair with the man I met while serving coffee at the Firehouse. We glanced at each other a number of times before either of us made a move, but finally, one Saturday evening, I left the GAA's second-floor kitchen and sat with him at a nearby table. After a few minutes we touched—knees, I think—and I boldly invited him home. And when he said, "Yes," I could hardly believe it.

That night in my living room we listened to Gregorian chants on the stereo and discussed Chinese history and the examination system for scholars in China. Perhaps it doesn't sound like the sexiest discussion, but it was wonderful—invigorating to learn that two men could use their minds and hearts as well as their bodies. The sex seemed to flow naturally from the music, the warm touch, the intonation of our voices, and, yes, even from our talk about the Chinese examination system!

Since that night, years have passed during which we have shared those moments of tenderness and intimacy that are the touchstones of all love affairs. Sex has waxed and waned, influenced by a multitude of experiences in our lives, some within the psyche and some the consequence of two people living, loving, and struggling together. There have been moments of fierce emotional confusion when the ghosts of early fears and the pains of early wounds haunted us. Demons of jealousy and envy tried to control our lives; old memories of abandonment and disappointment in love struck sparks of resentment. But then there were the quiet talks afterward, the divulging of secret fantasies and of hopes for the future. These were the tenderest of moments. They still are.

So little has been written about the lives of gay couples. While the interest of gay men in sex has been well documented, the problems they encounter in finding a lover, loving him, and maintaining a relationship have not. Novels and studies of gay life are generally big-city-oriented and deal predominantly with New York, San Francisco, and growing gay meccas. But what about the suburbs and rural farm communities? Are there many gays? Do they form couples? I had no idea, and neither did anyone else.

This monopoly by the urban media should be ended if we are to know what is really going on in the world, but the task is not easy. Rural and small-town gay lovers live private lives. They are highly domestic and don't like to be disturbed. While city gays adore publicity, country gays do not; while urban gays often want to generate the electrifying energy that makes some cities dynamic, many suburban and rural gays want to watch the embers in the fireplace burn.

So much about gay life written by gays is an illusion—the heroes of current novels are eternally young, hung, butch. The characters seem recent converts to the "Butch Reformed Church." But the real lives of people are much more interesting —and human. You'd think that no one ever had a lover who died, or had cancer, or wasted away from months in a hospital. From fiction you would never know the problems of gays, formerly married as heterosexuals, trying to create new lives together as homosexuals, with or without their children. But the truly useful lesson of life is that there are many unexpected styles of living and loving, many alternatives in organizing an existence. Few couples remain the same throughout life. As they age, most find themselves with more money, and the acquisition of possessions intensifies. A house is bought, or dreams of vacations to exotic places are realized. At various stages in a couple's life attitudes toward domesticity fluctuate—fortunately, whatever one wishes to do, there are other gay couples doing it. Although some gay militants want everyone enrolled in revolution, other gays are content to live a decadent bourgeois life.

Shortly after deciding to study and write about gay lovers, I received this letter:

> I read in *Gaysweek* that you are interviewing for a book about gay male lovers. I want to volunteer, since I had an extremely happy and constructive relationship of ten years, during which I lived with a male lover.

And the following day, a completely different letter arrived:

> When I was young I grieved that I never "found love." If my life's experience has taught me anything since then, it is that I have been more fortunate than anyone deserves to be in escaping such idiocy. Fate has brought me the dear friendship of a few fine persons, and not one of those relationships has been subjected to the devastation of "love." So you see it is unlikely that I could say anything of relevance for your study.

The discrepancy between these two points of view is the subject of this book. Each man wants the same thing—some form of happiness, a feeling of being at peace with himself; but one trusts another person to help provide it, and the other doesn't.

In some ways, it's hard to believe that anyone could possibly fulfill all the requirements of a lover. The burden is overwhelming. We demand sexual compatibility. We insist that the lover meet all our emotional needs, supporting us from time to time, understanding our emotional weaknesses and forgiving our outbursts of anger. We also ask lovers to "grow" with us, develop at a common pace, with neither partner advancing too far ahead of the other. Many of us have been exposed to the ideology of egalitarianism, which rejects role playing, sexual and social, in favor of the modern ideal of equal roles—in some cases, regardless of what we prefer. We must not compete, financially or sexually. We must face prejudice together, deal with problems of dependence and independence together, meet financial insecurity together, handle the fear of loneliness and abandonment when one gets ill or dies. Is it any wonder that modern relationships, regardless of the sexual orientation of the partners, are as fragile as they are? Is it possible that any two men can fulfill demands as stringent as these, and over the course of many years? Some can, but others are torn apart.

One man's love affair is another's cage. Jonathan Williams, a gay poet, wrote, "One man's queen is another man's sweathog." One finds love with one man alone, or a sequence of men throughout his adult life, while another sits lonely, bitterly bemoaning the coldness and artificiality of gay life. One man in the Midwest finds comfort, intimacy, and sex with another man in his town, while his neighbor finds only bus stops, tearooms, or highway cruising. In the lives of married gay men we discover the same disparity. One finds a lover who adds to his happiness, while another bitterly resents his wife and children, damning society for his lies and clandestine affairs.

Although research has begun on the lives of gay men and women, there is almost nothing published on gay love relationships. Marriage manuals and studies of heterosexual marriage fill out library shelves, documenting just about every aspect of married life. But of homosexual relationships there is no material. There is not one book, let alone a shelf. At first sight this absence of research may appear strange since gay couples are highly regarded in some segments of the gay community. But discrimination against gays, only recently challenegd, adamantly maintained that long-lasting loving, compassionate, and passionate love affairs were impossible in the gay world. So effective was the force of this myth that almost every professional in the social sciences, as well as many gays, believed it completely. Given those circumstances, investigating love relationships was absurd. One might as well have investigated the etiology of misery.

It's not likely that the "cause and cure" school will end the historical search for the proper techniques to turn homosexuals into heterosexuals. Most people don't give up their beliefs so easily, and this segment of the scientific community, allied as it is with traditional religious leaders, gives mutual support to the rightness and morality of its cause. But the issue for those of us engaged in sexual research is the stance to take in regard to the older theories.

It was my wish as a psychologist to examine the traits of male gay relationships that make possible the survival of such unions in an imperfect and even hostile world. In this task I have avoided defending gays against their detractors and instead directed my energies to understanding their lives as men and lovers. What was needed, I thought, was a new set of questions. The old and futile ones, concerning the cause and cure of homosexuality, should be replaced with queries that would help us design novel strategies of research, or re-examine dated observations in a new light. I was specifically interested in answering some questions suggested by my experiences as a clinician working intensively with gay men.

My point of departure was the assumption that there were universal stages in a gay male love relationship. I thought, for example, that if I could carefully examine the lives of gay couples I would find that all relationships go through similar stages. I reasoned that, as time goes on, a couple ages, becomes more financially secure, acquires property, and perhaps experiences changes in the sexual relationship. From the start I could easily identify two stages. In the first, the romantic stage of initial attraction, two men spend most of their time getting to know each other; in the final one, the period of old age, their love is secure, but they are increasingly beset by problems of failing health. But I believed intermediary stages could be found and that these would be helpful to gays as standards by which to measure their own love affairs.

After the first dozen interviews, I learned that gays had no clear idea of stages in their development. Instead, they knew and understood the major changes and crises in their lives, and it was these they wanted to talk about most. It was the nitty-gritty of gay love, and not abstractions about developmental stages, that had obviously occupied a great deal of time and energy in their relationships, leading at times to moments of intense intimacy or painful confrontation. I decided, therefore, to change my goals. Rather than clinically examining gay relationships in terms of a pattern, I decided to attempt to identify and understand the major problems that underlie them. I set out to be an explorer of gay couples, rather than their cartographer.

I was also interested in the effects of parents on embryonic gays. Since popular myth claims that parents have the potential for modeling what will eventually be a gay offspring, their every action has been microscopically examined as a contributing cause. This myth suggests that all children are genetically programmed to be heterosexual, but that parental error diverts the child into homosexuality. Most of the time the mother is identified as the villainess. Yet I was perplexed as to why the father had been so neglected. Did the early relationship between a gay son and his straight father have any influence on the ways the boy would look for love and the sorts of men with whom he would seek it?

Another neglected area involved the effects of early sexual experiences and their influence on later love relationships. I was curious, for example, to know whether having a boyhood lover (as I never did) affected adolescent and adult experiences of love, and whether coming out early was significant. I also wanted to know how religion shapes the attitudes of gay boys in regard to their sexuality.

My final concern was geographic. Since for the most part we have publicized only the lives of gays in our largest cities, I wanted to explore the varieties of gay experiences in many areas of the country, dividing my time among cities, towns, and rural communities. Life in a small town in the Midwest, say, with a homogeneous religious population might produce a different lifestyle from that of the frenetic city gays. The life of gays in the Midwest has rarely been publicized, but this coastal chauvinism toward the heartland of America should not interfere with our learning about diversity within the gay population.

Two other subsidiary issues have influenced my choice of goals. In the first place, I decided that this work would not be an investigation of love. It might as well be admitted: psychologists are probably ineffectual at writing about the indefinable, and love is most appealing because of its elusiveness. Love is for the poets, and for those who find themselves in a romantic state. Psychologists are nitpickers of the worst sort, desperately seeking to define what everyone else prefers to leave obscure. Psychologists also have the habit, learned after years of observing so-called lovers viciously mutilate each other, of looking at the "work" of a relationship: they observe the aftermath of falling in love. I can only say what every psychologist and every experienced lover also knows: falling in love is easy; it's learning to live with each other that's hell! This will be a book about men trying to live together.

No investigator is ever free from moral judgments. All research is influenced by the values and beliefs of the person who designs, administers, and interprets the research. Value judgments may aid the study by bringing richness and compassion to the material, or they may only illuminate the idiosyncratic prejudice of the psychologist. Many value judgments will be found in this study of gay men. I am aware of some of them, but probably not all. For instance, I have purposely avoided using words derived from morality: "Promiscuity," "infidelity," and "incest" immediately come to mind. Since it is impossible to divest these words of their moralistic connotations, I have tried to avoid judgmental terminology. But my values, like those of any other author, intrude at a number of places, and, in order to make it easier for the reader to spot them, I have confined most of them to chapters dealing with analysis and speculation, rather than case studies. In this way the reader is in a better position to understand and evaluate my bias.

The following pages are my attempt to understand the experiences of the 190 men who volunteered to be interviewed for this study of gay male lovers. Their stories are personal and may help to originate a new kind of gay history, the history of gay love and the experiences, the joys, and the frustrations in the search for happiness and companionship.

PART ONE

Childhood Years

CHAPTER ONE

Fathers, Sons, and Lovers

> I throw myself upon your breast my father,
> I cling to you so that you cannot unloose me,
> I hold you so firm till you answer me something.
>
> Kiss me my father,
> Touch me with your lips as I touch those I love,
> Breathe to me while I hold you close the secret
>   of the murmuring I envy.
>
> WALT WHITMAN

We modern people, no less than our primitive ancestors, need to bring meaning to a chaotic world. To understand the vagaries of individual behavior our ancestors sought explanations in the capriciousness of multiple gods or in the intrusion of an alien being such as an incubus who would take hold of a person's life, driving him in bizarre ways. In dramas of this sort, the victim's family members were mere unfortunate bystanders in the action; their only role was to flee.

In the twentieth century our need to understand the world is just as pressing, but we have looked elsewhere for explanations —not in an evil invasion, but in that modern toxin, the family. All the attributes of individuals, except perhaps the most obvious physical ones, are laid at the doorstep of the modern family, and complicated familial styles of communication are said to lead ultimately to either adult "normality" or ill health.

The origin of homosexuality has certainly occupied the thinking of many people in the twentieth century who firmly believe, more on faith than on evidence, that a homosexual identity can be produced only by a particular family constellation, most often described by the psychoanalytical school as a distant father and an overprotective mother. Other forms of family drama, even if extreme, are said to result in heterosexual children—perhaps abnormal in other ways. Investigators look for the "etiology" of homosexuality, a word not neutral in meaning, rather one that implies a disorder: to study the etiology of a stomachache is to imply a disorder in the bodily system; to study the etiology of homosexuality is to imply a disorder in the family system. We twentieth-century moderns, like our ancestors, seek to explain behavior that is psychologically disturbing to us. Homosexuality qualifies.

All of the psychological theories about the origin of homosexuality find fault in the family, assuming, perhaps incorrectly, that every child needs the same kind of care from parents, and that every child's interpretation of parental behavior will be the same. This assumption follows naturally from the belief that children are like putty in the hands of the family, neglecting the contribution of the child's own character to the communication process.

Implicit in the well-advertised psychoanalytic notion of homosexuality (and, indeed, in all theories about adult behavior) is the idea that the child is pure and malleable, his mind a blank page on which anything—likes, dislikes, desires, fears—can be written by his parents. According to twentieth-century notions, the child has virtually no personality of his own and no will beside that of his parents; his only option is to decide, consciously or unconsciously, whether to model himself after his mother, his father, or some combination of the two. Another misconception is that fathers invariably reject their gay sons. In fact, it is often *the gay son who has rejected the father*.

An athletic son has a relatively happy relationship with his father. He has patterned his life in traditional ways and enthusiastically trains for manhood. He enjoys athletics, competition, and he watches TV sports with his dad. He confirms and reinforces the masculine values the father was taught by *his* father years before; smelly sneakers, disobeying mother, and taking risks are all part of it. His friendships with other like-minded boys are similar to his father's experiences with boyhood companions, or even adult male companions. These sons neither reject nor feel rejected by their fathers.

Any boy whose interests and behavior conflict with the father's image of masculinity creates tension. A boy who is interested in books, ballet, or opera while his brothers are interested in team sports is bewildering to his father.

When a father tries to teach his son how to throw a baseball, he believes the son will enjoy this just as *he* did when his father taught him. He is not trying to force anything on the boy, and he is certainly not being hostile. But it simply may not work for either the father or the son; it's not what the boy wants, and he cannot be motivated to care.

Under these circumstances, fathers raised with traditional notions of masculinity are confused. The son consistently rejects the father's beliefs and values; worse, the son is not becoming a carbon copy of the father. Ultimately, the father feels rejected, believing that his son has abandoned him and turned to others (often to the mother) for support and training; he begins to fear the son and to feel alienated from him, then guilty for resenting his own child. What is revealing here is that the feelings of both father and son are identical: each feels the other as hostile, distant, and unloving. Since the two cannot talk honestly with one another, this emotional similarity is concealed.

Mothers, on the other hand, are not as important in the evolution of a gay child as we have been led to believe. Many psychoanalytic writers maintain that gay men fear being engulfed by women and suffer from a phobia caused by the smothering mother. This is myth. A gay man's problems in later life, particularly in dealing with love relationships, are more apt to center around the father than the mother. Most mothers are aware of the silent raging of this family battle. They most often support the son and perhaps have a better understanding of the boy's sensitive nature. A mother's attempt to maintain the stability of the family by supporting the boy causes family alliances to be formed—gay son with his mother, straight son with his father. But the most frightening feature of childhood for many gays was the distance between them and their fathers, and the feeling that resolution of the conflict was, and is, hopeless.

Let me be clear about this. There is a crucial difference between the origin of sexual orientation and the antecedents of the search for love. Our discussion is about the search for love. The problems between parents and their children have their effect on the child's eventual sexual adjustment insofar as problems within the family affect love relationships throughout life; this is true regardless of sexual orientation. The *origin* of homosexuality does not lie in father/son relations.

The Father As Phantom

Boys are easygoing beings, self-absorbed and fairly accepting of the differences between themselves and their parents. They do not expect parents to share their interests; some will even get angry at a parent's attempt to become involved. What boys do want, however, is love; and they want approval and respect from their parents. The gulf between a father and his son is created when the father cannot cope with the differences between his values and those of his son. This feels like rejection. Because of fear and a feeling of incompetence, both hide from one another. As the gap widens, they are haunted by the belief that they have made a mess of it. They become hostile or angry, accusing each other (quite justly) of various misdeeds. But these recriminations are in vain; they result in both being hurt and unloved. Although some gay men feel they have outgrown their need for the father's love, many gay relationships suggest otherwise. These relationships are usually characterized by the presence of a *phantom father.*

The phantom father is an internal person who lives within the son and is sometimes projected onto the son's lover. He is an idealized father whose image was formed in the early years of the boy's life, when the father was simply "daddy." He is the father who was desired then and is demanded now. This phantom father is impervious to time and experience; his image is rigid, and even when the gay man becomes an adult he continues to view his father through his childhood eyes.

The father of a gay man is a more complicated figure than a mere "role model." He is more than just someone to please or to receive love. For a significant number of gay men, the father (whether real or phantom) is a potential sex object—and perhaps their first fantasy lover. It is remarkable how rarely this has been stated either in psychological or gay liberation literature. Yet many gay men clearly remember their interest in the father's body and know that it was motivated by more than curiosity. Many wanted to touch their father's body; they wanted to suck their father's penis and have their father suck theirs. As boys, they imagined having sexual intercourse with their fathers. Some tried it, much to dad's chagrin. But since fathers rarely allow themselves to be seduced by their sons, the fantasy survives into adulthood and contributes to the image of the phantom father.*

Boys who have been rejected by their fathers often seek out other men to relate to—sometimes only sexually, sometimes only emotionally, sometimes both. The stories surrounding these searches can be touching or distressing, but the search itself is a good sign. It shows that the boy wants to replace the poor relationship between him and his father with another, more fully developed relationship; it is an indication of hope, and the goal is to make the boy feel more complete as a person. Of course, this effort to repair the torn contact with a father has its hazards. The boy who wants to love his father (but has not been allowed to) tries to love another man or boy instead. The danger is that he may confuse his feelings for his father with those for the lover—which often leads to adult tragedies in future love relationships.

One commonly finds the phantom father stalking in the background of gay male love relationships. Sometimes a lover is chosen as a replacement for the father, and it falls upon this lover to compensate for all the sorrowful memories of the past. He is burdened with a double role, father and lover; any transgression on his part causes a severe overreaction in his beloved (son and lover). Quite naturally, these complexities bewilder him. In other cases, the lover with the phantom father acts as father to his beloved in the ways he wishes his father had acted toward him; he turns his lover into himself. In both cases—turning the lover into the father or turning the lover into the son—the lover is assigned a role in a script not chosen by him. It usually doesn't take long for the misalliance of roles to end in helpless confusion.

Rejectors and Suitors

Someday parents will be accepting of their children's sexual orientation, and they will learn to judge them on their merits and their ability to lead productive lives. Even today there are some fathers whose love for their children goes beyond their need to produce carbon copies of themselves; indeed, there are fathers

* Would the fantasy survive to adulthood if there was sex between father and son? I don't know.

who are willing to touch their sons and accept them regardless
of a boy's different value system. There may not be many happy
families, but they do exist; so do fairly satisfactory relationships
between some gay men and their fathers. But most of us derive
from more traditional homes, in which being different (and
especially being "queer") produces a family drama. Disappointment and failure are hallmarks of boys who come from homes
in which the psychological distance is great. Kindly father or
not, the son wants to please him; ironically, the father wants to
please his son as well. But the years bring disappointment, the
son never endorses his father's value system, and the father,
sensing rejection, sees the embodiment of his failure.

Gay men respond to a father's rejection in characteristic ways.
As they mature, go through adolescence, and begin the search
for sexual and emotional fulfillment, the normal frustrations
and feelings of rejection are constant reminders of rejection in
the home. Patterns begin to form. The gay man becomes interested in certain "types," some of whom nurture his growth, while
others stifle it.

Two character types that develop in boys, out of the mutual
rejection between fathers and sons, are *rejectors* and *suitors*. Rejectors are men whose response to their fathers is anger (to
cover up the hurt) and bitterness. As adults, they come to believe that other gay men are deficient as humans, unattractive,
unsatisfactory as sexual partners, and disloyal. Asked about their
fathers, rejectors can point to a long series of indignities. Pessi-
mists, they've sworn off trying to make things better. There may
be some appreciation of the mother for being around to help
when the father failed, but there is none of the father. Beneath
the anger and bitterness, however, there is the rejector's knowledge that he has been a disappointment to his family, particularly
to his father. (The first son is usually the most vulnerable here.)
While he claims that other gay men are disappointing in love,
the fact is that he believes himself incapable of it. So pervasive
is this belief—sometimes quite conscious—that he often rejects
any lover who could love him as fully and faithfully as he claims
he wants. He feels that anyone who loves him must be a fool.

Suitors, on the other hand, are filled with romantic notions of
idealized love. They search for a substitute father to love. The

lover may be his own age, or the lover may be an older man: age isn't as important as the need to love another man and to take care of him, if need be, for the rest of his life. Just as rejectors are overly pessimistic about love, suitors are grossly optimistic; just as rejectors are certain they are unlovable, suitors are filled with love; just as rejectors believe that no one will ever *really* love them, suitors are positive that warm, loving men exist in the world if only they could find them. Finally, just as rejectors point to all their love affairs as evidence of the disloyalty of men, suitors remember how much they've gained from and grown with each passing relationship.

Some men can be categorized as solely and completely rejectors or suitors, but most are a combination. (For example, a gay man may reject authority figures—older men or men with business success—and at the same time act as a suitor toward his peers.) A suitor may respond to some physical characteristic of a potential lover but become angry without knowing why; a rejector may let his guard down one night and allow himself to love someone who responds to his bitterness with caring.

One commonly observed combination of rejector and suitor is the school yard comrade, the man who got along very well with his father as a child, the one who was a good athlete and a fine competitor. He grew up believing all the values about masculine authority, receiving many compliments for his achievements. Some "jocks" do become gay, and their gayness is often self-interpreted as a blight on an otherwise excellent record of masculine growth. These men (one also finds them in religious families) experience depression and lowered self-esteem when they recognize their homosexuality. Since they have identified so strongly with orthodox masculinity, they convince themselves that they have failed their fathers. Hence, after a boyhood of success, later adolescence convinces them that their masculinity has been a sham. Typically, as men they construct highly rigid boundaries between what is acceptable and unacceptable homosexual behavior. They define acceptable homosexuality in men by the same standards of masculine gender behavior they learned as a child and view as unacceptable the "effeminate" man with even the slightest suggestion of womanly manners. As gay men, school yard comrades therefore frequently become suitors toward highly masculine gay men and rejectors of any other gay men. Some of the homophobia in gay men probably results from this mixed type.

The more childhood baggage carried, the more perceptions of would-be lovers are burdened and distorted. We are all heirs to the emotional consequences of early family life, but gay men bear additional burdens since they suffer both societal prejudice and familial disapproval. For them, the barriers seem more impassable and the bridges flimsier.

Some may regard this view as overly pessimistic. Yet my view is not pessimistic but rather realistic, questioning the absurd notion that once you have found the man of your dreams the world will be magically transformed. Maintaining a love affair throughout life is difficult, and this is true regardless of sex and sexual orientation.

Teaching Romantic Love

No one innately "knows" about love and sex.* Contrary to the announcement by an army of embarrassed parents to an army of inquisitive children that they will learn about it "naturally" when they grow up, both subjects require considerable education and experience for their mastery. Our initial experience of both is often a jumble of ineptitudes and feelings of inferiority; many of us are still wrestling with misconceptions. Sex is almost never taught in any practicable sense. Progressive high schools sometimes give courses in sex education in which the "plumbing" system of sex is taught, but these classes are mainly devoted to teaching children to substitute Latin for Anglo-Saxon words. The child never learns what he really wants to know—how to have a good sex life.

Then there are parents who invariably leave a book—*The Teenager's Guide to Love*—on the coffee table; as a rule, these books contain little information youngsters want or need.

Teaching about love is another matter. Training begins at an

---

* I am willfully separating love and sex against all of my own training that sex is not complete without love. I do so for two reasons: love is an attitude of mind while sex is overt behavior, and they may or may not coincide; the drive always to make sex a part of love is intended to keep controllable the fires of lust.

early age, as soon as the child is capable of speech and effective motor coordination. This is the period of fairy tales and teddy bears, the period when inanimate objects around the house are alive in the imagination of the child. Fairy tales are a prime source of training about love. Prince Charming and Snow White, Cinderella and a host of other magical characters guide children into believing that someone special will one day be their husband or wife, and the future will be secure. Some gays are angry at the heterosexual bias of fairy tales, but my own view is that unrealistic expectations about love and lovers create more important problems.

As emotional dependence upon the parents wanes, the young gay boy reaches out to other figures in the world for affection, but the message is the same. Love and intimacy await those who are good; once found, they will last forever. Love stories in films, books, and TV all contain this message, while the advertising industry reaps financial rewards by selling magical potions to cure minor pimples and major acne, and to reduce all possibility of odor, guaranteeing that the young man will turn out a prince and not a frog. Alas! Many boys feel like frogs.

Gay and straight adolescents are trained in romanticism, but the obstacles to adult love relationships for gay boys are further increased because of their sexual orientation. Many adolescent boys who become gay are vaguely aware of the feelings stirring inside them. The word "homosexual" is foreign to them, and they are totally unaware that their desire to be with some boyhood hero/friend will one day turn into a desire for genital contact. Indeed, many of these boys avoid sex with friends, while future heterosexuals are involved in mutual masturbation. Such a boy will romanticize about girls, since he has been taught that the way to love is through women.

Gay adolescents aware of their sexual interests are placed in another, equally difficult position. Hiding their sexuality from age mates, gay boys are conditioned to believe that love and happiness belong to others; yet they dream all the more intensely, and their dreams isolate them further from the reality of love.

The underlying theme of all adolescent love fantasies is the concept of *the couple*, two people locked into a friendship so deep that life itself exists only by virtue of their bond. The couple is the reason for being, the motivation for living, and successful union is the only "real" measure of happiness.

Things might be different if fathers in our culture shared some of the responsibility for teaching their children about love; but our heritage of defining masculine and feminine precludes that. The father in the Western family bears practical responsibilities, significant functions such as making money, providing the home, and determining the structure of family rules. An interest in sex is another trait of masculinity. It is the mother who has been chosen to teach about feelings, introspection, and all the domestic responsibilities of the home. "Love" (as distinct from sex) is historically part of the woman's world, and the father is unlikely to teach much about it.

Of course, any son will learn about love from his father in ways the father doesn't intend. The boy will observe the relationship between his parents, and this will become a standard of comparison for his own experiences. In many American families, the relationship between parents teaches the growing boy the dangers of love.

Father/Son Fantasies

In some ways, gay men are extraordinary in their honesty about sexual desires and needs. Nowhere is this trait more obvious than in their memories of sexual desires toward family members, particularly fathers and brothers. One need only ask gay men about their sexual feelings toward their fathers to get a straightforward answer, combined with a mature willingness to examine the links that tie fathers and lovers together.

What is really interesting about father/son sexual fantasies and experiences is not that they occur, but that they have so rarely been discussed. Reasonable men can argue whether these fantasies are universal among gay men, but one has only to hear the reports of how sexually exciting they are to realize that father/son fantasies have long been repressed but still maintain their power.

When *Andrew*, now in his late twenties, was a boy, he slept with his father during a family vacation. One night, as his father climbed into bed fresh from a shower, Andrew touched his father's body and went straight for the genitals. Dad was out of the bed in a flash. The prescribed lecture followed—boys don't do things like that, girls' bodies are more interesting, and all boys grow up to love women, get married, and have children of their own. Andrew dutifully listened, sorry that his father had put on his pants, but satisfied himself by admiring his father's broad shoulders and strong chest. He'd heard the lecture before, and frankly he'd thought it boring the first time.

Andrew's father was an officer in the air force and consequently absent for long periods. Most of the time there was no male adult in the house. Then, when Andrew was sixteen, his father died.

As a gay man, Andrew's enjoyment of sex is as playful and daring as it promised to be the day he dived into his father's pants. He has always enjoyed sex and has no trouble finding compatible partners, but he always chooses the wrong potential lover. Somehow they all turn out to be unavailable in one way or another. Take Dick, for instance. Andrew met him at 6 A.M. at one of New York's leading gay discos. It was love at first sight.

> Just the sight of him was enough to start the adrenaline pumping. Besides being gorgeous, he seemed outrageously self-confident and charismatic, a real star. I had seen him once or twice before but had dismissed him as being out of my league—a con man, huckster, and snakeoil salesman wrapped up in an immensely charming package. He flashed his wide-angle smile at me, and I was sailing. So I became immediately obsessed and was determined to get my hooks into him.

The affair began. The sexual novelty and mutual exploration carried them for precisely three days. Then Andrew began to feel extremely anxious, overwhelmed by conflicting emotions.

> I was excited, afraid, exuberant, and insecure at the same time. When we were together I was uncomfortable, in fact, miserable, because instead of trying to enjoy his company, I constantly scanned every word and gesture for some sign of his feelings toward me. The more tense I became, the more aloof and preoccupied he became. I wanted him to respond positively to me, but he was increasingly impenetrable and confusing, which made me frustrated but more attracted than ever.

A silent battle between the men followed, with Andrew seeking warmth and caring from Dick, who grew progressively more distant. Silence turned inevitably into arguments, recriminations, and feelings of abandonment. One night, after an especially bitter battle, Andrew had the first of two dreams which were to change his life.

> I was in my apartment, sick and being attended by a doctor [Andrew was in psychotherapy at the time]. The doctor was transformed into a black-uniformed man who was rubbing his cock. I unzipped his fly and exposed not only the average-sized cock he was rubbing but also an enormous one which was dripping with come. I went straight for the big one and started sucking it. I woke up then and was so turned on that I jerked off, still fantasizing about the security of that enormous cock.

Andrew pays attention to his dreams, and he began to examine the similarity between his affair with Dick and others in the past. All his lovers had common characteristics. The men were physically attractive and charming, but elusive and unpredictable. At the end of each affair, Andrew had settled for "being a doormat, clinging to any debris which was tossed my way."

> I realized I had saddled Dick with incredible expectations that he couldn't possibly satisfy. Those expectations just about submerged Dick as a human being with all the problems, flaws, and insecurities of anyone else. He couldn't possibly have responded to me in a direct and positive way.

For the first time, Andrew was perceiving Dick as the person he was, not the one Andrew wanted him to be. Andrew was learning that Dick, through no fault of his own, was not capable of making Andrew happy. No one could have done so at this stage of Andrew's life. Then Andrew had the second dream. He was lying in bed, half-asleep.

> In a matter of a minute or two an image came which pictured two figures walking apart. A ghostlike apparition floated off to the left, and Dick walked off to the right. The instant I saw that image I started to cry. Not sadly, just emotionally. I got up. I walked around my apartment repeating, "Daddy, I love you. I miss you. Daddy, I'm sorry we didn't know each other. I love you. Good-bye." That was the first time I remember having those feelings. I cried more, and the image of the splitting figures came back, then was replaced by the dream

image of the two cocks. The images seemed to be super-
imposed: the apparition and the big cock on the left,
Dick and the regular cock on the right. I must have
stayed mesmerized by this for at least thirty minutes.

What Andrew understood, by means of the dream images,
was how he had confused his feelings for his dead father with
his feelings for Dick. The dreams helped him see the truth: He
couldn't give up unattainable men because the separation would
have been a reenactment of his father's death. The splitting apart
of the figures in the dream allowed Andrew to grieve for his
father's death, finally to say, "Good-bye." Andrew is now living
with his lover of two years.

Fred * is twenty-nine. He was born and raised in a large
southern city and came to New York for professional reasons a
few years ago. As a youngster he experimented frequently with
playmates his own age and even formed a "sex club." This was
at age eleven, when he had a special friend who was also a
founder of the club.

> We had a whole dialogue so that we could talk and ar-
> range sexual encounters, and nobody would know what
> we were talking about.

Fred admired this boy, who was a bit older and physically
more mature. Their sex was juvenile—mutual masturbation,
some sucking, and the common childlike pissing on each other.
Very quickly thereafter Fred became intensely interested sexually
in his father.

> He's southern, very handsome. When I was a preado-
> lescent, he was very affectionate with me, always pick-
> ing me up and everything, and I was having none of it.
> I was really claustrophobic with him about it at that
> time.
> After we moved, he had problems in his business, and
> he got very withdrawn, and he was miserable. I was
> thirteen at the time. Around that time I started getting
> real interested sexually. I had a fascination with pubic
> hair, which may have started with my friend because he
> was older physically.
> I was possessed by the hair on my father's body. He

* An asterisk indicates that the person named appears in the book
more than once. An index of these men will be found at the back of
the book.

had hair on his chest and a lot of hair going down his navel. I was glued to the keyhole a lot when he was taking a bath. I couldn't wait for him to take a bath. I especially started watching him when I was fourteen or fifteen. My mother was away on an extended trip visiting relatives, and I started plotting ways of catching him. I did things to try to get him interested like going out for football because I thought this would be a turn-on for him. I was obsessed with the idea of doing this for him, and I really worked hard on the football team.

I wanted to touch him. I wanted to touch the hair on his body. Go down the line from the navel. I wanted to put my hand right where his leg met his groin. I wanted him to touch my cock, to kiss me—on the mouth. I masturbated to all those things. It's strange—I don't remember feeling guilty about these things. I didn't have time to feel guilty. I was too busy trying to bag him all that time!

I would come home from football practice just exhausted, and I would position myself on the couch ages before he got home and sort of arrange myself, sort of undo one button of my trousers or undo my fly a little bit. Make it look like I was asleep. I just arranged myself to seduce him.

I also started cooking for him during that period. I took my mother's position. I started making it real clear that I wanted him to come upstairs to my room and say good night to me. I could get him to get in bed with me. He'd come up and he'd be tired, and I would offer to scratch his back or rub his back. Sometimes he would fall asleep while he was in bed. I was always trying to get him to rub my back. Sometimes I would go downstairs and get into bed with him if I could manage it, under the pretext of scratching his back again.

I finally did all the things I wanted to—kiss him, but from the back. I was in his bed, and it was a lengthy back rub. Each time I would get further around to the front of him, and I would concentrate on the hairy area, go under his arm and around his chest. Jesus, I remember touching a lot of sexual points, his nipples, and going down his stomach and his crotch. I didn't touch his cock, but I wasn't mainly interested in it. I was mainly interested in his skin and his hairy areas. But I did go around everywhere—real slowly. I don't know if he had a hard-on or not. I know I did. I can't remember if I came or not. I know I was close to it. It feels like I always was in those days.

It was fairly dangerous. It could have been embarrassing, and I was aware of that. He could—we have been leading up to it for weeks—but he could have turned around and said, "What the hell are you doing?" I was very scared of that, very scared of rejection by him. I didn't quite know why I wanted sex with him, why I was plotting all this. I didn't know what I would do if I got caught at the keyhole.

Then he made some move to indicate that the back-scratching was over. I think he turned from me, and I came out of my reverie and went upstairs. We've never talked about it, ever.

The next few years we had a terrible relationship. It all reversed again. We found it impossible to talk, and if we did, we fought bitterly. I hated his guts in my high school years.

I finished that season with the football team, but he never came to see a game. That was shocking as far as I was concerned.

Fred "came out with a vengeance" in high school and had sex with both men and women. Later, he went to live in New York City and met a man almost exactly his father's age. Fred was nineteen at the time.

I fell in love with him. It couldn't have been more obvious. I would have dreams that he was having sex with my mother. I would confuse the two in dreams all the time. I would slip and call him "dad." And he was severe with me like my father.

My being in love with him lasted forever and even to this day. He's still a good friend of mine. It was less important to him. Our affair only lasted a few months. I still love him. Sometimes I see him now, and I fall in love with him again—but sort of from a distance.

The aesthetics of hair. The idea of a bearded face next to mine or hair on the back of somebody's hand would get me real faint. Still interested in hair. At first I would go after men who had a pattern of hair like my father did—across his chest and a lot of hair down his stomach to his navel. The man I lived with had that pattern.

I'm just an expert at it. I can tell in an instant sometimes even if somebody was covered right to the neck, and I can tell what the hair pattern on their body is. I no longer have to have hairy people. Sometimes I can—the aesthetics, that one thin line from the navel. I like dark-haired people because their hair stands out from their skin. My favorite is black Irish coloring, because it's fair skin and very black hair on it so it stands out beautifully. When I have sex with someone, a lot of my concentration is on the feel of their hair against me, or if I go down on someone, my eyes are right on their hair. I always notice the different coloring in someone's sideburns, and the difference between their beard and their body hair.

Note how Fred's interest in hair began with his father and continues in his current sexual relationships. Today, as he says, he needs only the slightest suggestion of hair in the right places to excite his imagination.

Except for the brief affair described above, Fred has never had a steady lover. At the moment, he finds himself in love with two men. He corresponds with one by letter only, and they have never met. The other was a "dirty phone-caller," and the relationship was confined to phone conversations with S and M themes in which Fred played a masochistic role, frequently saying, "Yes, sir."

Beside it [the S and M] was me saying, "Please love me." The most thrilling part of the whole telephone scene was at the end of the conversation; he would say to me coolly, "Good night, sweetheart," and it would just make me melt.

Then one night Fred went out tricking, picked up a man, and suddenly recognized the voice.

I picked up my own dirty phone-caller!
I know myself better now. I picked up someone who couldn't be harder to get at, even face-to-face he was very hard to reach, and I had to be very cool about how I came on. Falling in love is very mixed with idolizing someone.

Albert's * story is one that is familiar to gay men. A son doesn't turn out to be the great athlete the father demands his firstborn to be. He terrorizes the boy for his athletic incompetence, making him feel ever inferior. One event stands out, because of its unmitigated brutality, in the life of this thirty-year-old man from New York City.

The first objects of affection I can remember was when

I was about six years old, I guess, when my mother bought me some puppets. There were four of them, and they had plaster heads. And I don't know—I guess they became symbols of affection to me. I used to sleep with them at night, play with them all day long, and take them everywhere I went. I used to have to hide them most of the time. I would stuff them in my pockets or in my coat, and I was told not to take them out of the house by my mother, because they would break, and by my father, because he was embarrassed by them.

I remember the night when I was sleeping in bed with the puppets—and I guess I rolled over one in my sleep, and it broke. It was my favorite puppet. It had sort of a clown face and a big smile. I know I had a name for it, but I can't remember it now. I guess I had names for all of them. And I was really upset. It just meant a lot to me, I guess. I didn't know what to do. My mother wasn't there.

My father was out in the living room, so I went out to him for help. I thought maybe he could glue it together and make it better. So I went walking out to the living room where he was watching TV. And I was crying. I was upset. And I remember walking out with the puppet in my hand and tears in my eyes. And he seemed to look really angry. And he asked me what the trouble was. And I showed him the puppet, how it was broken. And he seemed really angry. Then he muttered something about this doll that his son was upset about, and he grabbed it in his large hand and crushed it. And then he threw it in the garbage.

I can't understand how somebody I needed and loved so much didn't need me. I could never understand how somebody I loved so much could destroy the only objects of affection I ever had.

Albert's father was obsessed with the idea that his son had to be a "real man," the kind of boy he could be proud of. The process, of course, never allowed Albert to grow up his own way. "He used to call me a fairy or a faggot because I wasn't good at sports." If the family went on a picnic, the father would invite athletic boys to join them; he played with them, not Albert. He particularly liked a boy named Perry and insisted that Albert become his friend. Albert did as he was told and began an intimate friendship that lasted from kindergarten to the seventh grade. Perry was everything a boy was supposed to be, and Albert received attention from him that he could never get from his father. It began with mild sex games, but the symbolic importance of the relationship made it Albert's model for adult affairs.

> The big thing was to make each other get a "boner," as it was called, a hard-on. We would do things like go to the swimming pool and go to one end where there weren't many people. Perry would invariably put his hands in my bathing suit or just pick me up in the water holding on to me, and we'd walk around the pool like that for five or ten minutes. And I'd be in heaven, the idea of him touching me and holding me. He was so big and so strong.
>
> Oh, God, he must have been at least five or six inches taller than me [they were the same age] and much broader, but not heavy—athletically built. He was always the best athlete, the best baseball player. He was the person my father would admire whenever we played ball together. He was the one my father wanted to play with.

From the account Albert gives of the relationship, one suspects that Perry was a rather confident boy who took charge of the relationship.

> He acted very possessive, I guess. He would hold me whenever he wanted. He would grope me whenever he wanted to. It was very much a dominant sort of thing. And I loved every second of it. I was absolutely in love with Perry. I thought he was the greatest thing going, because he was showing me so much affection, I guess. It was the caring, the physical contact, the holding. There were always different ways he would hold me. We would make games out of it, piggyback rides or something. When you're that age, it's easy to find excuses to hold each other.

Then Sol entered the picture, and a triangle was formed. Like Perry, Sol was a good athlete, and Albert was soon alone again. The sissy was abandoned for the second time in his twelve years of life. Since then, Albert has been searching for a strong, protective man to care for him. It has become an obsession.

> I always look for a person who's strong. Not a physical type of strength; it's an emotional type. Someone who can handle situations when they come along, someone

who is very assured of himself. I can spot that kind of person in a bar.

It's like a magnet. All of a sudden I just feel all of that strength. I don't know how to put it into words. But if they have the strength, then I'll have it, too. Other times it bothers me to think I'm that way because I want to feel strong on my own; I don't want to feel that somebody is being strong for me. It's like wanting a mentor to take care of me, but not wanting it at the same time.

Albert found a mentor at the age of twenty-five—Gilbert, whose outward strength impressed Albert and who was interested in the arts. He became Albert's hero. They had known each other only two weeks when Albert moved in. It is uncanny how often the man who looks for strength in others consistently chooses a showy and domineering man, with a veneer of strength but little substance behind it. Gilbert was that type of man. A strong person is able to direct his own life and handle his problems; he doesn't need to raise his self-esteem by lowering that of others. The problems started as soon as Albert moved in. Their sex life was one indicator.

A lot of the time sex with Gilbert was demeaning for me. I would come home from work, and Gilbert would be lying in bed masturbating with a hard-on, and he'd say, "Quick, while I have a hard-on, get your clothes off and come into bed." And I would do it. I would just pull my clothes off and hop into bed, and he would fuck me.

Albert was to find that Gilbert would never turn him on sexually, but that he was always expected to service Gilbert. Disaster also awaited if Albert wanted to initiate sex.

I'd walk into his workroom and pin him against the wall, and I'd slip my hand into his crotch and start squeezing and start kissing him and going down his neck, and he'd go, "You're really turning me on, but I have a lot of work to do," and he'd just walk away. Then I'd feel crushed.

However, when Albert developed a crush on a friend, Gilbert became "ill," was horribly depressed, and talked about committing himself to an institution. Albert knew this whole act was designed to make him feel guilty about his relationship with someone new, but the intellectual knowledge didn't prevent it from succeeding.

> We might be having sex, and he would look into my eyes and say, "My God, I'd just die if you ever left me."

During our interview, Albert frequently mentioned how physically strong his father was, how macho and athletic, how he used to watch women look at his father admiringly. Then he responded to a question about whether he found his father physically attractive.

> It's funny, I've blocked that out. I was trying to think of that a minute ago when I told how the girls admired him. I imagine he was attractive. But that scares me. I imagine I probably did, because I'm shaking inside right now at the thought that I might have been. It really scares me.

Albert returned for a second interview a few weeks later to tell the following remarkable story, probably stimulated by our first discussion about his father.

> On Saturday I woke up in the morning with this tremendous hard-on. I was feeling extremely sexually aroused, and I wanted to masturbate. So I started to, but I realized that the thing I was being turned on to was an image of my father as a younger man. The type of image, I guess, that had always frightened me.
>
> It was kind of scary. It was the first time in years I had been able to picture him as a young man, to see him exactly the way he looked. And when I did picture him, it was the first time I ever allowed myself to be really turned on by his physique and the way he looked, his muscles and the entire thing. When I woke up, I found myself squirming around in bed thinking about that. I started to panic. I started to think, "Oh, my God, this is disgusting. You can't do this. This is your father. He's dead. He wouldn't like this sort of thing. He'd think you were a faggot." That hit me hard but not as hard as I thought it would, because the sexual drive was stronger.
>
> As I started to masturbate, the fantasy became stronger and stronger. I started to remember little things that had happened in the past. I remembered crawling into my father's bed, not really remembering whether he was awake or asleep, but imagining him now to be

asleep—and putting my hands into his shorts and feeling his cock. And I remember its being soft and getting hard. I don't remember his waking up or how long it lasted, just that I was excited and scared at the same time.

I know that while masturbating I was thinking of myself as a young child, maybe eight or nine. And the orgasm I had while fantasizing giving my father a blow job was the most exciting orgasm I can remember having. It was outrageous. I just shot across the room. I was breathless, and I sort of sat back waiting for the guilt to come. But there wasn't any. It was sort of nice and warm, and I laid back down and felt good under the sheets. And I felt—I felt—it was sort of the way I feel when people hold me and they're really strong. And I felt that way—you know?—I felt that everything was OK.

I fell asleep for about an hour. Immediately I started to have the same fantasy again. I was being turned on again by the fantasy of giving my father a blow job. I found it even easier to do the second time. Then I started to remember, or seemed to remember, an instant in my life where I seem to remember my mouth being on my father's cock. I don't remember if it was hard or soft. I blocked it out pretty quickly when it came. But it wasn't like the fantasies of masturbation. It was a visual memory, much like the first one about me slipping my hand into my father's pants.

After the second orgasm—which was really good—I sort of collapsed back, and I really felt close to him, felt really warm, and I felt like he was really there. Like he was holding me and like he was allowing me to love him. For the first time he was allowing me to love him. I felt like things were finally really good between us—even though I knew that he was dead and that the thing really didn't happen. It was as good as if it had happened. As though I had finally touched him—he had finally touched me.

The fantasy experience made a perceptible change in Albert's life. For a while he became as assertive as he had ever wished to be; this ultimately led to a job promotion. Then he became caught up once more in looking for "strong'" men. In his next affair he recognized the human vulnerabilities of his friend much sooner than he ever had before. In other words, Albert is still struggling, but in a positive way, looking for strength in the

only place any of us will ever find it—ourselves. It is to his credit
that he initiated the process himself.

Ian * is in his mid-thirties. He was born and raised in a midwestern city. In his early years he felt uncomfortable about his
homosexuality, so he chose to come to New York City where
he could learn to accept his gayness. He succeeded. During his
late teen years, Ian had a persistent masturbation fantasy that
symbolized his conflicts about men, particularly his father.

> When I was nineteen, maybe until I was twenty-one,
> I used to have these fantasies of Sparta. Like he was
> my teacher, the older man. I was a young soldier, and
> he was the older one. He was my patron. I placed us
> on the hillside far away from the battle, hiding in sort
> of a little cave, and he's holding me because I'm very
> frightened of the danger—and then we get very sexy,
> jacking off or his rubbing his hard cock against my
> rear, but nothing more.

Ian had a few early guilt-ridden affairs while still in the Midwest that always turned out to be misalliances. Then in New
York, after another bad experience in love, Ian fell into depression. The recent milestone in his life was the following sexual
experience.

> I was having sex with this friend. He's sitting, jacking
> me off, and I had my eyes closed and started to think
> of a porno story called "Father Figure" which I jack
> off to alone sometimes.
>
> It's about a man; when his mother dies he comes
> back home and when he was a child he used to ride
> on his father's back, playing "horsey." They're sitting
> in the kitchen and his father has been looking at him
> very attentively, and it's kind of a sexual situation and
> his father reaches under the table and puts his hand
> on his leg and moves his hand up and even eventually
> takes his cock out and starts jacking off his cock, and
> they have sex, and at the end of the story the father
> says, "I'd sure like to play horsey again."
>
> For the first time it occurred to me that it could be
> my father, and I visualized that and got very nervous.
> Then I thought about a photograph my parents had of
> my father when he was very young. He looked like
> Gary Cooper, and I was attracted to that when I was
> little, interested in what he looked like at that age and
> also because he was very beautiful. I visualized his

sitting at the table doing that to me, and it scared me again. It was my father at the age he was in the photograph, in his thirties. I was much younger in the fantasy, in my late teens, really kind of gorgeous, really pretty, and my father young, really sexy.

My father got up from the table after playing with my cock for a while through my jeans and came around the table and pulled the chair away and pulled my pants down. I remember very clearly saying, "At last. OK. Take it, I want you to do it." And it was this culmination of this desire that we both had had for a long time but had been ignoring. So he pulled my pants down and started working his cock into me. That was the most exciting part of the fantasy to me. His hard cock kind of screwing its way into me. And I popped off before he even got his cock in to fuck me. Just the thought of it going up inside me and starting to fill me up was . . . and his arms around me and his hands on my tits and so forth. And the intimacy, the closeness . . . which is a component of fantasies I've often had. Sitting in front of the big strong man who has his arms around me, sitting between his legs, jacking me off.

Ian has spent a great deal of time thinking about the repetitive disasters that characterized his three-year relationship with Werner and how he had contributed to the final breakup.

I really did turn him into my father. Aside from the way I behaved toward him, my responses toward him were extreme because of the way my father had treated me. When Werner froze me out and ignored me or withheld from me, it was worse because my father had treated me that way. That accounted for the fact that the last part of our relationship was such an unrelieved nightmare, I think, because I was really reliving the whole thing with my father in capsule form.

I learned a lot from my mother about how to deal with men, and so I dealt with Werner the way she dealt with my father. Instead of dealing with Werner, I dealt with him as if he were my father, and I had to use the same wiles that she used. Instead of saying, "You asshole, you won't talk to me," I manipulated him into responses the way I saw her do.

With Werner I was very troubled about a lot of things, and I needed help and I needed love, and the more troubled I was, the less I got from him, and the more guilty I felt because I didn't feel I had a right to ask those things from him. That he was my lover, but he was another person, and I was imposing them on him in order to get something else out of him because I was really mad at him. I still feel angry at him because he never responded. I feel that he was a rotten human being for not loving me in the ways that he could have loved me, for turning away from me completely, and that was what my father did to me.

Older men were more important to me than anyone my own age. I wanted approval and interest and also to manipulate them, I now realize, to use their power against them. I felt my father had betrayed me, and I wanted an older man in my power, to punish him for his weakness. For daring to love me, I think. It was a new kind of thing. I desperately wanted them to love me, but anyone who did show love toward me was weak. My father was strong, so anyone else who loved me, since I believed he didn't, showed their weakness. They weren't him. See?

One of the most commonly reported fantasies was thinking about one's father while masturbating. The story line most often heard was the father's entrance into the room while the gay son was masturbating. Then, instead of punishing the son, the father would join him. "I thought it would be terrific if he came in and caught me and also joined in," was the way one person put it.*

The fantasies and experiences of this group of gay men are quite commonplace; only now are we breaking taboo by discussing them. Neither the fathers nor the sons are unusual. But what of actual sexual experiences between a father and his son? Do they occur, or are the fantasies of gay boys forever relegated to private masturbatory story lines?

There are indeed occurrences of father/son sexuality, but they are very difficult to uncover, possibly because they don't occur very often or because interviewers are reluctant to ask. Only two examples surfaced in my sample of gay men. Whether this is an accurate estimate of its incidence in the population is im-

---

* Incidentally, this gay man, a twenty-two-year-old from the Midwest, became upset about his homosexuality in college and went to the college physician for help. "Stop eating eggs," he was told. Now, that's a new one! Fortunately, while leaving the doctor's office, he met another student who was put on the same diet. He now lives with his lover of six months.

possible to assess at this time. The two experiences are quite different.

Philip * is a musician, a man in his mid-thirties, born and raised in the Midwest and currently living in a large southwestern city. He has just decided to live apart from his lover of six and one-half years, in part because of his desire for varied sexual experiences. Philip knew since his teens that his father and uncle were gay.

> My dad and I didn't have a very close relationship when I was growing up because he couldn't understand my professional interest in music, even though it was a middle-class family. At the age of thirteen, my mother talked him into having that conversation that dads often have with their sons—about the facts of life. Well, I already knew that from the age of four. But I played dumb so I could at least hear what he was going to say. When he started talking about condoms, I pretended that I didn't know how to put one on, which was absurd, but I did it anyway.
>
> I sort of indicated that I didn't know how to use a rubber. So he showed me. So I had an erection. He demonstrated it on me. I got a hard-on. Being out and active for three years already, I could read his responses immediately. Shortly after I unveiled myself, I saw he had an erection. His hands were shaking. He was probably afraid that he was going to reveal something about himself. We ended up masturbating each other.
>
> I felt very mixed about it. I was excited from the obvious standpoint of having another sexual experience, and the fact that it was my father excited me. The negative aspect of it, the confusing aspect—this was the most positive of our interactions, and sex remained the only positive interaction we had throughout my high school years.
>
> We had sex together maybe a couple of hundred times. It was always mutual masturbation and sucking, never anal intercourse. We tried, but I wasn't ready to be entered at that time, and I wasn't interested in it. And he seemed a bit reluctant. Often I would just place my penis between his thighs and ejaculate that way. There was no kissing in those days, but as I matured, as I became an adult, there was more genuine affection, but this was only after I left home.
>
> To the best of my knowledge my mother doesn't

know we've done it together, but ironically enough my dad was arrested for gross indecency in a public john in the same place that I had been arrested a number of years prior to that. So she found out about him.

That's a hard question to answer [the effect of having sex with his father on Philip's life]. I don't think it's been a negative influence. It was just very confusing as I was growing up as a teenager because it was the only positive interaction we ever had. We were fighting all the other times, about my career or about chores around the house. He knew I was gay. I think he felt concerned that my life would be filled with hardship, and once he confided in me that he probably wouldn't have gotten married if he'd known what he knows now about himself. He probably would just have remained single.

Philip's experience with his father raises a number of intriguing questions. For instance, what is the experience of gay married men who are attracted to their sons? How do they handle their feelings, and especially how do they confront homosexuality when it occurs in their children? Presumably not all gay fathers have sex with their sons. And what of the lives of gay fathers who suppress their homosexuality but see their sons living an active, happy gay life? There is no research of any kind on gay fathers, but one hopes other investigators will confront these important questions.

The next account of a sexual experience between a gay son and his father is even more unusual. It is also psychologically damaging, probably the most destructive family pattern described in all the interviews. In all likelihood, the father was psychotic, and once again the experience of the child profoundly affected the adult's perception of the world.

Walter * is now twenty-five years old. He was born and raised in an extraordinarily poor family in a rural farming area of the Midwest. Walter is the youngest of five children. He describes his father as "an emotional sadist."

He committed incest with my sisters, all three of them, from the time they were three or four until they left home.

Walter's mother was aware of her husband's rape of the children but, as one generally finds in this kind of family constellation, did nothing. The children soon learned that their mother maintained a hands-off policy regarding her husband's molestations.

> The first time he molested me I was about twelve, and I had stayed home from school because I was sick; Mother had gone to the grocery store or something. And he called me into the bedroom and said he wanted to show me something. I knew what it was all about. I just sort of sensed it. It wasn't anything he said, but I sort of knew it was coming. And he tried to get me to screw him.
>
> He greased us up. Lubricated my cock. And he had me get on top of him, but my cock was too short. I didn't feel anything; I don't even think it went in. But when it was obvious that it wasn't going to work, he decided to try and screw me—and he was not gentle. Just thrust it in. It hurt. I felt a combination of guilt, excitement, and anger.

This was not the first time that Walter's father had imposed his sexual will on the children. Besides raping his son and daughters, Walter's father tried to force him to have sex with a sister while the father looked on. (Walter was six.) The father tried this on a number of occasions, but the children were never able to complete the sexual act because of their age.

Walter's first masturbation fantasies involved older men, and he had a few sexual experiences in adolescence. But then Walter's strict religious background (ironic in his family) made him feel guilty about his sexual desire for men. In high school Walter made the first of six suicide attempts.

> By taking an overdose of my father's sedatives. I guess I didn't want to kill myself. I just wanted someone to know that I was having problems. I wanted to let somebody know I needed help.
>
> I felt angry at my father. I felt it was his fault that I was gay, because he wasn't the model figure a father was supposed to be. I hated him intensely, and sometimes I still do. The suicide attempt was my way of getting even with him. In a small town like that, anyone who attempts suicide is obviously sick. And of course the neighbors would talk. Not that they weren't talking already, because my father would play around with my sisters' girl friends, so everybody knew.

In 1966 Walter made what he calls the first "real" suicide attempt. He took 1,500 milligrams of Valium, drank a fifth of vodka, and went for a walk in the park.

> I wanted to die watching the sunset. How romantic. I was sick of everything, tired of struggling. I was miserable. I didn't want to work. I felt it was useless. I was tired of the relationships I was experiencing, mostly one-night stands. At least two different men a day, sometimes all the way up to four a day. Ten guys a week. So I went to a friend's house, and she took me to the hospital, and they pumped my stomach out.
>
> I guess the main reason I felt so worthless is that I had been programmed in the Pentecostal Church to believe that if I was not living a holy life that life would be worthless and that therefore I would be worthless. So when I left the church I felt that my whole life was wrong, that I was wrong, and that I would never amount to anything.
>
> I didn't want to believe it—but the church was the first experience of having people loving me for what they thought was myself. But in actuality they didn't love me, they loved what they wanted me to be. At the time I didn't realize that—I didn't want to realize it. I felt this life wasn't worth it. I felt this life was a ball game, and I didn't want in.
>
> I used to think that most homosexuals were sick, degenerates, that they were living life wrong. I felt that heterosexuality was the way to do it, that was the way it should be. I didn't have a very high opinion of gays. I can see why. The gays I knew were those I met in the park, and that was strictly on a sexual basis.

During the ninth grade (age 15), after another suicide attempt, Walter was confined briefly in a state hospital. When he returned, he found that one of his sisters had told everyone in the school about the hospitalization, "and I was an outcast."

Walter's later teen years were a series of tragic episodes. Briefly summarized, they include being kicked out of the house by his father because he had joined the Baptist church (his father was a Methodist), a stint in a Pentecostal Youth Redemption Center, wrist slashing, and the bizarre experience of a man trying to make Walter his "slave." His last suicide attempt occurred one and a half years ago. "I'm really amazed. A year and a half is a long time," Walter mused.

Walter is now involved in his first love relationship. His lover knows the relationship is tentative at best. Walter has never before had sex with someone more than once, and he distrusts anyone who wants a monogamous arrangement. Walter has also become a masochist and fears bringing that into his relationship. The two live in a local hotel, afraid of taking an apartment and settling down permanently; both sense that the relationship cannot last and avoid any action that will make the breakup more painful than it has to be. At present there are too many ghosts from the past intruding on Walter's emotional life. His personal struggles are severe. For the first time he's trying to find a way out of this labyrinth of self-destruction, but in the meantime he is incapable of trusting anyone.

Confusing a parent with a lover is hardly unique to gay men. It happens consistently in the lives of heterosexual men and women. Ask any woman about her husband, and the probability is that you'll hear endless stories illustrating how often he wants his wife to be a mother; the husband can offer evidence to show how strongly his wife wants a father. Searching for parent substitutes in our lovers is a trap for everyone. Even worse, many parents demand that their children do all the things they couldn't accomplish to please their fathers when they were young; these demands are unreasonable, and they are doomed to failure. If anything, gay men are probably in a better position than straight men to examine themselves and their feelings about love relationships. In gay relationships, it's honesty, both to oneself and to one's lover, that creates the sparks and the solidarity.

The fantasies and experiences of the gay men in this chapter demand an explanation. If it is true that a gay man's father is more important in his life than his mother—in contrast to the prevailing myth—there are significant implications for our view of homosexual love. Some people will applaud the theory as evidence that homosexuality is exuded like some form of toxin in the family. There are still many, both professional and lay people, who search endlessly for the holy grail, the "truth" about the etiology of homosexuality. Unfortunately, a large number of gay men must be included among them; they need a "cause" to justify their lives, a "thing" to blame, because they have not yet found justification for the love in themselves. While professionals may jump to a new explanation of homosexuality, some gay men will only find a new person to "blame" it on.*

The experiences of the men cited in this chapter provide no evidence that fathers, or anyone else, create either homosexual or heterosexual children. Some men persist in the idea that their fathers have made them homosexual, but we can identify gay men who have not had troublesome relationships with their fathers, and others who have resolved father/son conflicts. Certainly it would have been helpful to have interviewed the fathers of the gay men whose stories have been recounted in this book, to have learned their experiences and how they perceived their sons. No one has ever done this, and no theory about the effect of father/son relationships on future love can reach even an approximation of the truth without investigating the father.

Many gay men experience their fathers as ghosts from the past. They are still angry and resentful over painful childhoods, and they view the father as a kind of alien, an enemy to be repelled. Still others wait patiently for their fathers to show signs of love. These two types of gay men are somewhat similar; they expend energy thinking about their fathers and how they want them to change. What is different is how they react as sons. Men who justifiably hate their fathers for brutality and cruelty find they cannot escape the paternal influence on their feelings and behavior with other men, as well as on their self-esteem. Whether they still hope for love, act indifferently, or hate, these men are tied to the past, haunted by memories, fantasies, and wishes. They distort their images of themselves and their lovers, though some are more aware of it than others, being more capable of confronting and changing the distortions.

What is elusive and difficult to resolve in the lives of gay men haunted by conflicting feelings toward their fathers is illuminated by the realization that there are two sons and two fathers in every couple. Each gay man looks at his father through the eyes of a child, hoping and expecting that the man his father was, say ten or twenty years ago, will change, will become a better father than in the past. He ignores the fact that his father is

* The best response I ever heard to those who want to blame their homosexuality on someone else came from a bit of graffiti in a subway corridor. Someone had written, "My mother made me a homosexual." Underneath was the response: "If I give her some wool, will she make me one, too?"

now a middle-aged or old man who may have forgotten the events still so vivid to the son. It is a developmental problem; all the memories and feelings of the son originate in childhood and are carried into adulthood with an energy of their own. It is as if the gay man carries around a child's reality, a child's perception of the world in the midst of adult characteristics. He insists that his father change, that his father go back in time and make up for problems of the past. But the father cannot; he doesn't understand what he did wrong so many years ago or what changes he can make now; he is not the same man or the same father. The only way he can change is if the son alters his behavior. When the son learns to depend on himself, not his father, then the father can learn who this new adult son really is.

The sexual fantasies reported in this chapter support the idea that some gay men want present-day love from their fathers to make up for the past. In all the sexual fantasies recorded, the father and son moved back to an earlier age, and the sex took place in the past, while the gay man experiencing it is in the present. In my interviews with gay men, I rarely found anyone who wanted to act out his fantasies with his father now. The fantasies serve the purpose of giving form and life to the phantom father, thereby letting go of the past and moving on to adult goals.

The phantom father can interfere with love relationships in any number of ways. First of all, he influences self-perception of masculinity. A second effect is his distortion of our perceptions of other men, creating a belief system about other men's behavior and motivation leading *us to act toward men as if the distorted view of them is correct*. For instance, someone like Albert still believes that a strong, loving father will appear and protect him, and he is forever disappointed to find the men he chooses are never as strong as he wants them to be. Ian is still angry at his father; he looks for men who are weak in order to expose them and get even with them. Neither can assess the real assets and liabilities of the chosen lover because of distorted expectations.

These distorted expectations show up in a number of ways. On the simplest level, one expects a lover to make up for one's deficiencies; but sometimes a lover demands that his partner take on deficiencies as if they were his own, and this is a task no partner can ever accomplish. At other times, the father/son distortion is manifested in a situation in which the lover, consciously or unconsciously, notices an attitude in his partner that reminds him of a similar attitude demonstrated toward him years ago. He attributes the same motivation to his lover as he did to his father, and he responds to it like a hurt child. The final level of distortion occurs when a lover takes his father's role, acting as his father would in a given situation. This happens most often in displays of anger or depression. In all these cases, the partner is confused and mystified.

Distorting a lover because of the relationship with one's father is bound to end in disaster. Certainly no one takes kindly to having his motivation distorted, and no one wants the responsibility of atoning for the deficiencies of another, even a lover. At first, the idea seems like a compliment, the fulfillment of the desire to be needed, but eventually it makes the atmosphere stale and stuffy. The lover begs for a breath of fresh air, a chance to be himself, and rejection follows.

Perhaps the most frightening aspect of the phantom father relationship is the way it imprisons the lover: he is made to feel that he has been bound in chains and told never to grow, never to expand his horizons, never to see his partner in a different light. Always the shadow of the father looms. No lover can endure so pernicious an influence, and a rush to break the chains is not only inevitable but necessary for his own psychological existence. If the lover makes the break, it is interpreted as abandonment and fulfills the prophecy.

Homosexual love is not always a replaying of the father/son relationship, but the relationship between father and son is crucial for future success in love. Some gay men have not been able to give up their demands for father love; as a result, they expect their lovers to fulfill dual roles. Other gay men do not have this problem; either their father/son experiences did not create a barrier for the future, or they have learned how to pull apart their distorted perceptions of a lover and judge him for who he is, assets, liabilities, and all. Some can do this alone, while others learn after a positive experience in psychotherapy. The young suffer the most since they are first to discover, usually the hard way, how they can make or break their own love relationships. Older, more experienced men have realized (one hopes) that their love is not always altruistic, that some of the selfish motivations attributed to lovers in the past are characteristics of themselves as well. They are less judgmental about lovers today.

The difference between "mature" and "immature" men is apparent in the quality of their breakups. Mature men understand what happened, realizing how personal growth in either partner changes a relationship in ways that make its continuation a fraud. Leaving one another can be a moment of mature judgment, each lover understanding how he has changed and what to look for in the future. This understanding is worlds apart from lovers who break up and live with bitterness for years. They have learned nothing.

CHAPTER TWO

Boys in the School Yard

We two boys together clinging,
One the other never leaving,
Up and down the roads going, North and South
   excursions making,
Power enjoying, elbows stretching, fingers clutching,
Armed and fearless, eating, drinking, sleeping, loving.

WALT WHITMAN

The school yard is the training ground for adult male behavior. Proper masculine attitudes will be learned there, and the rewards for following and the punishments for violating adult male values will be meted out. A new fantasy world will be developed to replace the feminine one of early childhood. Here boys participate in the fantasy of achievement and victory, engage in the competitive excitement and the hero worship of older, more competent boys. The younger must approve of and admire the older, even love them in the way young boys are allowed to love older ones—who, of course, reject them. Boys cooperate in this school yard, but only for purposes of competition: the goal is to be a member of a team not only to beat the other team, but to outshine the teammates. Parents call it play.

The school yard is not the same as the playground, which is the province of teachers, characterized by maternal control, fairness, consideration of feelings, perhaps even the rudiments of the democratic process. The playground during school hours is an extension of child's play. Mother took her toddler to it partly for him to play, but also so she could meet other women who wanted to get out of the house, too. In the playground, Mother made the rules and chose the game; she was always there as arbiter whenever scrapes or arguments broke out in the long process of childhood. But the school yard represents a move away from the care and protection of Mother and into the world of men, a movement from childhood into adolescence.

The ethos of the school yard—even the division between those who play there and those who do not—separates boys into rough categories that continue throughout life. Highly valued traits such as competitiveness and aggression and most particularly the ability to win (regardless of the cost) are early learned and practiced here. But there are other traits developing in the boys as well, traits that will be important in their adult lives as workers and lovers. Some are displayed openly, like the sexual provocativeness of adolescents challenging each other to "blow jobs" or jerking off when the little kids aren't around; others are more subtle and more powerful.

The school yard reinforces the standards of budding masculinity. Changes from feminine to masculine domination can be seen as the boy grows up and takes his place in areas reserved for the older, tougher boys. At the top are the postpubescent adolescents who choose where they will play and with whom. They are winners by virtue of their strength and aggressiveness. Adventure colors their imagination. In their internal story lines they charge out against enormous odds, win the struggle, and receive the worship of the community. They visualize the adoration of younger boys, but more important is the esteem of older men, for they wish to become men themselves.

For older boys, the imagination must also entertain danger, preferably to life and limb, with small injuries welcome as proofs of manhood. Adventure, hero worship, danger, physical endurance, and exhibitionism are the major themes of male fantasy in the school yard.

The younger boys are still feminized in varying degrees, still under the tutelage of their mothers. Since domesticity is the characteristic of the feminine imagination, "playing house" or any kind of play in the home is feminine and controlled by Mother. When the imagination of young boys produces monsters, the creatures invade the home, and the boy needs a protector. The pubescent boy, however, is not satisfied in having a monster-free home; he goes out to slay the monster. If there are no villains in the world, then the boy is forced to create them.

Still under the care of their mothers, younger boys are not yet aggressive enough to compete with other boys. The differences in mother or father identification can be observed in costume. Father-identified boys are dirtier, wear older clothes, and seem oblivious of their age or condition. Indeed, age and threadbareness of clothing are sometimes an important symbol to the boy; interference by the mother in his costume is seldom tolerated. But younger boys must be careful not to get too dirty; they are still subject to Mother's disapproval.

The muscularity of children changes with age. Though older boys have finer muscle dexterity, it is the gross body movements they practice most in the school yard. They exult in the energy of total power, the thrill of hard body contact. They scratch, develop a new type of walk, and play without a shirt—perhaps tied around the waist or thrown in a pile with the other artifacts of male supremacy. Endlessly they touch their muscles and crotches in a narcissistic display of masculine power. Even the odor of their clothes, the smell of sweat, is a sign of masculinity and sexual potential. It's a very sexual scene, with older boys strutting about the school yard, posing for each other, competing with each other—and yet enticing each other repeatedly in this homosocial environment.

In the school yard, the young boys admire the acting abilities of their superiors. As they observe the aggression of the older boys, they learn what kind of physical contact is acceptable, and how to grimace and get up with dignity after an injury; they discover the right way to finger their muscles and genitals. They admire older brothers and their friends both in and out of the school yard; many of the younger boys worship the older ones as heroes.

The school yard, then, is a metaphor for the process of training boys for adult male gender roles. As described here, it is a reasonable picture of the early lives of many men. But men who were brought up in rural areas and either walked long distances to school or were driven there by school buses or parents couldn't play in the yard after classes. For them the school yard may have been the family farm; the playmates may have been brothers and sisters or kids from the next farm. Their play may have been cutting firewood, or driving the tractor and harvesting crops. Here boys work alongside "real" men. The city boy will play basketball and admire one particular professional basketball team, hoping to watch it play when it comes to town; the country boy will clean his .22 caliber rifle as his father cleans the shotgun. In the fall, they hunt together with other men and their sons; whoever downs the first deer of the season, or the largest, or the animal with the most "points" will be worshiped as a hero by the boy. The scenes may be different, but the process serves the same goal—to end the period of Mother's control and replace it with the values of the father.

Male Gender Roles

Masculinity is an attitude or belief about how behavior conforms to or differs from the acceptable social norm. Much of the training of children concerns the distinction of masculinity from femininity; along with this distinction they are taught the punishment for blurring it. For instance, walk up to a small boy and ask, "Are you a girl?" He'll probably snap back, "No, I'm a boy!" This child is saying he's learned that he is the same as one class of people—boys and men—and very different from another —girls and women. He may not know that male and female genitals differ, but he does know that boys and girls look and act differently, and that boys shouldn't act like girls. This behavior, apart from physical characteristics, is what is meant by *gender roles*.

Four different kinds of boys can be roughly identified, all of whom have learned the rules of male behavior but who vary in acceptance or rejection of them. These boys are *comrades, outsiders, sissies, and romantics.** They are characterized on the basis of their feelings toward masculinity and toward male playmates. Almost certainly, these roles influence the selection of partners in future love relationships.

The nucleus of life in the metaphorical school yard is formed by comrades, pairs of boys who share the same values and compete with each other. For them, school yard camaraderie is the model of male relationships. It includes closeness and caring, the comrades becoming friends and spending much of their days together. These boys are often high achievers. The parents of these boys often become friends as well. But always in these male-identified boys, adventure is the primary characteristic of

* This classification of boys, like all classifications used in this book, should be viewed as a way of perceiving the differences among people, rather than as an absolute division. It emphasizes how young boys tend to perceive themselves because of their experiences with other people.

their relationship—to do something out there.

City boys compete with each other or against pairs of comrades in the school yard; suburban boys soup up their cars to be hotter than any other in the neighborhood; and rural boys hunt together or wander off into uncharted woodlands. In all cases, the quest is the same: to do something out there together. Their task as comrades against the world binds them together.

Louis is thirty-two. He was born and raised in New York City, where he still lives. At twenty-three he was married and had two chidren. He had been having homosexual experiences outside his marriage, and when he told his wife about his double life, they decided to separate. As a youngster he had been a fine athlete.

> I got along swell with my dad. We were very close because I was the firstborn son, and he showed me a lot of attention. I don't know why, but I was very popular around the block and in school. Maybe it was because I had good coordination, like being able to throw a ball far and accurately. I was the captain of my Little League team, too.
>
> I guess you would call me a competitive kid. I was always trying out for school teams, and winning meant a lot to me. I had lots of trophies in my room. I still have a couple of them somewhere. One of my best friends—his name was George—we used to pal around together all the time. He was just about as good in sports as I was, and we used to compete against each other a lot. It was one of the ways we had fun together. There was nothing sexual between us. In fact, we always used to call each other "fag," but that was just something that all the guys used. I'm not even sure I knew what it meant, although I did later.

On the periphery of the school yard stand the outsiders. For these boys, the school yard is ground zero; status decreases as boys move away from the center of the yard. Boys in this category are poor competitors; they experience themselves as weak. They cannot compete successfully against school yard comrades and hence are not chosen early for any team. Sometimes they try hard, but lack of skill or an incapacitating fear of failure upsets their coordination. They miss balls, run to base awkwardly. In short, they aren't a good bet for any team, and the other boys let them know.

These rejected fellows are unattractive psychologically to themselves because of a deep internal conflict between goals and abilities. They aspire to be atheletes (or whatever the status activity of the area) but are rejected for their failure to perform. Ultimately, they both hate and admire their heroes. Sometimes they identify with the athletes in the school yard, seeing them as strong men, potentially powerful allies whose friendship infuses them with a bit of masculinity. When such a friendship occurs, their self-esteem rises. If not, they begin to search for the man who will infuse them with masculinity and make them feel all right.

Sometimes the rejected athletes behave in a negative way, seeing the hero as a fraud who wins games or excels at sports unfairly. They seethe with jealousy and anger, believing that they could succeed if only . . . Their excuses are endless, their denial of failure complete. Instead of taking pride in real accomplishments or developing unusual skills that others do not have, they feign abilities envied in others. They are not generous as boys, and later as men in love—if indeed they can ever love. They are likely to view their unfolding homosexuality as another episode in a long record of injustice.

Ed is twenty-two. He was born in a conservative New England town and now lives in New York City. He's lived with a lover for the past year or so, although their relationship is a bit strained because of Ed's periodic depressions (he calls them "the blues").

> I was a runt. The other kids were always bigger than me. Jim, my lover, is bigger than me, too. I never quite understood it, but my hands and legs never worked the way other people's hands and legs work. I had no coordination at all. I could throw a ball, but it never went where I aimed it. Then I would play baseball and swing at the ball, miss it, and hit my shins. It sounds like a joke, but it wasn't for me. I felt like shit because of it.
>
> Who wants to play with a kid who strikes out all the time? I mean, all the time? And I always tried hard. Maybe that was the problem—I tried too hard. And I always admired the jocks, the kids who were popular because they were good in sports. All the other boys liked them, and I wanted to be their friend, but it

didn't happen too much. I was also deathly afraid that
the kids would call me a sissy.

I get the blues a lot because I've never gotten over
the feeling that I'm not as good as other guys—other
men. Wherever I am today, I want the "in crowd" to
accept me, and if they don't, I get upset. I also don't
like effeminate men.

Even further away from the nucleus of the school yard are
the sissies. Their paths rarely cross those of the comrades. They
don't get in each other's way, for neither has anything the other
wants. Because their personal sense of values is primary, the
sissies are not much interested in abiding by the rules of others.
While they are *non*conformists, they should not be confused
with *anti*conformists who would be happy to conform but reject
the rules, for they feel themselves rejected by the rule makers.
The outsiders, for example, may develop into the latter group.
Being homebodies, but not necessarily mama's boys, sissies'
rooms have all the things they need for developing a private
fantasy world. They paint or work at crafts, they cook, and they
enjoy playing with their sisters. Generally afraid of being hurt
physically, they are unlikely ever to participate in any athletics.
If forced to play ball in school, they strike back by deliberately
striking out, or by running to second base first, or by laughing
when the team is serious. How else can they fight back? Often
chosen last for such games, they prefer not to be chosen at all.

Depending on age and experience, sissies may think of themselves as partly or wholly feminine, or just as boys with finer
sensibilities. They often don't accept the idea of exclusively
male and female preoccupations, and frequently prefer the company of women. Their fantasies are distinctly what the world
calls feminine.

There are also boys who are not real sissies at all, but pseudo-
sissies. While pretending to be against sports and competition,
pseudo-sissies may become athletic in their adult years. While
their jock-type brothers may settle down as managers of Little
League teams pushing ten-year-old boys around, the pseudo-
sissies may end up fine tennis players, avid cross-country skiers,
or the most dedicated of joggers. Not until they become adults
do they discover that sports don't belong solely to a team of
foul-mouthed boys, pushing and shoving, having to win or lose.

As adults they learn that the expenditure of energy in athletics can be rewarding, particularly in sports more suitable to their frame or temperament. They can be good team members if there's fun in it, but they're unlikely to want to defeat others. They may, however, compete fiercely in other areas.

Craig is twenty-eight. He lives with his lover of eight years in Chicago. He was born into a very religious family, although his parents were never able to get Craig to believe or practice the religion. Somehow he comfortably ignored it for his own more promising world.

> I was not only not chosen, in school as a boy, to be on a team, I wasn't even present at the choosing. This avoided the embarrassment of a teacher forcing one or the other teams into accepting me, and me in agreeing with the respective captains, since I did not want to play those games. I suppose some boys really like those games. I did not. I preferred to play with the girls, not because I necessarily liked girls better, but because I preferred cooperative rather than competitive games, nor did I like the anger and aggressiveness on the playground. I really didn't like team things.
>
> I suppose I was what is generally called a sissy, although I certainly wasn't a "mama's boy." But I did do all those things that boys are not supposed to do: I kept clean, my room was clean, I never collected filthy frogs, and I thought about pretty curtains. Later, I thought about love. I have always cared about love. Fortunately, I was wise enough to have chosen and live with a man who also never collected filthy frogs.

Finally, there are the romantics. While comrades use their energies competing and exhibiting themselves to the world, while sissies learn about the home and quiet pursuits, the romantic boys exist only for each other. They discuss with one another their feelings, their fears, and their hopes; they reach out to one another for solace and support. What characterizes them best is their strong desire to be together. Their bond is love, sometimes spoken but more often not. In many cases, their relationships are more important and more intense than any that they will experience in adult life. Although romance may be found among some comrades and sissies, it is much rarer and more fleeting. Romantic boys not only want to be together, they want to be apart from everyone else—camping in the woods, building tree houses, setting up tents made out of blankets in the basement. All boys do these things, of course, but the romantics will want only one other boy to join the fun.

Keith is nineteen. He was born and raised in a suburban town near a large midwestern city. He's now a freshman at a large southern college. This year Keith has met another man, the same age, in his college dormitory, and they have started a relationship—under the noses of the other men in the dormitory. It isn't the easiest way to be together, since they need to hide their youthful passion by occasionally dating women (of course, they double-date) and by carefully monitoring their reactions toward each other in the presence of roommates.

> My family used to do a lot of camping when I was young, so I got accustomed to nature—you know, the woods, sleeping under the stars. I used to think of the stars as my friends—friends who came out at night to watch over me.
> Sports wasn't my interest. There were too many kids. Maybe I couldn't relate well to so many, I don't know. But I always had a best friend. I can't ever remember not having one. Just before puberty I had this friend, Ken. We went everywhere together. It didn't make much difference what we did. I was very accommodating. We used to talk about a lot of things —how we felt about our parents or school, or what we were going to do when we grew up. And sometimes when he slept over my house, we'd cuddle together— but we never told anyone about it or talked about it. He eventually moved away.
> I started having sex in junior high school. Just playful stuff. But it was always with just one person. Even in those days I was monogamous! One thing I've noticed. Throughout my childhood, these friends—I felt closer to them than I did to my family.

The play of boys is one of the primary ways to teach what masculinity is about, and the school yard is the training ground of this learning. Most writers have given the major responsibility for this task to the parents, whose contribution should not be minimized. But I think training by peers is more powerful than training by parents. The first important lesson for boys in the long process called socialization is to learn the appropriate gender role—to be a boy, and then a man. This is the first of three crucial concepts that influence the development of a boy into a fully productive, functioning homosexual, with the willingness to be loved by another man and to return that love.

Behind the individual stories of the lives of homosexual men lie the recurring themes of gender role, coupling, and intimacy. Jock or sissy, gay or straight, raised in the metropolis or on the farm, each man finds these three themes influencing his life, and even, in some cases, controlling it. These themes form the basis of all love relationships, providing room for the resolution of conflicts or weapons with which to do battle. Gender role, the idea that certain attributes and perceptions of the world are either masculine or feminine, is the central theme and the one learned first. Coupling and intimacy are the other themes.

Coupling and Intimacy

The idea of being half of a couple (to children this means adult marriage) must be very confusing to many boys, since they witness at first hand many marital interactions which often include resentment, anger, selfishness, alcoholic rages, and lovelessness. Some readers perhaps need only to remember their own childhood to agree that the marriage model presented by their parents has little to recommend it in the way of intimate bliss.

Nonetheless, the boy is programmed to believe that by becoming a solid member of a team of two, he'll gain a loving and compatible companion for life. The training from childhood is incessant, the goal, marrying an ideal woman to continue the chain of life by producing little boys and girls of his own. Perhaps this is part of the reason young boys can have so much sex with other boys and never consider it "real sex." Even as small children they believe that "real sex" occurs only in marriage.

Children are taught that by having a married mate, they will be socially, sexually, and psychologically fulfilled. The failure to marry, they come to believe, is obviously an indication that something is wrong with them; they learn early that being chosen for love is the single most important thing that will happen in their lives. They are further taught that, once chosen, they must remain with the beloved forever. (However, the popularity of divorce has opened modern children to other options.) Children are also taught to confuse sex and love. The sexiness, the horniness, of a growing boy is not approved by his parents, his community, or his religion.* The boy quickly learns by his own experience that sex can be had without any need for love, even though traditionally considered impossible or a sin. Fortunately, most boys reject this adult hokum of no sex without love and continue their forays with even more secrecy and far from the eyes of meddling adults.

Behind the storybook adventures and competitive strivings of the school yard comrades are profound feelings of closeness. A boy's love for his companion is one of the strongest ties of his life: memories of these boyhood affairs are touching to hear, and separations from comrades are a painful part of many men's histories. For all the hostility they may have shown to those they considered outsiders, particularly to sissies, there was often more warmth and love in these childhood attachments than in their present adult relationships.

Sex play begins with the comrades as well. This is not the funny sex play of younger boys, who play doctor or have contests to see who can throw the furthest trajectory of urine across the bathroom. The sex play of comrades is more serious, more adult in the sense that it is motivated toward genital satisfaction, rather than exhibitionism. Comrades sleep together frequently, sharing each other's houses with the full permission of their parents, who either dismiss the idea of sex between the boys or allow it as part of growing up. Touching games are popular, leading inevitably to the crotch and mutual masturbation. Sometimes sex play will progress to mutual sucking, less often to fucking. What is interesting about sex play between school yard comrades is that, although there may be love between them, it is rarely expressed verbally, especially in a sexual situation. The fun-and-games veneer overrides the emotional. The novelty of sexual pleasure and orgasms, together with the funny comments about where to put "the stuff," keep it from becoming more than a game. Comrades use their own and each other's bodies willingly for the sake of exploration only. They don't kiss, of course. That would be very serious.

* Mother disapproves severely, but father winks at it, remembering his own past and accepting his son's need to "sow his wild oats"— heterosexually, that is.

Since sex is the universal sport of boys, its meaning for them is very different from its meaning to an adult who is apt to take sex very seriously. Two boys in a rural district can swim together in a lonely stream, wrestle in the water, rub their genitals against each other, and comment on each other's "boners." They can pull off each other's bathing suits, get out of the water, and masturbate each other to orgasm. The school yard comrades don't think of these games as homosexual. To them, sex is one more game they play with each other—just a different kind of sport. It isn't until much later that it becomes associated with homosexuality. They don't understand it clearly, but homosexuality, or being "queer," has something to do with being like a girl, and they have devoted quite a bit of energy to maintaining their boy status. As a matter of fact, many of them don't even consider these early acts as sex. They say, "We're just messing around." They mean it, and it's true.

A couple made up of comrades is first concerned with personal independence and adventure, and then with sex. For a comrade, a spouse of whatever kind will be modeled after his adventurous boyhood comrade. Sex will be both challenge and competition. The seduction of another man or woman equals having a car with the most horsepower under the hood. The physical will not frighten him, but conflicts pose problems since introspection, at which he's not much good, will be needed to resolve them.

The outsiders badly need to become coupled. For them, a mate represents something more important than love; it means acceptance and respect. They have spent a childhood admiring the competence and popularity of others without developing their own special talents. Hence outsiders dream of union with popular images, such as clean-cut American youths, athletes, good dancers, life-of-the-party types. At the same time, they block from their consciousness all other types of boys as unworthy— like themselves. Outsiders dream of moments of intimacy, sure that if only the admired boy were to allow it, they could make him happy. But this dream is an impossible one: the outsider *needs* the admired boy to make *himself* happy. What he really wants is to receive, not to give.

The outsider's division of men into admired masculine ones as distinguished from despised weak ones (like himself) leads to exasperating problems in love for himself and his beloved. He may choose a heterosexual man to love, campaigning with obsessive energy for love from this one man. It's remarkable how often this quest is obsessive in some gay men; for a few it's only a plateau on the road to coming out, but for others it becomes a vocation, and one obviously doomed to disaster.

Beneath the claims of love for the chosen man, one can hear the demand to be loved, an insistence that the beloved infuse some of his energy and skill into the outsider. It's much like filling a bottomless bag, not likely to encourage feelings of mutuality so necessary in any love relationship. In adulthood, outsiders pretend to be giving, when in fact they want to take from the beloved, who eventually realizes that he's been caught in a trap of dependence with his freedom to give or to withhold severely curtailed.

Outsiders needn't live so hazardous a life. They can change their behavior with relative ease by looking for and taking pride in their own special skills. As a rule, outsiders, like other boys and men, receive compliments from time to time about many different talents. While others believe and take pride in the compliments, the outsiders reject them, unless they come from status people. When they recondition themselves to accept compliments, to take pride in themselves—and to judge the status people more carefully—their psychological posture and self-esteem rise.

Then there are romantic boys. Although the romantics take more than one form, they all share some characteristics: they are aware of their closeness in a way that comrades are not. The romantics are more sympathetic to coupling since their earliest fantasies and experiences are consistent with their social conditioning. Comrades are loyal, but romantics love each other consciously, powerfully, believing their love will last forever. They are the ones least likely to brag about sex, talking instead of closeness and sharing. For them, nurturing is at least as important as getting laid.

Romantic boys in rural areas live in an ideal environment. There's always a place for them to go to be alone. They can swim, walk in the woods, explore deserted houses, or drive through winding country roads—they're licensed earlier than city boys. City boys have more technical problems in finding ways to be alone, in getting away from brothers and sisters playing the stereo too loud or spying on them.* It is difficult to meet often enough; each must take special lessons after the school day, the bane of city sophistication and overscheduled children.

Romantic boys aren't trying to beat the world; conquest holds no attraction for them. They're not interested in being noticed and admired by others; they just want to be together in boyish games or quiet pursuits. Although romantic boys strive for independence from their parents, they are dependent on each other and wouldn't have it any other way. Like the comrades, they avoid the domestic side, unless it's cooking and cleaning when camping together.

While the sissy is essentially different from the romantic, he may share one important trait, looking for love with a friend. Like that of the comrades and the romantic boys, the pairing of sissies also becomes a model for future love relationships. Sissies are highly domestic in their activities, working, playing, and thinking about the home and their place in it. Some of these boys remain at home much of the time for safety, since their nonaggressiveness makes them victims of more masculine age mates. The aggressive kids beat them up; the romantic boys just ignore them. If they're lucky, these "feminine" boys will have like-minded friends, but often they're alone with their own creative pursuits and highly developed fantasies. Many of them are loners and discourage friendship. There's little or no adventure in them, and they won't play outside in the cold.

The sissy often has a well-developed idea of what a couple is. In his self-absorbed fantasies, he views the couple as a stable unit held together by love, rather than sex. Physical excitement for the sissy takes second place to feelings and introspection. To the sissy the couple is marked by longevity; he's not interested in one passionate affair after another. He'll weather any storm and compromise far more than needed (sometimes more than wished) only to keep his love relationship going. But just as the school yard comrade neglects his romantic side—for him sex cements a relationship—so the sissy exaggerates it until he resembles a troubador singing to a chaste lady. It's not that the sissy ignores or is afraid of sex, but he won't evaluate his lovers

* City boys commonly retreat to basements and roofs for privacy.

by their performance in bed. The school yard comrade wants to get his rocks off; the sissy wants to know that his lover cares.

The sissy has one advantage over the other types of boys. He's already different and marked as such. Most likely, he has already suffered for it, sometimes at the hands of his own parents, often his father. If and when he understands that he's gay, he's unlikely to be as upset as his more masculine counterparts, whose homosexuality defies their striving for manhood. The sissy may be quite relieved, believing it a confirmation of his place in the world. Although like-minded boys make the best couples, sometimes through strange circumstances a comrade and a sissy will become close friends, but it usually ends in disaster, at least during the period of adolescence. It's not easy for two boys—one aiming for marriage and the other for adventure and excitement —to find common ground.

In very large families in isolated areas, brothers may make up a couple, even if they're of different ages; or in more populated areas, two brothers suffering from parental neglect will find solace in mutual support and sex, but only if they are like-minded boys. Contrary to common belief, older brothers do not hate younger ones; there is no necessary dislike of the young. What they reject are the reminders which the younger brothers present of earlier mother-dominated values. The comrade-type older brother doesn't want another boy around who hasn't yet learned the ways of being a man, knowing that his younger brother will snitch on him for every violation of family rules. The older brother wants to violate the rules to proclaim his independence; the younger tattles to prove his identification with domestic conformity.

There is no documentation on the nature of coupling in children, though it is obviously an important issue. Children form a concept of what a love relationship means long before they ever have lovers. Obviously parents and grandparents serve as models. All the bedtime stories, animal cartoons, and every aspect of propaganda directed at the child teach him that he will become one half of a special unit called a couple. Only years later will he hear of other kinds of relationships—three-ways, transient affairs, and the like—but by then the basic programming will have been complete. He will have a set of expectations of how members of a couple should relate to one another, resolve their conflicts, and define obligations. Much of this is learned from the parents and their relationship, but the nature of the boy and his childhood love affairs are often neglected.

It would seem natural that the definition and experience of intimacy vary among boys. Intimacy, this stuff of closeness and shared expressions, this tenderness that dissolves the psychological boundary between two people, is discomforting to the boy motivated by adventure. When he is young, he knows he doesn't like "the love stuff"; when a bit older, he avoids boys who don't properly control their feelings of affection. He may feel intimate, even sentimental, but he'd rather show it with some boyish gift than express his feelings in words.

On the other hand, romantic boys want to express intimacy. They want to hear that the boyhood lover (some even use the word) cares for them more than anyone else in the world, and they want to say the same to him. Sometimes they kiss, and at night they dream of being with their friend. To the romantic boy (how the world has ignored him!) no symbol of status or any of the things that money can buy equals the cherished moments together.

Of course, intimacy causes explosive problems in love. The realities of a relationship with its normal bouts of anger, pain, and guilt violate the ideal of a conflict-free intimacy. Comrades desire only occasional intimacies, while romantics dream of nothing else. There's seldom a problem if like-minded boys get together (comrades with comrades, romantics with romantics), but the rare relationship between a romantic and a comrade spells trouble. They often lack any common language of the emotions. In the bad old days of rigid sex roles in gay relationships it wasn't a problem since one could be the man and the other the woman. Modern egalitarianism makes that old-fashioned, and such a couple may find it uphill work resolving the myriad conflicts that spring up from misinterpretations of each other's behavior.

Boys change through experience or by emulating the behavior of some man they admire, a man who differs from their fathers and their earlier heroes. They continue to change in many ways until patterns are set in adulthood; even then, change is possible and occurs frequently. But if we take into account geographical and socio-economic variations in communities, the general pattern discussed in this chapter seems accurate enough. The central thesis is certainly valid: our childhood experiences with love and sex profoundly affect our lives as adult male lovers.

CHAPTER THREE

Coming Out and Young Lovers

> For I, that was a child, my tongue's use sleeping,
>   now I have heard you,
> Now in a moment I know what I am for, I awake,
> And already a thousand singers, a thousand songs,
>   clearer, louder and more sorrowful than yours,
> A thousand warbling echoes have started to life
>   within me, never to die.
>
> WALT WHITMAN

> I had this feeling inside that needed
>   something to come out.
>
> BOBBY, age sixteen

Since children are affected by their early experiences and carry them into adulthood, first sexual encounters contain a wealth of information. They influence and often determine success or failure in adult sexual life. For some, memories of these playful early days are invigorating, a source of excitement and wonder; even occasional rejections produce no untoward consequences. But some boys grow up in more restricted environments and learn nothing about their sexual selves; the little they discover shames them.

Left to themselves, boys experiment with sex. It usually begins when two friends who are bored (boys are forever claiming to be bored) start wrestling, touching, and grabbing. They would probably do the same thing in a culture in which sex and elimination were less shameful. There is a limit to the extent to which any society can stop young boys from playing with each other; as soon as the adults aren't around, young hands move right in to touch and explore.

Coming Out: Early Years

It is hardly remarkable to find that sexual experiences can begin before the age of ten. What is interesting, however, is how often gay men noted that their early sex experiences had special qualities for them, feelings of being different in ways they couldn't understand at the time. They now believe that these sexual contacts were the formative ones, with one man even claiming to have to come out in the sandbox as a preschool child. The following two men serve as examples:

Douglas is twenty-four. He is a black man from a southern Baptist family and was raised on army bases. He currently lives in a large midwestern city.

> As a child of three I was always aware that I was dif-
> ferent. I wish I could explain it, but I can't. I had very
> vivid fantasies of being kidnapped by these two men
> dressed entirely in black leather, and they would take
> me out of my house, just drag me off to a base and sit
> me in a corner, and they would force me to drink beer
> and smoke cigarettes, which to a child of three was an
> abomination. And I was aware that this wasn't the
> kind of thing you shouted about, "Hey, Mom, look
> what I discovered." But I was sort of excited being
> there with them, being there, alone with them. I en-
> joyed it, I was getting off on it. Definitely.

In the following vignette, it is obvious that sexual feelings in early childhood, though diffuse, still affect the child. Bobby de-scribes an emotional sexual need not yet attached to genital release.

Bobby is sixteen. He was born and raised in a southern college town. Last year he ran away from home with his twenty-eight-year-old lover. They now live a transient life, drifting from place to place, hiding from the police.

> *C.S.*: When did you start having sex?
> *Bobby*: When I started feeling horny.
> *C.S.*: What age was that?
> *B.*: Six or seven.
> *C.S.*: What did you do?
> *B.*: Nothing. I never did come or anything. I had this
> feeling inside that needed something to come out.

Most, though not all, the early sexual experiences reported were so benign. There were a few cases in which some form of molestation occurred, leaving brutal memories. Nathan's story is the most shocking example of this.

Nathan * is forty-two. He has been with his lover for eight years. He grew up in a small town in the South in a family with a strong Baptist tradition. Family violence prevented Nathan from disclosing his worries about sexuality.

> When I was five, one of my neighbor's sons (he was fifteen) brought me into a shed. I remember him being on the floor with his pants down, kneeling, and that he forced me (held me by the head) to give him a blow job. It was at that moment that my mother called me; she called and called me, and I always responded to her calls. I was forbidden to go out of the yard without her knowing where I was, so I knew I was going to be punished no matter what. He wouldn't let go of me, and he came in my mouth. I don't remember being repelled by the odor of the come, but I can remember, very vividly remember, finding the crotch smell terribly offensive and I would suspect very unclean. And for many years after that I found the idea of having mouth/genital contact very repelling.
>
> As soon as he climaxed he warned me that if I ever told anyone he would beat the shit out of me. And when I went back to the house I couldn't tell my mother because I didn't know how to describe it. I just knew it was wrong. I felt guilty because I wasn't in the yard where I was supposed to be. It wasn't just that he had threatened me.
>
> Then it happened again in the foster home when the man of the house (I was ten) made me do the same thing, on two occasions. They were about six months apart. I didn't know what was supposed to happen. I remember it seemed to take forever, and I couldn't understand why. I was confused, and I didn't like it.

While some gay men report sexual experiences very early in life, it is more common for gay sexual experiences to begin in later childhood, after the boy has entered school. If he is going to have gay sex in his youth, it's likely to begin anywhere from the fifth grade to the junior high years. It is interesting to note in the first two stories how pleased each of the boys was to participate in some form of sex with other boys. The third story illustrates the loneliness of certain first experiences. The impression given by the respondents is that sex will unfold as natural exploration unless adults intrude with religious or social demands. Male-to-male sex in childhood is rarely guilt-producing.

Lawrence is twenty-eight. He has lived with his lover for three years. Both were raised in the same rural farm community of 11,000 people and now live in a larger town of 20,000.

> I think I was always gay. I think the first cock I ever saw was my father's, and it excited me even though I couldn't relate to what it was that was exciting me. And I just went with that every chance I got.
>
> I would never do anything sexually at school. I would bring friends home; I would bribe them, saying that they would get something other than what they were going to get. I would say we were going to look at my father's *Playboy* and then take them right into a sexual situation. I would ask them if they wanted a blow job. I was about eight. They would say sure. And they would do the same.
>
> I felt that I was very special—odd. I was more aware and more in touch with feelings and sensitivity. And I felt gifted, better. My sexuality always set me apart and made me feel better than other guys.

At the age of twelve, Lawrence's parents sent him to a military school, perhaps as a way to curb his sexual appetite since they had barged in on his school-pal sexual scenes on a number of occasions. But young military behavior is no less sexual than the adult variety. It was a utopia for Lawrence, and he had sex at least once a day during his stay at the school.

Marlin * is fifty-nine. He was born and raised in a wealthy, upperclass family in rural England. He has lived with his lover in New York City for fourteen years. During his early years, Marlin lived with his mother, a lesbian, and her lover, "Aunt Jane."

> Aunt Jane moved in with us in 1926. She died after World War II, God bless her soul. It wasn't that I didn't like Aunt Jane, but when she was drunk she was unbelievably foul. She was just like a witch when she got her liquor, sounded like a fishwife. But my only resentment toward her was that she was brought up excessively Victorian. If you can imagine a big bull

dyke sitting in a tailored suit, sitting with her legs straddled, pumping on an old cigar, with these big, pink bloomers—kind of a weird sight.

I just knew as far as I was concerned women were taboo. The idea of going to bed with a woman nauseates me. I'm sure fuck ass is the thing to do. I mean the entrée for us is a good screw, and to fuck cunt is disgusting as far as I'm concerned. I could appreciate what straight men could see in them, but for myself, I tried it once. I fell asleep.

How old could I have been when I started? Five? Six? I can remember who it was. He was American. He wore those little britches which we used to call "plus fours" in England. Belted jacket in the back, very funny.

I suppose he must have been twelve. James used to take little Iris—that was the bitch's name, little red-haired girl—take her down in the coal cellar. In those days every house had a coal cellar. And she'd pull down her trousers, and he'd tickle her puss. And that's as far as it got. And I thought, "This is excessively boring." So one day I said to James, "Why do you bother with her. All she does is giggle when you touch her. Now you touch me and I'll touch you, and we can do things." So we ended up blowing each other. But when we blew it just tickled, so we had to stop. But it served its purpose.

Then there was another boy; can't remember his name. He used to wear a kilt which I think he had no right to wear at all. He wasn't Scottish. I think he just wore a kilt because his mother liked him in kilts. But I liked him in kilts because he used to wear no trousers underneath. So then I went into more advanced sex, from sucking to rimming.

When I was eight I was sent to a boarding school, and my lover was the prefect [age fourteen], so I became his fag, which has nothing to do with being a faggot or being gay. That means you serve this man; you have to clean his shoes, prepare his bed, and all this jazz. Then he became head prefect which means he had his own room, and of course his fag would have a bed in his room, because that way I could take better care of him, which I did.

Once I thought he was cheating on me, and I was yelling at him. "You cheat on me with kids, eight years old." I was nine at that time. And I threw an inkwell at him. Made a mess of the room. I found out years later that the master was outside listening and wanted to give me a good caning, but he was laughing so hard he couldn't keep a straight face to do it.

By the way, I found out later that he married some bitch, three kids and as dreary as all hell. It wasn't too many years after (I think it was 1933), I was playing the lead in some play and he had come to see the show, and he came backstage to see me. And I said, "Remember the old days?" And he said, "You bastard, we were schoolboys." I said, "If you want to put it that way. But we had one hell of a time for schoolboys!" He was from quite a dreary upper class. Very pompous young man, perfectly straight.

Bernard * is thirty-two. He was born and raised in a small conservative New England town. He can't remember how early his homosexual feelings began, but he can remember intense loneliness in his early years. For whatever reason, he waited until his early teens for his first sexual experience, which occurred with an adult man who acted in a teacherly role toward Bernard. Bernard has never had a long-lasting relationship. His pattern is one of intimate contact with another man that generally ends after a year. Because of their inconsistent emotions toward him, Bernard never trusted his parents.

I'm one of those men who does not remember *not* being homosexually stimulated. Before I started masturbating I had a boy baby-sitter, and he would sleep in my bed. I remember going bananas over his body. We used to invent games we would play in our jockey shorts. I used to ride him like a horsey.

I was fourteen when I first went to a Greyhound bus terminal. This guy came over and invited me to his room, and I went. We were undressing, and I'll never forget holding a sock in my hand, saying, "I've never done this before." I didn't know what to do. And he sort of looked at me and said, "Sure!" But finally I got the message across, and he did what I always thought was a wonderful thing. He said, "OK, then I'll show you." And that evening we did everything there was to do. I sucked him, he sucked me, I fucked him, he fucked me, all the normal sexual things short of S and M and water sports.

This guy was very helpful. He said, this is KY, this is how you use it, this is why you use it. Things like that. This is how you suck cock. Don't do that. Do this.

Bernard made a habit of going to the Greyhound bus station after that first experience, and the men he met invariably assumed that he was a hustler. He never asked for money, but they always gave it to him. For a long time Bernard was very indiscriminate, going to bed with the first person who talked to him.

> At first I used to spend the money, but then it got too much. I had no privacy at home, and I was afraid that my mother would find the money and start asking questions. So eventually I would preaddress envelopes and send the money to the Museum of Fine Arts as an anonymous cash donation. I always loved the place.

Sometimes the first sexual experiences, or the most important early experiences, occur with brothers. There is no question that sex between brothers is common, and rarely if ever are parents aware of the sexual contact. In most interviews for this book, the sex was a form of experimentation. There was no report of anyone being forced to have sex with a brother, and by and large these activities stopped abruptly when the straight brother started becoming interested in girls. Bert, in his interview, expressed a casual and emotion-free attitude about sex with his brother and other friends.

Bert is twenty-three and was raised in a farm town in the Midwest. He attended a small school where thirty-two children in eight grades filled the one-room schoolhouse. Bert's first sex occurred at age ten, with his brother, age thirteen. It began with mutual masturbation and sucking to orgasm, but then they progressed to Bert's fucking his brother.

> It was really easy to get something going. My brother and I, we lived on twenty acres of land. We used to go out to the woods and play around, take our clothes off, run through the woods, have sex; some neighbor boys would do the same thing. We'd go in the barn and play around in the hay. Suck each other off. A lot more petting, kissing, touching, feeling with them, but no fucking with friends.

In a few cases a gay boy needed love from his brother as well as sex. Invariably the brother broke off the relationship at adolescence, and the gay boy felt abandoned without understanding why. In these instances the pain of being rejected lasted well into adulthood.

*Chris,** age twenty-one, was born and raised on a farm in a sparsely populated midwestern state.

> Ever since I was old enough to realize that I was sexual, I had fantasies about men. I always dreamed of being with a man. I was probably around ten or eleven when it started.
>
> And I would discuss it with my folks. Look, I have these feelings when I go to bed at night that I want to sleep with a man. Tell me why do I feel this way? And they said, "It's wrong, you don't do things like that." Consequently, for a long time I felt that God had made a mistake, and I was meant to be a woman, in order to sleep with a man.
>
> I began having sex with my brother at night. He was two years older than me. It was mostly mutual masturbation. It was wonderful. I loved it. But as time went by and we both started getting older, my brother finally cut it off because he felt he wanted to relate to girls.
>
> We were extremely close when we were together in bed, and the rest of the time we never talked to each other. It was total separatism when we were away from the bedroom. When we were in the bedroom, it was just a very different, very emotional, very intense thing. I felt very close to him, and I wanted to hold him and kiss him because he was a male. He was about the only person I knew that I could do that with, that would be willing to let me do that, too.
>
> Consequently, I loved him very much for that. He made me feel very good. He had a very gentle touch, and he was somewhat aggressive to me at times, but he never went overboard. He made me feel as if I belonged in this massive scheme of things.
>
> When my brother finally said no, it completely shattered me. I didn't think I was going to be able to go on. I was really scared because I didn't have the security of having him there anymore. I was being told very bluntly and very coldly that, since we were brothers, what we were doing was wrong, and that we were both old enough that it was time to stop. He had to do his thing, find his own life, and I had to find mine. It was very scary.

Chris was teased incessantly in high school because of his effeminacy. It was during this period that his masturbation fantasies took shape.

> They were usually about very macho men being aggressive with me. Big men with hairy chests, much older than me, in their thirties or forties. I would fantasize about them being extremely aggressive with me, throwing me around, just really putting me in my place, so to speak. Just totally dominating me, so to speak. A dominance/submission thing, that's what it was. They would lay on top of me, and they would lick me and caress my body, lick my entire body until I would come.

At sixteen, Chris was raped while hitchhiking; four years later, he was raped again. The rape experience became an obsession and ultimately led to resentment and suspicion toward men.

> The experience tore me up—a lot. After I returned home I was completely withdrawn, celibate for almost a year. I didn't love women. I didn't want to fuck with women. I'd already done that, and I didn't like it. I didn't want to have anything to do with men if they were going to be that way. I had always fantasized about being treated that way, about being raped, and yet when it came right down to it I didn't like it at all.

Chris's experience is not necessarily the same as those of other gay boys raised on a farm. Gays who live on either coast have an idealized image of farm boys and their early lives since freedom and opportunity characterize farm life to the outsider. The following two examples of farm boy sex are more common. In the first example, the sparseness of the population lends an opportunity to experiment with boyish abandon; but in the second, isolation is perceived as a prison. Both are frequent experiences of boys who grew up in rural areas.

Madison,* age twenty-three, is a farm boy who had sex (mutual masturbation and sucking) with a younger brother for a period of about one year. The little brother is now married and a "Jesus freak." As far back as he can remember, Madison used to fantasize about older men, men in their twenties like those who worked on the farm. His first gay experience, outside the experiments with his brother, occurred at age twelve

with his twenty-two-year-old scoutmaster, an affair that lasted
for two years.

Living in a small town has advantages, especially since distances are great and parental observation difficult. As a teenager, Madison slept with almost every boy in town; in some
cases, he had sex with every brother in the same family.

> It started when we were camping. I would always end
> up sleeping with somebody, and we would fool around.
> For some reason I always knew how to get them
> aroused.
> Most of the time it ended up as jacking off—jacking
> each other off. I also started fucking with a friend. I
> don't remember how we started doing it. I just remem-
> ber he'd come over every morning after my mom would
> leave for work. He'd come and climb into bed with me.
> I was about eleven or twelve. The last time I had sex
> with him, I was about sixteen.

At sixteen, Madison had a lover, another student in his high
school who had been voted "Sweetheart of the Year" by the
female students. That relationship ended when Madison refused
an invitation to live with this lover. He went to college instead.

> I thought it would never last with a man, and I didn't
> want to be hurt. I thought it was just sex, that they were
> going to leave when it was finished, just using me. I felt
> very used, like they came to get their rocks off, for
> them, and there was nothing for me. It was different
> with Roger, but it was a small town, and he was so
> afraid of people learning anything. It was so quiet. But
> we did make it at church a couple of times.

At college, Madison began hustling. Eventually, because of
guilt and religious scruples, he married a woman.

Julius * is forty and lives in a very small rural town in the
northern part of the Midwest. He came from a large, poor
farming family, with no running water or toilet facilities in the
house. At the age of six, he began helping his father skid logs
on the farm. He began masturbating in the third grade, usually
to fantasies of the men who worked with his father.

> When I was a second-grader a cousin came to live with
> us. He was eighteen. One day in bed I asked him what
> "fuck" meant, because I had heard it on the play-
> ground, and he showed me. He laid on me and humped,

and then he masturbated and he climaxed. It was the
first time I'd seen come. He said that his brother had
showed him, and I was interested. I was very attracted
to him, very much in love with him. I loved his big
cock. It may not have been an oversize cock, but I was
a second-grader, and when he had an erection it was
big.

I wanted him to hold me. I wanted to touch his body.
He kissed me and he hugged me in bed. Just sleeping
next to him I would have a hard-on. Sometimes I would
wake up in the night and be excited. I would touch him,
get as close to him as I possibly could, and sometimes I
would try to take his cock out of his underwear so that
I could touch it. But I was afraid to because I didn't
know what he might think about it. He only stayed a
month, and I was very sad when he left.

There were a few fleeting attempts on Julius's part to make
contact with some men who worked on the farm, but all of
these were rebuffed. In one case, he was reported to his mother,
who threatened to "cut it off." At the age of thirteen Julius
turned to animals.

I got turned on by the dogs. We had dogs on the farm.
I got excited watching them copulate. Upon exploration, I discovered that the male dogs enjoyed being
jacked off and the female dogs in heat enjoyed being
fucked. I also used the cows and the horses and sheep—
both male and female.

It was in high school that Julius became aware of the "queer"
label, and he tempered his activities. When he finished school,
he longed to leave home and go to a city where he could search
out other gay men. He left for a Rocky Mountain city and
worked there for nine months.

I wanted a father image, somebody older than myself,
middle-aged. Somebody that would have very strong
feelings for me and make me feel like a child, pick me
up and hold me. Let me sit in his lap, tell me everything's all right, that he'd take care of me and provide
for me. I went to lots of bars, but all I ever really got
were diseases. So I came back here where I feel more
relaxed away from other people.

The crowd here is very small. There's a lot of hen-
pecking and bitch-fighting going on, and so consequently all these people don't like this person because

of something they did or something they said. And this
person has ten friends that don't like somebody in this
other crowd. So I live in a hick town and just more or
less avoid the whole thing because I don't like that in
the crowd, either. It's no better than people who trick
fifteen times a night.

I realized that my fantasy isn't readily available, and
in most situations I get better sex from masturbation
most of the time and staying at home. Sometimes with
animals, too.

Coming Out: The Later Years

There are many reasons why certain men will wait for many
years after sexual development to come out into the gay world.
In some circumstances, the man suppresses his homosexuality,
knowing full well the extent of his gayness but refusing to have
gay affairs. Under other circumstances, a man may be totally
unaware of the smoldering fire, feeling only some vague discomfort. But in extreme cases, all sexual feelings are repressed
and the man lives a mostly asexual life.

Geography is also important for coming out. There are
areas of the country that are geographically isolated, in which
information about homosexual feelings or experiences is never
openly discussed. In such a place, a gay boy is likely to learn
later than his city friends of his homosexuality and be more
likely to believe it an aberration. The following two midwesterners live in the same small town, nestled in the midst of rural
"cowboy land." The closest city is a town of 20,000 people.
There are no gay bars in this particular state, and there seems
to be no gay community. The two men reported here, Russell
and Joseph, have never met, even though they live within a
few miles of one another. Both demonstrate how geographical
isolation interferes with accepting homosexuality.

Russell is twenty-five. He was born and raised in a midwestern
state in the midst of wide canyon country. By the time he was
five, his father was an alcoholic, and later his mother began
to drink as well. "She couldn't leave him," Russell said, "so she
joined him." He has been living with a lover (his first) for
eleven months.

When I was in my senior year in high school I couldn't

stand to be around other people. So a week after I graduated I moved into the canyon, two and a half miles inside the canyon, with no people around. At the time I didn't know why, I just had to, and I didn't want to know why. I just knew I had to get away from everybody. I always knew that there was something going on with me. The fact is, I was getting away because I was a homosexual, because I wasn't feeling good about myself.

The time in the canyon was like trying to say, "OK, well you've got to get yourself excited about women," because all of my fantasies when I jacked off were about men. Once in a blue moon I could somehow fit a woman in there.

Then there was a flood in town, and a lot of loose people moved into the canyon. They were young people my age, so I became friends with them. There were women who took off their clothes in front of me and did everything for me, and I didn't get it. As I looked back on the situation a few months later, I got beet-red in the face and thought, "My God, how obvious can it be?"

Last year I came back for Christmas, and one night my older brother and I were alone in the room, and he went down to get himself a six-pack of beer, downed it real fast, and said, "What would you think if I were to tell you that I'm gay?" And it was like a rush went through my body, and I just sat there for a while. Then I said, "I'm gay, too. I think I'm gay, too." I cried all the way back to the canyon. I had been fighting the fact of being a homosexual for years. I had become a recluse. I went out to the very end of the canyon and lived there and never came into town for anything. I'd fought it for years. But when my brother told me that he was gay, then I thought that I can be, too, because I had always looked up to him, and I saw him as an example in the family.

Joseph is twenty-four. He was born and raised in the Midwest. Like Russell's, his parents were alcoholic. He had his first sexual experience only a year ago. He has not yet repeated it.

I've never told anyone my masturbation fantasies. I guess you would call it a fetish. The fantasies I had would be sort of on a western level. I thought a Marlboro man type of look, very macho. That sort of thing appealed to me.

> When I was very little I always wanted a pair of cowboy boots, but I couldn't get my father and mother to buy me a pair. They claimed it would hurt my feet. Around junior high I finally ripped off a pair from this other kid's house.

Joseph continued to masturbate to his leather and western fantasies throughout adolescence. He was certain that no one else had such fantasies. The homosexual label was absent until college, when Joseph began to have fears that he was a "double pervert." The fact that he began to see himself not only as a homosexual but also as a western fetishist led him to attempt suicide. One year ago, Joseph met a man, and they had sex.* It was not a fulfilling experience.

> I couldn't enjoy it. It didn't feel good. I suddenly started really looking at him, like, "What am I doing?" I felt like a cheap slut. I felt, "Do I really like this guy, do I know him? I'm using him, and he's using me." And I didn't know if I really cared for that.
>
> But then, after we both paused and were just lying there, I liked the fact that there was another person lying beside me in bed with his arms around me. That was really nice, a really good feeling, I'd never ever done that before.

There are some men whose early lives were devoid of any kind of sexual experience or feelings. These men haven't reported anger at controlling parents or the repression of society. They were simply unaware of any sexual needs in themselves and of the sexuality going on all around them. Myron is a humorous example of this personal sexual repression; Seth reveals that sexual repression occurs in the lives of some farm boys as well.

Myron, age thirty-three, was born and raised in a large midwestern city. He has never had a lover or lived with another man.

> Sex was something I always heard people talk about, but I had absolutely no idea what it involved. I knew there was a way people got together to procreate, but I didn't know much more about it than that.
>
> I can remember that I always wanted to see male statues. I can remember a lot of things that had to do with male nudity that I enjoyed but that was not sexual

* They met at a gay dance held once a year. It was the only gay social event in the state.

to me. I'd blocked that part of it, somehow.

I must have led a very sheltered life. I did not have a lot of friends. The friends I did have did not talk about sex a lot, or when they did I just tuned them out.

The first time I ever came, I was twenty-two. I was a security guard in the Air Force. I had been moved to Okinawa during the Vietnam conflict, and I was guarding tankers fueling bombers on their way to bomb something. At this point in my life, I guess the suppression in my life was really taking its toll.

I was on post one dark night, and I got the idea that I wanted to walk the post nude. I stripped down naked and then put back on my web belt with the gun at my side, and my rifle over my shoulder, and my boots. And I walked one length of the post and back, and on the way back I had a hard-on. It was a real turn-on. I was marching naked, with my guns and boots and a hard-on.

I was worried, very worried. I didn't want to get caught. I started running back. There weren't many people around, but I was paranoid, and I started running to get my clothes, thinking, "Why am I doing this? This is crazy. I'm going crazy." And I accidentally brushed my hand against my hard-on, and I came.

I had never experienced it before, so it was a terrifying experience as well as a wonderful one. I really remember being frightened. "What have I done?" I thought. But at the same time I wanted to know how to get that feeling again. And that's how I started experimenting with masturbation.

From then on Myron masturbated at least six times a day. Just three months after his first ejaculation, Myron was on a base in Texas when a fourteen-year-old boy began to follow him around. For days the boy would follow Myron and talk with him.

About the fourth day he asked me if he could give me a blow job. I said, "Of course not." Plain and simple, you know? I probably was terrified of it. I don't know. I had never had any sex up to this point. I would have liked to see him nude, but the idea of doing something hadn't occurred to me.

I had heard of blow jobs. I had heard people talk favorably about them. I had a vague idea of what they were. I knew it involved mouths and cocks.

One day I took a shower, and I had a towel wrapped

around me. He said, "I really want to give you a blow job," and by this time I was getting very curious, so I said, "OK, but I want to see you nude." So he took off his clothes. He was nude, and I had a towel wrapped around me. And he said, "Just lay down on the bed, and I'll do the rest." And so I laid down on the bed, and he did the rest.

After it was over he wanted to talk about it. He asked me if I liked it. I said, "Yeah." He said, "Will you let me do it again?" I said, "No!" And the next time was six years later.

Seth,* fifty-two, was born and raised on a farm. He and his lover of twenty-five years live in a small southern town with a population of 5,000. They have no problems with the local community.

I missed all that stuff. When I read Dr. Kinsey I realized I missed out on all the things farm boys are supposed to do. Sheep never interested me at all.

When I was young I kind of felt that sex was overrated. It just wasn't the big thrill I had anticipated. I developed a couple of strong attachments with boys at the university, but nothing happened there.

My first sex was at nineteen when I was stationed in Honolulu, in the Army-Navy Y. I went down to the men's room and read the graffiti on the wall, and it came to me that that was what I wanted. That turned me on. The next day I had my first sex.

The next ten days I learned a lot of sex because I was too shy to say no. Anything they wanted to try on me; I really didn't know how to say no.

In any group of "late bloomers" there are some men who are homophobic—men who hate themselves for their own homosexuality and frequently hate the men with whom they have sex. Some of the accounts of geographical isolation and sexual repression noted above are examples of this from the teen years, but these men overcame their initial fears and depressions. They were able to perceive them as childhood errors that could be abandoned for mature sexuality. It's not clear exactly how they did this, perhaps through the warmth and kindness of the men they met.

The two gay men whose interviews follow are still homophobic, still angry at their homosexual selves. Their lives are filled with personal conflict and fraught with pain and loneliness. The third man changed only after falling in love with another man.

Simon is twenty-five, a student at a southern university located in a town not far from where he was born. He has very mixed feelings about homosexual men. His early homophobic response was to fall in love with a straight man, a common trait of homophobic gays, and a temporary one for some men during the coming-out process.

When I was a sophomore in college, my roommate was a swimmer—college swim team—and he was straight. He and I were very close. I didn't realize at the time what was going on. I had a terrible crush on him; I was madly in love with him.

Sometimes he'd go away, and I'd sleep in his bed. It was a very erotic situation. We were living in a small room. We were just talking one night, and we must have gotten around to sex. I said, "Let's masturbate. We're here in this little room. We don't have to worry about being caught or seen." I said I just wanted to feel free to masturbate. He said, "That sounds like a good idea." So we were both lying there with the lights out, jerking off in our beds.

We had been talking that night, very heavy things, talking about our feelings. It just got very intense, and the floodgates were opened. He said something. If I were a homosexual. I said I'm not sure. I was mortified. I wanted to go on with it. I never slept with him, just jerked off. It was like everything just short of physical contact.

One night he wanted to sleep with a girl, and I said I'd be happy to sleep upstairs. He said no, she's going to leave. I asked him ten more times, and he kept saying no. So I went to bed. After a while they got into bed, fooling around. After a while the clothes started flying out. I don't think they were actually screwing. I was lying there so jealous; I really hated her. I don't think I slept a wink that whole night; I was angry and envious, but I was very careful not to show it. I really loved him, and I still do. I'm going to be at his wedding this summer.

The thing that concerns me is—I wonder is that kind of thing possible with a gay man. I wonder if what I'm looking for, the closeness, is something that I can't have. I don't seem to feel the same thing toward the typical gay people I meet. Is it a hopeless mismatch?

We can't find in each other the thing we really need.
It's kind of discouraging. I don't know if it's true or not.

Eric, twenty-eight, was born and raised in a well-known
southern beach community. He has never had a steady lover.
His first gay experience was at nineteen, and it was not emotionally or sexually fulfilling.

> Even now when I think about sex—I'll be in circum-
> stances and I'll think about it—somebody's edging up
> to me to be involved, and I find out that it's their first
> experience, and I say, "Good-bye." I won't. I don't
> want to put somebody in a situation where they may
> regret what they did afterwards and they're sort of ex-
> perimenting.
> First of all, I don't think I've totally accepted myself
> at this point. The difficulties living a gay life or what-
> ever. I think the main mixed feeling is that I'd still
> like to get married and have a family. Children are
> important to me. I've thought even in the past to adopt
> kids. It's part of life to help fulfill the life of other
> people and help someone grow. Like planting a tree.
> I came from a family that didn't relate to one another
> very well. I was told I was loved, but I sat over a dinner
> table last night with a bunch of people who said very
> little.
> In a social manner I often come across as being aloof
> and cold. I can walk down the street as close to a non-
> lascivious manner as one can get, and there's nothing
> going by.
> I'd like a lover who can communicate honestly,
> openly, a sense of humor, a positive person, sensitive
> to people in general. Sensitive, able to grow. I'd just
> have to say mature. Age isn't important. Generally I've
> been with someone who is a little older than me. In re-
> cent years it would have been my age. Somebody I've
> felt could have more experience than me, could teach
> me, in terms of life.

Clayton * is thirty-nine. He was born, raised, and still lives in
New York City. Though he has lived happily with his lover for
the past twenty-one years, he went through a common homophobic pattern after high school. He became "trade" for money,
a part-time hustler. It was only after meeting and falling in love
with his current lover that the homophobic pattern was altered.

Right after high school I was palling around with this

married man. He used to take me to the naval bars around the navy yard. We used to go out and drink beer. He introduced me to these so-called queers who'd do us and give us five or ten dollars; then we'd go out and drink all night and take women home.

It was strictly letting a queer suck you off. Some of it was fun; some of it was horrible. But he was there, and I was young, and I would say to myself, if he's going to do it, how could I not?

I found that once in a while I'd have the urge; I'd go back to the sailor bars, hoping something would happen. But I would never do it for nothing. I realize now that it was because I had to prove to myself that I was only doing it for the money. But the truth is, I was enjoying it.

I joined the naval reserve even before I finished high school. I was still seeking out people with money to pay. And at this point already I was more experienced, so I didn't have to go to the sleaze places. And I was still having relationships with women, too. If I got twenty-five dollars, I would spend ten dollars on a woman. I don't know why. I guess again I was proving to myself that I wasn't a homosexual.

I spent two years in the navy, and a few months after I came out I met Irving [his lover]. After the first night, which was not sex, but after the first night meeting this person, I knew I was a homosexual.

Young Lovers

The accounts presented above were mainly the experiences of youthful sexuality without emotional attachment and love. The reports that follow are quite different. In their early childhood years, these men fell in love with another boy or man. At no other period in life does love between two males seem so absolute and uncompromising. Young boys fortunate enough to have had an early lover have a distinct advantage; they understand the power and joy of emotional and sexual compatibility. Generally speaking, boys who have had affairs with other boys find love in adulthood easily; they also appear to be less emphatic about sexual demands on a lover, tending to place the quality of the relationship above sexual perfection (which does not mean that they are uninterested in sex).

At no time did I find an adolescent relationship that lasted into the adult years, although I frequently heard of them. The general pattern of these young affairs seems to be a period of emotional and sexual intensity, terminated abruptly because of parental interference or the fears of one of the partners about the newly discovered label of "homosexual." As a result, young lovers almost always learn early about emotional loss, and it was moving to see how often tears appeared during the interviews when men began to talk about an early love affair.

Phil * is thirty-two. He was born and raised in a small desert town in the West, and he has been living with his lover for the past two years. At sixteen, Phil began a relationship with a friend that lasted for five years. It started when he had dinner at the friend's house, followed by sex because "It was the most natural thing to do." Then came double-dating with the local girls. After taking the girls home, Phil and his friend would make love to one another.

> We never spoke of it. For at least five years. Sex was something we strictly did at night and never talked about. And the double-dating of girls, somehow it was important to us to keep that facade up, even with each other.
>
> Most of it was masturbation. Toward the end, the last year or so, some oral sex, finally some anal sex.
>
> I went to college a year ahead of him, and he came to live with me and try to pass a qualifying course to enter college. That was creating a strain, more so for him than for me. I think that by that time I was beginning to come around a little to the fact of the gay thing, but he wasn't. I was beginning to accept it, let's put it that way.
>
> Suddenly in the dead of night he packed his bags and left to join the navy. I caught up with him, and we had a five-hour conversation. It all came out that he was scared to death that he wasn't going to hack it in college. There must have been some references in our conversation to the gay thing. I can't recall how we referred to it, some oblique way, and we both knew what we meant. I'm sure it must have been in the conversation because I did have an awareness that it was pressing in on him hard.

The discussion did no good. The frightened lover joined the navy, and they never saw each other again.

Like many other young men of his age, Phil was only vaguely aware of his homosexuality. A guilt-free pleasure in homosexual experiences, both emotional and sexual, is frequently found in young men and boys without the realization that the label "homosexual" applies to them. This paradox might be explainable by the stereotype that all homosexuals are like women, and since these boys know they aren't like women, they may therefore come to the conclusion that they can't be homosexual. But there was a point at which Phil suddenly and dramatically became aware of his gayness. He had been called up for the draft and, during the physical examination, was asked to fill out a questionnaire.

Have you ever had chicken pox, mumps, measles, and all that jazz. And the very last question was homosexuality.

I had been checking mumps and so on. And I thought, "Yes, by God, I am." So I checked that box. We turned it in immediately thereafter—no chance to change my mind—and it was really an impulsive decision. It was probably the first time I had ever faced myself, really come to grips with it.

I thought, "My God, I've really lost my senses. What are they going to do when they know I'm queer?" We're all standing in a room, and a sergeant is sitting there at a desk, and you line up, and the sergeant has the exam forms, and as every person comes up he wants to know when you had these diseases (chicken pox, mumps). And he says this in a loud voice in front of the whole room.

I'm about eighth or ninth in the line and just about to shit. My God, he's going to go through the measles and mumps and then say, "Are you a faggot?" You can imagine the turmoil I was going through. I walked up that line, not knowing what the hell to do. Outside the window they're marching, "Hup, two, three, four." And sure enough, that's what he said. He went through all the things, and then he stopped dead in his tracks. The whole room got quiet because he was saying absolutely nothing. Then he said, "Oh! So you have ho-mo-sex-u-al tendencies." He got total attention. You could have heard a pin drop. And I'm standing there just freaking out. I said, "Yes."

Then he said—I'll never forget this—"Are you active or passive?" And I thought, "Active or passive? What the hell does that mean?" Oh, I thought, I'd better make it active. I'd better make it like I do it all the time. "I'm very active."

Part of the reason that youngsters can participate in gay sex but not define it as homosexual is related to the idiosyncratic way they arbitrarily say that one thing, like sucking, is OK, but another, like kissing, isn't. Kissing is probably one of the most significant signs of homosexuality in youngsters, and as long as the parties don't kiss, with all the "mushy" stuff, there is no conflict. Sex and love continue but are defined as conventional masculinity. Loran's experience with a childhood lover is a good example of this.

Loran * is twenty-seven. He's a "navy brat" who was quite content with his homosexuality. For the past eight years he and his lover, Nathan, have lived together in New York City. At fourteen he met his childhood lover.

> Drew was my best friend. I met him through school and the Boy Scouts. He was a close neighbor. At that point in my life there was nothing I wanted to do that we couldn't do together, so that we shared almost everything. It was so easy to be with him.
>
> It started with the two of us masturbating, looking at *Playboys*. And then it led to more intimate contact, anal intercourse, but never any kissing. The first sex just sort of happened, mutual masturbation. I wanted it to happen, and Drew seemed to. We had anal intercourse almost immediately. That was what dominated the relationship, both ways.
>
> I tried to kiss him, but he wouldn't allow it. His attitude was no, no, we don't want to do that. That will make us queer. I think this is what he actually felt. And he would never allow that kind of affection, and yet we had a touching relationship. My consciousness at that time was that gays were really individuals who wanted to be women, and I had no desire in that direction. I didn't know anybody who was gay.
>
> With Drew, we would go out with women and come home and have sex, or we would go camping and have sex at night. There was no sense of guilt or remorse about it at all. That sticks out in my mind now. It's really amazing to me to hear all the horror stories about growing up gay. With me there was never any sense of trauma, never any reservation, and even though

Drew wouldn't let me kiss him, I could go out and kiss women.

The relationship between Loran and Drew ended when Drew became interested in girls.

There are some boys, like some adult men, who build loving relationships easily. They always seem to find the best traits in another boy and respond to their special friend's needs effectively. Mike was that kind of boy.

Mike is thirty-four, born and raised in the East, and in all of his adult life has never been without a lover, although his love affairs don't last more than a few years. Mike's experience shows us how an interest in a particular physical type can begin during the formative sexual years and continue into adulthood. At least it did for him.

> My first sexual experience was with my cousin Freddy. It started when I was six and Freddy was eight. He was a triangular, well-built boy with a Neanderthal face. We would have sex with a vibrator and masturbate each other with it.
>
> We did some pretty crazy things. We'd tie each other up. The adults would be upstairs, and we'd go downstairs where he'd tie me to a chair with my clothes on, and then he'd take my cock out. Then I'd tie him up. I think I was more interested in his cock because he had a bigger one. Once I can remember we were in my basement, and he got the bright idea we should pee on each other. We didn't do that very much. We'd do a lot of long masturbation, prolonging it, sometimes for hours. I still do.

After one of these prolonged masturbation sessions, Mike's penis was sore, and he asked his mother what he should do. The whole story came out, and Mike was prohibited from seeing Freddy for two years. They never had sex again.

> I was absolutely distraught. It was the worst thing that could have happened. I was like an only child. I had a sister ten years older, my father died when I was five, and my mother had rheumatic fever when I was seven. It was a miserable house for a kid. I had no friends because she wouldn't let me out to play, and Freddy was my only link to the outside world.
>
> After I told my mother, Freddy and I met only at

family gatherings, and then we were very tender. Once we were lying on the grass looking at Whitman's *Leaves of Grass*. We didn't say very much. We sort of said to each other without saying much, "Gee, that was pretty bad." He was still a little angry at me because I told, and yet he forgave me. I remember saying, "Couldn't we do it again?" He said, "No." I don't know how he said it, but what he meant was, "I want to do it with girls." It was really nicely said, but the message came across.

When I was with him before, even after he said no, I'd more or less tell him everything that was going on, except that there was a little distance after the no. I knew I couldn't tell him all that I wanted to do sexually. Sex sort of became a nonsubject with us. But I still longed for the way it was. Just lying down next to each other with as much of your bodies touching as you can and with your hands just feeling lightly the parts of the body. It's like—it's almost literally being very close—and just being like that and moving around a little bit and being very excited by that.

Mike's method of masturbation during those young years was much the same as it is today. He rarely allowed himself to come. When he approached orgasm, he would hold back until the feeling subsided, then continue for hours on end.*

I was waiting for someone else to be there. I'd hold off till someone else came into my life.

Then in seventh grade Mike met Conrad. Their affair lasted for five years. Conrad came from a large and very poor family, and Mike and Conrad would baby-sit for Conrad's younger siblings. Sex started when they put the children to bed; then they'd play strip poker. In the next few months, the children were put to bed earlier and earlier, while the card games got progressively shorter.

We'd spend hours lying next to each other, fondling each other, these enormous erections, just getting a lot of pleasure out of that. We'd love to touch each other's bodies and see how delicately we could do it till the other person would just squirm. Literally just writhing in pleasure—we'd do that for a long time. We kissed, but not very much.

* A technique that could lead to prostate problems.

He looked like some of my later lovers. Smooth body, short cropped hair, tight body, funny face, that character look. A character look in the sense of being a spontaneous nonintellectual or nonmind-oriented person, like a sort of *Lord of the Flies* boy—I mean the one who was the leader of the cult group in the story. Someone like that isn't like me; they're more physical, impulsive. They act more on how they feel. They're good sexually. They throw everything into it.

You know, just about all my lovers have been "Neanderthal"; they all looked something like Freddy.

Only once did I find an example of young lovers who separated without interference from adults. Alan felt that he had to get away from his family. To escape his home, Alan also had to leave his lover.

Alan * is thirty. He was born and raised in rural New England and has been living with his lover for the past two years in New York City.

I had a lover when I was twelve years old. He was two years younger than I was. It was very private, and we were sort of terrified that someone might find out. But we felt a strong attachment. I would call it a lover relationship. It was a very special thing. We only saw each other when we knew we were going to make love. We didn't talk about it, we didn't speak in terms of love necessarily, but it was very passionate. We started thinking in terms of Route 66 type things and cars.

I sort of felt protective in a way, and at the same time he was teaching me things; he was much more open than I was. He liked kissing and hugging and things like that, but then I would want to do something else, take a hike or something, but he would want to continue. We would have sex in the woods, and it would go on for hours.

Where I was living was very rural, hundreds and hundreds of acres of woods. No threat of being caught or anything. We were so isolated in the woods. We would say things like I really love you, but I don't think I ever used the word love.

I'm really grateful that this relationship happened. I really felt good about it. I still do. Grateful in that I was very young and it was very natural; there wasn't so much guilt or fear of being caught. It was because it was natural that I'm grateful.

He was really cute. I really saw beauty in him. He

was a really nice person, too, soft-spoken. And I guess
I'm grateful because of the fact that it was part of my
childhood, and it is something that I can look back on.
When I left home, when I ran away (I was fourteen),
I stopped by to tell him. He was the only person who
knew where I was going or what I was doing. It was
the last thing I did before I left. I felt badly about
leaving him, but I knew that I had to. I was crying on
the way down to the highway to start hitchhiking. I
wanted him to go with me, but then I didn't. The Route
66 thing—leaving. But there was something real about
it. It was more than just a fantasy. It was a real conflict. I really sort of wished that he had come with me.
I didn't ask him, but in the back of my mind I thought
it would be nice, but I thought it was impractical, too.

Most men can remember special friends in their early sexual
years, as well as the wish to develop sexual and emotional relationships with them. During the interviews many men wondered where their childhood loves were today, what kinds of lives
they lived; they especially wondered whether friends and early
lovers turned out gay themselves. Two men in this sample had
the opportunity of seeing their childhood lovers again in adult
life, and their experiences are revealing.

Steve * is fifty-four. Born in the rural Midwest, he was raised
on an Indian reservation where his parents worked for the Indian Service. From the age of eight to fourteen he had a love
affair with Kevin. They slept together, caressed each other, and
indulged in mutual masturbation and oral sex. Kevin's parents
sent him away from the reservation to a Seventh Day Adventist
religious school, and when he returned he told Steve that sex was
something they shouldn't have.

There were many elements present in our relationship.
I loved him dearly. He was my closest friend, my total
confidant. I was very much in love with him, and it
was physically pleasurable also.
Then I met him again fifteen years later. I was in
Denver, living with a former lover. Kevin came to Denver, had contacted my parents and gotten my phone
number and called me. We met. It was terribly depressing. He didn't look like I remembered him. Our
relationship was rather strained. I believe he knew that
I was living in a homosexual relationship. He was married and raising a family in the meantime. We seemed

to have very little in common, and I felt sort of depressed. The whole meeting—I would rather have not had it.

Kevin made it clear that he was gay, heterosexually married, and unhappy.

Pat * is forty years old. He's the only child of a farm family from the South. His parents were poor; there was no water or electricity in the house. At thirteen, Pat started a love affair with Roger, who was also thirteen. It lasted for the next three years.

> We were sleeping together at his house or mine three or four nights a week. We were both in the band and went on these great trips where we would sleep together.

The relationship involved a great deal of kissing and affection as well as sex, and Pat reports that he was well aware of being very much in love with Roger, but totally unaware of the word "gay" or its meaning.

> When I was sixteen, all of a sudden I came into biology lab, and he had moved. He had taken a girl partner. And he wouldn't speak to me. It was terrible. I went berserk. I really made a scene right there in the classroom because he wouldn't speak to me at all. For the next three or four weeks I was in a living hell. Then I slowly got over it, and I began looking for other boys, but I couldn't find any.
>
> About ten years later I went back home to visit. And I had this terrible toothache, and I went looking for a dentist, and there was this sign—with his name on it. So I just walked into the office. And the secretary said, "Why, yes, if it's an emergency he can see you." And I walked in, and there he was.
>
> He gave me this look and got me into the dentist's chair. When he was working on my tooth he said, "You know, I'm married. I have kids. And I'm absolutely miserable. I wish I had known."
>
> He's gay, but he really fought it. And then he explained the whole thing—what happened in the biology lab. Some of his friends told him that they knew I was queer and he had to stop hanging around with me —and he was a very macho image. He just made up his mind not to be gay, and he fought it for several years until he got married.

In both cases cited, the childhood lover turned out to be gay, but there is no reason to believe that this is always the case. It can be assumed that the greater the emotional commitment expressed between childhood sex partners, the greater the possibility that one or both will become gay adults. However, the amount of sex between them is not a good indicator for predicting adult homosexuality.

Observations on Coming Out

If we step back for perspective, we may see that these stories provide insight into various stages in the development of the gay boy into the gay man. The earliest and most perplexing observations bear on the origins of a boy's homosexuality. There is disagreement in the professional community over this. Some believe homosexuality begins very early in life, while others believe it blossoms after puberty. The data gathered in this study clearly indicate that homosexual development begins at an early age and that it is different from the heterosexual development of the straight boys who are early sex partners. It precedes the labeling process. Nor is there sufficient cognitive development for an "identity" of the homosexual with all the expected behavior that any sexual identity demands. My suspicion is that the rules of behavior that are tied to the role of "homosexual," the identity of a person qualitatively different from other men, are preceded by the early experiences of the gay boy, and not the other way around. Those who insist on believing that homosexuality is formed later and is therefore changeable at a later date are listening closely to the sexual experiences but not to the emotional hunger of a gay boy—his desire to love another boy and to shut off emotional communication with the outside world in a way that no straight boy does.

Early sex play includes almost every possible variety of sexual activity. Most boys seem to be masturbating even before puberty —though some learn later with a friend. They also participate in genital sucking, anal intercourse, and tying each other up. When they get bored with this, they sometimes piss on each other. The forbidden is alluring.

Most boys seem to demand constant excitement and exploration. They insist on it for one simple reason—it's fun. There is rarely any indication that they think there is anything wrong with it. Their problem is more practical; they know they need to avoid the prying eyes of disapproving adults. Adults always interfere with the excitement of childhood—the dangerous, adventurous aspects of childhood, when children invent games which they know instinctively no adult will condone. The forbidden aura probably makes the games that much more exciting.

For boys (gay or straight), early sex play seems perfectly "natural"—just another game to while away the time. Adults describing these early encounters never suggest that as boys they thought of them in any other way. Pejorative words come later when the boy learns that adults have very strong feelings about how the body should or should not be used. Some boys learn this earlier than others, and some care more than others.

This time of childhood and adolescence is the playground of later love, and the lessons learned will be played out in the adult years. A boy learns to judge himself and others by discovering the good boy/bad boy dichotomy. It begins very early, when the toddler starts to knock things over or spills his food; he is taught that some things he does are good while others are bad. But in some families no distinction is made between *doing something bad* and *being bad*. As a result, a bad act is viewed as a symptom of inner rot, as an inborn characteristic that needs to be exorcised in the name of goodness and social conformity. In these rigid families the boy grows up believing that he is unworthy of love. In other cases, religious doctrine influences the way he perceives himself. It succeeds in teaching the boy that his body is untouchable, so that when he experiences sexual desires he feels sinful.

Peers also teach the good boy/bad boy dichotomy, but there's more variation in their behavior. While some childhood peers are influenced early by the judgmental attitudes of their parents and religion, other peers are experimenting with their young lives and daring to be adventurous. Boyhood friends can alleviate a great deal of suffering for the youngster by teaching him new ways to view the world and his body. In some cases, they can completely turn around the deleterious effects of the most repressive family.

One of the characteristics of boyhood sex is its reciprocity. There are no active and passive roles. They may say, "You do it first," but the boys never think of their sex play as either masculine or feminine. They have hardly learned enough of adult rules to make such judgments. Later they learn the association between gender and sexual activity and will either play or reject the appropriate roles, but in the early years they try everything they can think of. They haven't yet learned that the "active" role is synonymous with power and control, and that giving up this status will lead to humiliation by their peers.

Straight boys are also interested in playful sex. From their accounts of sexual play, one would think that every straight boy has had some boyhood experiences with another boy. Except for kissing, which does not appeal much to some children, straight boys usually do the same things the gay boys do. Sex is merely the expression of powerful physical needs. For instance, sex between brothers has always been common; it includes mutual masturbation, sucking, and fucking, often without the slightest need to develop a real sense of affection beyond the brotherly relationship. In fact, brothers may have sex during the night and fight with each other during the day. It doesn't seem strange to them since no emotionality is intended by the sex. It is a very distinct male trait to be able to separate sex from emotional commitment, and boys appear to learn the distinction early.

What is the difference then between gay and straight boys? Gay boys differ from their playmates, but not in their sexual behavior. In general, gay boys are serious about the business of physical contact in a way straight boys are not. They feel different from their friends. The claim made by some gay men that they were aware of their homosexuality at an early age appears to be true. Listening carefully to their stories, one realizes that a deep sense of love and commitment often accompanied sexual interest in another boy. There are many references to tender feelings toward older boys and young men, and here, too, there is a desire for closeness that is qualitatively different from what one would expect from straight boys. Straight boys can play sexually for a while and then give it up; it is merely play to them, merely "getting it off." Gay boys also seem to see and study the male body more closely than their straight counterparts. They are not only genitally aroused; if they could (and lots of them try while others learn very early not to), they would admire the entire body as a source of pleasure. But many of them appear to recognize just how different their motivations are from those of their straight friends, and one of two things invariably occurs. One type of gay boy will become an initiator, leading the other into game playing more deeply; he is the one who will insist that they remove the undershirt placed as a barrier between mouth and penis while sucking, the one who's constantly inventing new strategies for getting friends over to the house for sex play. He is insatiable, oftentimes manipulating, ever persistent, and never takes no for an answer; whatever rules he may have learned about sex from adults are forgotten or rejected outright. The other type of boy is more circumspect. He, too, knows how different he is from his straight friends, but, instead of being excited by them, he is reluctant to exhibit his interest in their bodies. He shies away from them, while never forgetting how much he wants them. This boy always feels that something is not right, although frequently he doesn't know exactly what. He realizes that he is more serious than his friends, but, in contrast, he feels he has to hide it. This stratagem occurs to most gay boys at some stage after puberty when their straight counterparts are starting to get interested in girls and modeling their behavior after adult males.

Some gay boys, however, begin the concealing process considerably earlier, experiencing a constant tension between their desire to feel and hold their friends and their need to keep this hidden. Consequently, they tense up, don't take chances, think a lot before making a move and, by the time they've thought it out, either have decided against it or lost the moment. As adults, memories of fumbled opportunities plague them.

As the gay boy ventures beyond the family circle and into the world of other boys, he is forced to meet the challenge of athletics. Curiously enough, what delights straight boys often repels and depresses gay ones; it is extraordinary how consistently gay boys reject athletic competition. The reasons are obscure. They reject the kinds of sports so highly prized in our competitive world— team and body-contact sports like baseball, football, and basketball. There are gay athletes, as we all know, but most gay boys refuse to play the competitive body sports that are taught so obsessively in our schools.

These gay boys might be more interested in athletics if they were only a mode of self-development in which he could compete against himself, rather than with a group of foul-mouthed, bullying boys. No doubt many straight boys are also uninterested in body-contact sports and are as ill-served by the schools as gay boys. Professionals who have noticed how often gay men refused athletics as boys have not been aware that their observation is as much a comment on the incompetence of the schools' athletic programs as it is on the nature of the gay boy.

The onset of puberty is often marked by the first orgasm, and boys seldom know what it is. The first ejaculation is not only a surprise, but more often than not it is interpreted as a sign of illness. Boys think it is "sick piss," "cancer of the penis," or any of a host of other ailments that mysteriously appear in the midst of previous good health. Few men report knowing what it was, yet they invariably overcame their apprehension, tried again, and the pleasure of the orgasm finally convinced them that it was a good thing.

At puberty, a gay boy's experimentation may end or increase, depending on a number of factors. Probably the single most important is whether the boy feels comfortable among his peers. The boy who is comfortable will continue the experimentation with another boy or boys—the famous "circle jerks." This degree of comfort is probably more comprehensive than mere sexual comfort. It is a general measure of how well a boy relates and whether he feels equal to his peers. This all-around comfort makes sexual play more acceptable for all, and these boys are most likely to continue this adventurous spirit into adulthood, demanding a high degree of physical sexual satisfaction from lovers. The other kind of boy—one who upon entering puberty feels more distant from his playmates—is more likely to make up for his lack of experience through fantasy, with the likelihood that his fantasies will be more romantically directed than those of his reckless friends. Of course, these are general directions that are intensified or diminished by the influence of the other factors that ultimately affect adult behavior.

A second important factor is the boy's concern with parental approval. Some boys not only know "it feels good" but have every intention of continuing their sexual experimentation regardless of what any adult thinks of it. Perhaps they have their own set of standards of acceptable behavior, or maybe no standards at all, but they seek out sex and avoid parental interference. Other boys react differently. They filter their feelings through the adult network, and even if no one has explicitly said, "Don't do that," they know their parents wouldn't approve and reject their own feelings as bad. The straight boy who wants to participate in sex with friends has no psychological problem about it. If he can't do it because his parents wouldn't approve, he is merely disappointed; he doesn't feel the pain of the young gay, who not only wants the sexual release but solace and affection as well. The gay boy pays a price for knowing that he needs the kind of sexual contact that has been labeled bad even before words like "queer" and "fag" have any meaning for him.

Turning to boys who went beyond experimentation and engaged in sustained affairs, we find that, without exception, every man interviewed who had an emotional investment in another boy saw the relationship end, almost always because the other boy either rejected it or moved away. The gay adolescent wants nothing more than to continue his sexual and emotional relationship with the friend; but the friend is most often probably straight, and at some point he will decide that he can no longer continue to relate sexually with a male. Certainly most straight boys begin to become sexually aroused by girls, yet heterosexual interest cannot suffice as an explanation of the sudden rejections straight boys deal the gay boy. The straight boy realizes that, whether he goes with girls or not, he must stop all same-sex fooling around. The adult masculine creed demands it. By this point, sexual roles (i.e., active and passive) have become connected to the ideology of masculine and feminine, and the straight boy's reputation, or worse, his own sexual status, is endangered by continuing this activity.

In addition, we have already learned from the stories of young lovers who saw their childhood partners again many years later that the rejecting "straight" boy may also be gay but refuses his role because of community pressure. The need for peer approval, the acceptance of religious regulations, and the fear of disappointing one's parents all contribute to rejecting the gay lover and the gay role. But gay boys do not understand it. They have been rejected, and the rejection is never forgotten. This is the moment when the gay boy is most apt to feel that there is something wrong with him, some flaw in his character. He mulls over the counts against him—the rejection by his loving friend, the distance from his father, and the constant harangue about sex and sin. At an earlier age he thought that his behavior was sinful; now he comes to regard his character as sinful. It is here that he seeks the guidance of other males. For gay boys the search is crucial and a role model very hard to find.

Gay boys frequently look for older men to show them what being gay is about or to be initiated into gay sex. For many, it is a necessary part of the coming-out process, a transition from childhood to adulthood, and not the beginning of a lifelong pattern of sex with older men. Some boys look for an adult who will assure them that their feelings are acceptable. Frequently, the boy is not primarily interested in sex, although here, too, variations exist. He wants reassurance, and though some boys are able to get it just by talking with an adult, others can accept it only when sex is included. The sex is often irrelevant and, except as sexual lessons for the boy, not of great importance. But the comfort and reassurance are of monumental significance. The boy trusts and learns from the man, offering his loyalty in return. Most boys who have had such an experience go on to find a partner their own age.

There are cases of sexual exploitation as well. Not all men are considerate of the feelings of the adolescent, and though most gays do not exploit the young, there are those who do. Although there is some reason to believe that some of the exploitative men are straight, it's almost impossible to be certain whether a particular adult in someone's experience was gay or straight. Exploitation is more democratic, and an exploiter is seldom concerned with the sex or sexual orientation of the exploited. Being exploited by an adult man does not inhibit homosexuality in a boy, even when the experience is particularly brutal, but it does create a mistrust of adults, particularly of men. When it happens to a gay boy, the attitude of mistrust is generalized to include all men. When such a boy becomes an adult, he may be inhibited sexually and ready to do battle at a moment's notice. If he's wise, this kind of boy will choose a gentle lover who will allow trust to develop over time, instead of demanding it quickly and driving the boy away.

We are left with two other phenomena that originate in childhood: the homophobic gay man and the sexually unaware gay. The homophobic gay is quite easy to identify. He adores the high school athletes, wishes he could be like them, and believes that homosexual men are incapable of love and feeling. He is sure his life would be worthwhile if only that straight man he loves would get in bed with him. This seldom happens, but the obsessive wish continues, sometimes for years. Another variation on this theme is the "If I love men, then I must be a woman" interpretation of gayness. This changed gender interpretation is clearly an indication of a belief that a man cannot love another man. A third homophobic reaction, probably the most common, is the "I don't like those feminine types" statement heard so often, especially in the gay business community. It is a reflection of one of the most oppressive aspects of male culture—condescension toward "softness" and the "womanly." Since all these methods of rejecting gay men are also modes of rejecting a part of oneself, they can be viewed as equally homophobic, though some are more incapacitating than others.

Finally, there are the sexually unaware, the men who at the age of twenty or twenty-five "suddenly" discover they are interested in men. Examples abound, though most gays from cities such as New York find it incredible that such people actually exist. They believe a man can suppress his homosexuality but not be unaware of it. They are wrong. Talking with gay men from other geographical areas, men who grew up in environments less conducive to examining one's sexual life, it is apparent that men can be prevented from even knowing that they are gay. This is particularly true in rural communities far from the centers of urban life. It happens where the ability to acquire information about the world is tightly controlled.

Growing up requires a boy to define the ways he is similar to and different from others in his community. He must also learn the degree to which differences in behavior are tolerated and the punishments meted out for undesirable behavior. In a sense, the community defines his psychological, vocational, educational, and sexual alternatives. These alternatives will be embodied by various members of the community. In a heterogeneous community, one in which many different religious groups, life-styles, and socio-economic levels are represented, the sexual training given the boy by the family has limited effect. For instance, take an adolescent boy living in the heart of New York City. In his apartment house are dozens of boys his own age, from families with different religious and ethnic backgrounds, and he learns a little about all of them. His school fellows are even more diverse, encompassing boys and girls of all ethnic, racial, and social groups. He spends a good deal of time going with his family or his friends' families on trips and vacations, is exposed to cultural events, and, if religious, is likely to have a sophisticated version of those beliefs. Tremendously varied news sources, from the multitude of radio and TV stations to newspapers and magazines, are available to him. With such an array of information and opportunities for experience, the family of such a boy can hardly control his mind or behavior, except in the most limited way. He not only sees alternatives but tries them, and if his family objects, there will be other adults to applaud him.

It is quite different in other sections of the country, particularly the Midwest, although any small town or rural area can limit information about alternatives for its population. Information is hard to get, and the potential gay boy fails to learn about his sexuality. There are many communities where the population is extremely homogeneous. In religion, they are all members of the same church, be it Baptist, Pentecostal, or any other fundamentalist group.*

Radio and TV in these homogeneous communities reflect the values of the area. Very little, if any, diversity can be seen on the local TV stations, since they refuse to broadcast any program that might offend their audience. The schools allow no diversification, and teachers in homogeneous communities are often less prepared educationally than their big-city counterparts. The school is not likely to teach anything that conflicts with the local morality, and teachers are watched closely by parents and church groups.

In such areas, the teachings of the families are heavily reinforced. In a sense, the entire community is an extended family, and everywhere the boy travels in his town he hears the same message and the same justifications for the required behavior

---

* The fundamentalist religious groups differ from the standard popular religions; they reject church tradition, the writings of the church fathers, and in a sense are highly anti-intellectual, relying on "testimony" as the proof of God's power. The educational training of the ministry in these religions falls below that of the major religions, and tends to be insular.

pattern. When it comes to sex, the message is, "Don't." Sexuality before marriage is viewed as alien, and hysterical, repressive demands are made on the growing child. In the absence of dissenting voices, he internalizes these demands so effectively that he comes to regard sex as a foreign invasion to be warded off.

When information control is enforced so severely that all sexual feelings are smothered, and when premarital sex is damned so feverishly, sexual alternatives seldom enter the thoughts of the youngster. When sex is prohibited and effectively controlled, a person cannot find out who or what he is. Case studies of midwestern and southern adult gays frequently reveal how they married without thinking it strange that they didn't love their wives. Many could not have said at the time whether they were homosexual or heterosexual. They married simply because it was expected. In such a setting it is possible to repress homosexual feelings completely.

Others repress them, but incompletely. A boy may have sex with some married men in anonymous settings, men who are fearful of being discovered by their communities as gay and of suffering as a consequence. In an extreme example, one of my respondents had a long affair with a married man known to him only as "H." This restrained and uptight model of homosexuality can easily convince a boy that it is indeed something alien and unnatural. The community teaches that homosexuals are people who want to be women, and the potential gay boy knows that's not what he wants. He cannot see himself as one of "those" people, and so he easily rationalizes his sexual interests as "a stage," or "I just want some affection from a man because my father was an alcoholic." The masturbation fantasies of men like this are frequently immature, laying stress on affection and tenderness, while the genital component is attenuated or nonexistent.

Communities are changing. The heartland is no longer the walled camp it once was, and homogeneity isn't as complete anymore, even in the smallest of rural towns. Gay liberation organizations have sprung up everywhere. The clergy and teachers are better educated than ever before and therefore exposed to alternative ideas. The coming-out process allows boys to choose gay role models more wisely than in the past, and they can visit the urban gay meccas they hear about so often. Today no one needs to remain in an area that is repressing sexual development. The country is becoming culturally integrated, signaling increased chances for homosexual boys to find men to love. Even those who grew up in repressive areas can learn new ways. We see the interesting phenomenon of young gay men showing older men where to meet other men in the gay community. Those men who take advantage of this aid from the youngsters generally find a new source of strength and a widening of their horizons.

PART TWO

Major Issues

CHAPTER FOUR

Excitement Seekers
and Home Builders

How many painful disillusions would be saved if, instead of thinking themselves obliged to say "I love you"
men would content themselves with saying "I desire
you . . ."

RENE GUYON

The rapture of love consists in feeling ourselves so meta-
physically porous to another person that only in the
fusion in both, only in an "individuality of two," can it
find fulfillment.

ORTEGA Y GASSET

There are two general categories of gay men—excitement seekers and home builders. Not all gay men are totally one or the
other (in fact, most gay men are a combination of both), but
each gay man is usually motivated more in one direction than
the other. An excitement seeker is one who emphasizes novelty
and change, rather than stability and longevity in a relationship,
preferring to evaluate other men on the basis of sexual compatibility. He avoids dull experiences and doesn't accumulate
personal possessions; he values his mobility and independence.
On the other hand, a home builder is one who looks for permanence in a relationship, who wants to plan for the future with
another man. He judges a relationship more by the degree of
intimacy achieved than by the level of sexual excitement.

Excitement Seekers

It is customary in our society to see an excitement seeker
through the Victorian spectacles of psychoanalytic bias: a man
who cannot find another man to love and live with is neurotic
and stunted, with the absence of a lover a "symptom" of his in-

ability to bear the intimacy of love. The assumption, swallowed whole from our heterosexual ancestors and passed on by our parents, is that true health and happiness come only from the partnership of long-lasting love. All this is based solely on fancy, denying all the evidence to the contrary in present-day society.

An alternative to the "mental-health deficiency" theory is one that sees excitement seekers as men with a high degree of masculine trait identification, whose reluctance to commit themselves to domestic love affairs reflects masculine identification rather than neurotic instability. While straight men identify with athletic contests, some gay men identify with the competition in the sexual arena. Both represent a deflection away from the home, emotionality, and permanence and a movement toward variation, competition, and adventure.

The following six men are typical of excitement-motivated gays, each showing how the thrill of sexuality is as important as the physical release.

Adrian is a forty-nine-year-old New Yorker. He came out when he was eleven and quickly began to participate in anal intercourse. Since then, as he puts it, "I have slept with thousands of people." He has been with his current lover for the past eight years and previously had a lover for six years.

> I have a lover, but we don't put any stress on fidelity. That's not the driving force in our life, but we don't lie to each other.
> Marriage is wonderful and warm and affectionate and all kinds of terrific things. One of the things it isn't is exciting, and I guess I just don't want to let go of that excitement. I've never articulated this before, but —I love the hunt. I love going out finding sex. I love cruising. I love going to the baths, cruising, prowling. I think of myself as a prowler—almost catlike in the way I would stalk someone. I'm not the most physically attractive man in the world; I'm not big and muscular. I'm twenty-five years older than most of the people, and I really like seducing and getting people to come home with me or doing it with me in the baths.
> I love the sex itself, and I love to suck cock. I love to turn other men on because that turns me on, too. Sometimes my lover and I can have sex seven times a week, sometimes once every two weeks. We like to make love to each other a lot. I'm a good wordsman so

I'll paint a fantasy picture—quantities of guys doing
things to us and with us, and I get him off on this a lot.
I'll be sucking his cock—talk—suck—play with your
hand. You can do a lot of things, and you can keep this
feeling going. I'm not into fucking, but I'll play with
his ass, rim him, shove my fingers up his ass, and create a big cock for him in his head with my fingers.

Ron is twenty-eight and lives in a southern city. He spent a
number of years having sex in public rest rooms and prefers the
excitement inherent in a dangerous place to the comfort (as
others would see it) of the bedroom. Thirteen years ago he
put a "glory hole" in a college rest room.

My glory hole is still there. More cocks have been
sucked off in that hole than anywhere else in town.
I'm proud of that. The excitement. It puts pressure on
you timewise, builds up the sweat because the whole
place is really hot, and these guys come in and they
want to get it over with fast. Especially the straight
guys who are coming in just for a blow job. That
makes it real exciting, and they don't want to get
caught.

I had sex in school in the tearooms, but that had
nothing to do with my social life because I divorced
sex from my social life altogether. It had nothing to do
with love and friendship. I was horny all the time,
and I had an erection all the time.

You'll never find me in one of those lover-type relationships, no one-on-one possessiveness. I know where
you're coming from when you say it doesn't have to be
that way. I know you're the doctor, but I see very few
relationships that work, where there isn't jealousy and
possessiveness, where people can be secure in themselves. I don't see how I could ever expect one person
to fulfill all my needs for the rest of my life. In fact, I
can't see one person fulfilling my sexual needs right
now. Period.

Sure, I've seen gay marriages. I think it's great for
them if they can accept it for being a terminal thing
just like anything else in life—which they don't. When
they get married they think it's forever, and when they
break up they go through all this pain. And I don't see
it's being worth all the pain they go through. I just
don't see the one balancing the other. I've seen suicides, depression, hostility, anger, hate—love turning
to hate because they put too many ties on each other.

I've seen some relationships where they really love it
because they love to yell and fight and scream and all.

Vernon is twenty-eight and has lived in New York City all
his life. He's one of those men who was not upset to learn of his
homosexuality. He developed a love affair at sixteen with a man
who was thirty-three, a relationship that lasted for six years.
Sex was its mainstay.

> We never talked about love, not in six years. I don't
> know if I ever told him I loved him. There was a bar-
> rier on that. One of the things that really turned the
> relationship sour was that he really wanted me to talk
> love, and I wouldn't because I didn't feel it.
>
> I was required by the rules of the relationship to tell
> him every gory detail of everything I did with everyone
> I went to bed with. It was an offense to the relationship
> if I held back. Sometimes he'd jerk off while I'd tell
> him.
>
> I like sucking cock. I developed a technique to make
> other people come easily. I can go into the park and
> suck off ten people. Sometimes I wouldn't have dinner.
> I'd go in there hungry and catch my dinner on the
> hoof. I thought of it in hunting terms, in terms of
> catching food, tracking in the woods, feeling very
> much like a large cat—trapping them and reeling them
> in.
>
> After our relationship ended I began a new one that
> lasted for five years. I was happy to find that he was
> very cool, cold physically and mentally. He was the
> icicle I was always looking for, as cold as I was.
> Through the whole five years together we never talked
> about love. Maybe toward the end we admitted we
> were lovers. Our relationship was based on friendship.
> Love is for men and women.

Larry (age twenty-two) and *Jason* (age thirty) have been
lovers for seven months. They are both students at a large midwestern university. They do not live together and have never
maintained an exclusive sexual relationship. Both feel that phallic size is very important.

> *Larry*: I like a man with a fairly large cock. It seems
> more manly to me. There's also a challenge involved
> having oral sex. Then take fucking, for example. I like
> to feel a cock inside of me, not necessarily splitting my
> sides, but I like the feeling of a large one inside of me.

The sensation is greater because it's tighter—it fills up more space.

If I'm sucking on a small cock, it's like there's nothing there. I like the feeling of something going down my throat, being able to wrap your hand around it at the same time.

Marvin (age twenty-nine) is a New Yorker who has never had a lover. Except for his adventures in sex, Marvin is quite shy and unassertive.

I always find something wrong with the person after the second date. Any reason will do: not butch enough, not intelligent enough, don't wear the proper sneakers, too much hair on their ass, or collect antiques, or I don't like the color of their carpets.

My expectation is that sex should be as good the second time as the first time. If it isn't, I'll be disappointed and then I lose interest in the guy. I only like people who give hot sex.

I went to the baths last Friday night. I was really horny. But every time someone really attractive appeared at my door, they didn't come in. It wasn't an interesting night.

C.S.: No sex?

Oh! I got fucked eight times, but it wasn't hot.

Linus is in his fifties, a native of California and a perfect example of how upset an excitement-motivated man can become when he finds himself involved in a love relationship. This middle-aged man has always preferred sex with hustlers, who usually add their own variety of excitement to the affair. Linus writes about the experience in a humorous way.

My last relationship lasted seven weeks. It was one of my longer ones. A relationship has always been traumatic. Success can be measured as mere survival—getting out alive, without physical violence, property theft, destruction, blackmail, arrest, or litigation.

This last affair ended in hospitalization. I almost fainted in my office one Friday afternoon. I was able to regain enough composure to drive myself to the emergency room of a local hospital. There they told me that my blood pressure was high. It actually rose and fell like mercury in a thermometer.

The doctor was young and blond and, I think, gay—

cute, in any case. I told him that I thought my condition was due to a "domestic" situation—a guest who had stayed longer than I expected. The doctor winked and smiled and never even referred to "her." He must have been gay—a safe assumption where I live.

I went home and told my friend that I was about to have a stroke but that it could be prevented if he left at once. He asked, "You mean I'm hazardous to your health?" I replied, "We're probably hazardous to each other's." This reply was in the tradition of California egalitarianism. It was also masterful, based as it was on the principle that two faults are better than one for breaking up relationships.

He moved out the next day. He was too stoned on Valium even to move his body that night. The pressure went down in two days. So far I haven't had a stroke. I haven't even missed him very much. There was a brief nostalgic interlude of Gershwin and Sinatra when I was trying to miss him, but even that music elevated my pressure.

I've strengthened my conviction that I am a person for whom lovers are extremely dangerous. If lover relationships could be bottled, I would demand that the FDA have them labeled, MAY BE HAZARDOUS TO YOUR HEALTH.

Noticing the "cute" doctor while death may be imminent is very typical of the excitement-seeking person. Linus reports that his affairs now last no longer than one night and that his health has never been better.

Men primarily motivated by the desire for excitement have a number of characteristics in common. By far the most important of these is their enjoyment in catching someone sexually in what they frequently call "the hunt," "the chase," or "the seduction." What is striking is that the excitement of the pursuit is at least as rewarding for them as the sex. Without competition, without the thrill of knowing they can win or lose, sex is viewed as dull. It's easy to become moralistic about these men, to call them promiscuous, but that would only be a demand that they obey an arbitrary social standard.* We would also be overlook-

* Gay men are often accused of being "promiscuous." The word should be stricken from the sexual vocabulary. If we believe that sexual pleasure is a part of the good life, then a wide variety of experiences should be encouraged, including sex with men of various

ing their contribution to the gay community. In general, they are not exploiters (though some individuals may be); rather, they take pride in their sexual performance and make every attempt to provide their transient lovers with a memorable sexual experience. They are frequently excellent teachers for the inexperienced, and more than one person who is just coming out has reason to be grateful for the patience shown him by an excitement seeker who taught without making emotional demands.

When they do acquire a lover, sex is prized as a physical experience, but any expression of intimacy is restrained. Sexual complications (say, some sexual dysfunction in the lover) are usually resolved by tricking out, instead of showing patience and compassion. As a rule, excitement seekers are very demanding sexually. They often need a constant escalation of sexual experience, frequently getting tired after they and their partners have reached their limit of sexual kinkiness.

Characteristic of such gays is a reverent attention to masculine symbols. Both straight and gay men are obsessed with masculine symbols; both show off sexually, exhibiting themselves either in direct or symbolic ways. In this respect, excitement-motivated gay men are more like straight men than gay domestic types. Penis size is tirelessly discussed. One man commented that a big penis "is a treasure." It is extremely difficult for these men to form an attachment to any man who does not measure up physically, no matter what other characteristics he may possess.

Another masculine trait is independence. Freedom is very important to excitement seekers, and they are highly sensitive to any attempt on the part of a potential lover to interfere with this. For them, perhaps, a relationship can end only in freedom or slavery. Dependence on a lover is a mystery; they cannot fathom how others can endure a relationship in which one person influences the actions of the other. They look with horror

---

ages, shapes, sizes, and "types." And why not sex with women as well? Most of us have learned that having sex with another man is one of the best ways to get to know him and to learn from him. Frequent sexual experiences are a form of education, and we should accept that. Thinking of sexual experiences as being "promiscuous" is merely a way to deny the opportunity for learning.

on the possessiveness and jealousy in dependent relationships, in which they see backbiting, deliberate attempts to hurt, accusations, lying, depressions, and suicides. They prefer relationships in which each lover has the right to control his own body and to have sex with other people; they do not see this as a rejection of the lover, since they don't expect one person to satisfy all their sexual needs.

Excitement-motivated gay men are not very domestic. They are not likely to be thrilled at the prospect of choosing new wallpaper for the apartment or rearranging the living room. For them, domestic chores are too contrived and confining. In contrast, their favorite activity, "the hunt," is a spontaneous experience in dealing with circumstances as they arrive; this constitutes a measure of the excitement. Long-term planning with a lover, making the home more pleasant aesthetically, even cooking a fine meal for a few other gay couples, all these are likely to be viewed as a ball and chain around their necks.

One of the more surprising attributes of excitement seekers is that age seems unrelated to the characteristic. One would expect young men to be more thrill-motivated than men in their thirties and forties. To some extent this is true, since younger men are still learning sexually, but the fact is that many young men want domestic love affairs, while some middle-aged men are just as excitement-motivated as a teenager with a new driver's license. It would be a very difficult task indeed to show that domesticity and excitement invariably increase and decrease with age.

What actually seems to happen is that more mature, experienced, excitement-motivated men make better choices of lovers than they did when young. With age, they become less demanding and less critical, no longer insisting their lovers obey rules they themselves break. They also become more honest, learning to choose lovers who have similar beliefs about sex, independence, and possessiveness. When they can make these choices, their relationships seem to be as successful as domestic ones. In a sense they do become more domestic than in their youth, but without giving up the demand for excitement.

Home Builders

One can easily see how the major values of domestically oriented men differ widely from those of excitement-motivated men. These are the gays who form most of the long-lasting relationships, although it should be understood that the length of time two men have lived together is not necessarily an indication of the quality of their relationship. Duration is a measurable objective fact. Whether the relationship between lovers is worthy of emulation is a value judgment that varies according to one's standards.

*Alan,** age thirty, has been with his present lover for six months. As a teenager he had a long-term affair with an age mate. After arriving in the New York City area, he lived with a lover for twelve years in a basically monogamous relationship. Much of their time was spent refurbishing the house they bought together.

> After I left my lover I did a lot of tricking, but that was very unsatisfying. The sex was fun, but then I always wanted to do something with the person. But they weren't interested in anything but sex. A sense of continuity is very important to me, and I missed that when I was just tricking with people.
>
> Because sex is such a small part of life, really, and when you get into that mode, sex becomes the whole meaning of life to you. Tonight I'll have this hot number, tomorrow night I'll have that hot number—and that's it. You can't really see too far into the future. But I think in terms of a long life. It's nice to have someone to share everything with, besides just someone in bed.

Earl, age forty, and *Vincent,** age fifty-five, live in a small town in the West. They have lived together for eight years. Vincent lived with a lover for eleven years until the lover died. Earl had a few affairs when he was younger, but his relationship with Vincent is the longest.

> *Earl*: One of my masturbation fantasies has always been where I'm the stronger one and someone is weaker than me, and I go and rescue them from some situation and pick them up in my arms and carry them off. I was influenced a lot by the movies that I saw in the forties and fifties. I lived in a small town, only one theater, and exercising my fantasy life was going to this theater. I had this fantasy about picking somebody up and getting onto horseback and riding off, someone smaller and weaker than myself. I was mothering them and nurturing them and protecting them from dangers and

this sort of thing, and having them dependent on me.
I suppose this is one of my biggest fantasies. I've never
really been aware of it till just now.

What I like to see in a man is a beautiful blend of
the masculine and the feminine, and not having one
overwhelm the other. There's always this feeling I have
with Vincent to let a softer part of my nature come out,
not feminine, but softer. It's been very liberating to be
able to do this.

But I've always had these fantasies of someone being
very vulnerable and being able to open themselves up to
another person and reveal all their weakness and feelings as well as their strengths, and the other person just
laying there and revealing themselves to you.

I suppose this has been romantic and Gothic in some
ways, but this whole idea of rescuing somebody and
making love to them and comforting them, easing their
pain, swooping down and taking them somewhere.
There's never been much verbal content to these fantasies. It's more like a silent movie in a way. Perhaps it's
just something very romantic, but that's about it.
Vincent: It's all about wanting a home, some sort of
regularity where both people simply worked, came
home, you know, regular hours, a regular life.

I've always wanted to scream to the world: I have
a lover, and we have a home. That was more important
to me than our sex life itself. So with my first real lover,
who died after we lived together for eleven years, the
only thing that ended it was his death. I think he felt the
same way I did.

Vincent explained that he and Earl stopped having sex after
two years. Earl has outside sex at a local gay bath, which he
prefers to bars. "There is so much playing around and hypocrisy,"
Earl explained.

I think this is very common, and this is one thing that
your study may bring out. That many gay relationships,
particularly between two males who have been together
for many years, where they have passionate sex for
maybe the first two or three years, then it sort of dies
out. And yet they stay together because there are other
very important, very crucial things that hold the relationship together. All the other departments, the non-
sexual aspects of life, like the emotional and the financial
and the social. This is the way Vincent and I are. We
don't have a sexual relationship anymore, but there are

these other important things that hold the relationship together, like love and affection, and having a house together, and security and companionship. These are ultimately the things that are the most important to us.

One of the most important things in a relationship is whether your partner is a homebody or a bar type, the type of gay person who likes to go out and socialize a lot and go to bars. This is contrasted with the stay-at-home, the homebody. And I think that to have a good relationship that you have two people who are homebody types and want to settle down and have roots, a home. Some people say, "I have to go out every night." I think that's why they break up, when one person is a homebody and the other's a gadabout. I feel the same way about people who run from job to job. Anyone who flits from job to job is the same as anyone who flits from bed to bed.

Ramon,* age twenty-five, returned to New York City after an abortive coming-out experience with a straight friend. In part, the experience may have been due to two factors: his reluctance to accept his homosexuality and his masturbation fantasies, which include being tied up by a soldier or a cowboy, gagged and beaten. At twenty-two, he began to accept both his homosexuality and his S and M feelings. Soon after Ramon was rejected by his straight friend, he met *Charles*,* age twenty-seven. That was eight months ago, and they are currently living together. Their first night together was a memorable experience.

> *Ramon*: I really wanted to be held that night, to have someone grab me and hold me in their arms and say it's all right, there's nothing to worry about. You're here, you're beautiful. He paid a lot of compliments to me that night, and I needed it. When I woke up the next morning I thought it was just going to be a tricking experience. Charles struck me as the kind of person who wasn't going to get tied down, someone who had a different man every night.
> *Charles*: Ramon was constantly in motion that night, constantly grabbing my body in different places and being passionate and holding me and obviously wanting me to hold him and do things to him, to kiss his body all over, to lick it, to play with his cock and grab his ass and fuck him. I must have fucked him five or six times between two and five A.M., all in different positions. And in between there were nice interludes of hold-

ing each other, and talking, and complimenting each other. Then we fell asleep for about an hour or so, and I got a phone call, and after that I fucked him for another two hours before we went off to work.

Ramon: I have to say I've always wanted a place of my own. I've always wanted a place where everything was how I imagined, or sort of my dream castle. Shelving or pictures on the wall that I really liked or furniture I admired.

I guess I'm very domestic in that sense. The only other place of my own that I had, except for at home where I shared a bedroom with my brother, was at college. I've always wanted an apartment of my own. I wanted a place to entertain, to have parties, and invite people over. A place where me and another man could shut ourselves away from the rest of the world and just listen to records and have peace and quiet. I guess it makes me feel that—it sounds crazy—that life is worth living just to have a place with somebody that you really care for, that you love.

Charles: I used to be a very promiscuous person. But now I feel secure enough to share more of myself, giving and receiving love. I was promiscuous because I was afraid. I wasn't going to trust in one person. I used sex in a control way. I had people who were very attracted to me, and the way I would handle that would be by rewarding them sexually. But I kept my distance. I had a lover once who was very scared, so that was safe for me. Ramon isn't safe. He's hot and passionate, and he can hurt me easily.

This is an interesting couple because each man changed his life-style after the relationship began. Charles considered himself a "night stalker," always proving his sexual prowess and never allowing himself to become emotionally tied to another, very much the excitement seeker. Ramon, on the other hand, always fantasized about homey things. But their life-styles may change drastically in the future. The hint of this possibility can be seen in the way Ramon forced Charles into making a commitment to fidelity very early in their relationship. He did it by means of powerful sexual challenge. Ramon had just come from having dinner with a couple of Charles' friends. He decided to stop off at one of New York City's most popular back-room bars.

Ramon: I was in the back room, and who walks in but

two of Charles' friends, the ones I had dinner with that night. And of course it's very dark in there, so I sort of made the point of having sex with one of them. I was against the wall, and I wanted him to come over so I could pet him or grab his ass and have him start fondling me. And he did. He came over, and we sort of just touched, and then either he sucked my cock or I sucked his. I don't remember which.

Then after I had sex with him I introduced myself. "Remember me? I'm Charles' friend." I hoped that the next morning they would call Charles and say, "Guess who we saw in the back room last night?" I knew they were going to see him the next morning, and I wanted to make him real mad and jealous, which it did. You see, he was going out with another guy that night, and I didn't see why he should, so I decided to make Charles feel as miserable as I was.

Charles: They told me about it the next day. I felt very jealous and anxious. I didn't know what to do. At that point the whole tricking thing was very ordered, and it was what I wanted. I had a lover before for about eight months, and we lived together in an apartment. And it was awful, it was terrible. I was off having fun all the time, and he was home not having fun. And I didn't want to get into that again. I knew that being monogamous had led to a lot of problems in the past. To claustrophobic relationships, clawing and hurting each other. I didn't want to do that again.

But the thing I wanted was Ramon. That's what came through that day, and I was willing to pay whatever price he demanded at the time. I agreed for us to live together, and I made the commitment to him.

Now, eight months later, Ramon is afraid that he himself will find someone and run off. Ramon is starting to wonder what he's been missing by not having sex with other men. It began with curiosity about Charles' previous sexual life.

I'd want to know about some of Charles' tricks from the past. What was he like in bed? What did you do? I guess I was looking for a comparison with me, that I was the best.

There are also times when I feel that Charles has been to bed with hundreds of men, done everything. I haven't done that. Maybe I should, to find out what it's like. Then other times I think I have such a good relationship with Charles, why destroy it?

Ramon is becoming more motivated sexually and less interested in domestic affairs. One could reasonably hypothesize that
Ramon will soon insist on a "polygamous" arrangement. The
likelihood is that Charles will agree, and if they both structure
their relationship around excitement/motivation, the lover arrangement will work. But if Charles refuses, the relationship is
bound to end.

*Stephen,** age sixty-one, and *Jonathan,** age seventy-two, have
been lovers for thirty-two years. They both worked for the same
institution in New York City, from which they are now retired.
They first met in the steam room of a servicemen's residence
after World War II. As Stephen puts it, "I walked into the
steam room as naked as a jaybird, and Jonathan's first remark
was, 'I admire your tan.'" It wasn't until a month later that
they had sex.

> *Stephen*: I fell in love with Jonathan a couple of weeks
> later. It was my twenty-ninth birthday, and Jonathan
> gave me a book that I wanted, and I had hardly given
> any hint at all. I was so impressed that he wasn't upset
> that I had a mind. He was very thoughtful, and he could
> be counted on to stay within bounds.
>   We were never the best sexual partners because we
> were both lacking in knowledge and perhaps not the
> best suited physically. We're both very heavy hung.
> *Jonathan*: Our sex life was never very wild.
> *Stephen*: Never very wild. We never heard of some of
> the things that people do until a few years ago. Most of
> our sex was fellatio. And Jonathan isn't the kind of per-
> son who will say I love you. He never has in thirty-two
> years.
> *Jonathan*: I don't believe in going around and blaring
> all this stuff. I'm from Maine, and we're very tactful
> with each other.
> *Stephen*: I think there are two kinds of people. There
> are the kind that want emotional and romantic highs,
> and no matter what book you give them for living to-
> gether, they can't do it. Then there's the kind who are
> domestically inclined, like us, who will sacrifice sex
> and emotional highs for compatibility.
>   From the time I met Jonathan, I was never in love
> with anybody else. I may have slept with more people
> than he has, but I was never in love with anyone else for
> five minutes.

It was only after eleven years that Stephen and Jonathan decided to live together. The reasons for maintaining separate apartments are a bit obscure. Perhaps it was some reservation about commitment, or affairs both were having with other men. It was certainly not an interest in looking for another lover.

> *Jonathan*: I knew there couldn't be anyone who could replace Stephen.
> *Stephen*: Incredible! This is the first time in thirty-two years that Jonathan has said that. I knew it, but he never said it.
>   For many years I had trouble accepting Jonathan's low sex drive. And if Jonathan had sex with someone else I was very upset, not jealous, but frustrated because I wouldn't get any. There were times with a lot of tears and slammed doors and weeks of not seeing each other. But when I accepted it as final, it became easier, but I went through many sexless years, and I assumed my sex life was over. Then one year we were in Italy, and I found out it wasn't. Now I go to the baths, and I'm still amazed, don't understand what young people see in a man my age, but they do.
> *Jonathan*: I think it's wonderful.
> *Stephen*: I only go about once a month because there's too many other things in my life so I can't fit it in. For instance, we're giving a party this week; then we're preparing to go on vacation next week.

Edgar,* age sixty-five, and *James*,* sixty-two, have been living together for the past forty years. They spent most of that time living in and around the New York City area and now reside in a pleasant home in a well-known beach community. James was experienced sexually when they met, but Edgar was not. James has always felt that homosexuality was the most natural of feelings while Edgar was in conflict about it.

> *Edgar*: I didn't know what a homosexual was. When I first met James I was so naive. I said, "Men actually live together?" I thought it was something you did in the dark. I was more sheltered than he was.
> *James*: We had a rather long and chaste courtship because of the difficulties in those days of not having a place to go. We were both quite young and living with our families. It was several years before we were inviting each other to one another's homes and staying over

weekends. We went to the movies or the theater. Sometimes we would lock ourselves in the bathroom together
or kiss on the back staircase. It was at least a year before we ever took our clothes off together. It drove us
nutty for the longest time.

Edgar: It didn't drive me nutty because this was something so new and wonderful that it filled my whole life,
which was sort of empty before.

James: There was something of the rescue squad in me.
I was going to provide the comfort and warmth that he
had been missing.

Edgar: And in those days I didn't like sex that often,
but I do now. I felt it was vaguely repulsive, except
when you were so hot you couldn't control yourself.

James: The first time we had sex he acted like the
princess, and I did him.

Edgar: I liked him so much that I tried to stop him. I
thought it was wrong. He was such a wonderful person,
I thought, how could he degrade himself? Then James
wanted me to do him, and I refused. It was years before
I would do that. Maybe ten years before I really started
to enjoy sex like I do now.

James: Some people's lives are centered around sex.
Sex is central to my life, but we have so many other
things that occupy us as a community effort.

Edgar: And we've both remained friends with our
families, and that takes a lot of time, too. We entertain
them, and they entertain us.

Edgar and James were together for twenty years before they
had anal intercourse together, and this was stimulated by the
presence of a third man. "I was not demanding," says James in
an understatement. Until James' recent illness, they had sex
regularly; as a matter of fact, Edgar has found that his advancing
years have increased his sexual drive. He's more interested in
sex now than ever before.

James: I've seen the decline of sexual interest in young
guys and married couples. Maybe three or four years,
and it's over. I suspect that this happens in a relationship that is built one hundred percent on sex. If there's
nothing else there to tie it together, I suppose it does
wear out after a while. Whereas we've built all sorts
of other bonded interests right from the beginning. We
both love the theater, we both love music, we are both
passionately attached to our possessions and whatever
house we happen to live in at the time, and that became

part of our personalities. I suppose it's ordinary; people used to think of us as one person—Edgar and James. One name was never mentioned without the other.

Edgar: We started out as if we were going into a marriage, and we followed the same rules married people are supposed to follow.

James: Well, up to a point.

Donald, age fifty-two, and *Seth*,* age fifty-two, were interviewed the week of their twenty-fifth anniversary. Both were born and raised in small rural towns, and they've lived these past twenty-five years in a community of just a few thousand people in a southwestern state. Donald was married and has a son who visits them frequently. He's also a strong believer in Christianity. "I never lost faith in Christ, and I never will," he says, though Seth doesn't share his religious fervor. Donald was one of those men who married mostly because the woman wanted it.

> *Donald*: She said she couldn't do without me. I said, "Well, I don't really love you in the way you love me." She said, "Oh! God can take care of that." She was a bit flaky in that area. But, after all, she had been a Christian all her life, and I felt she knew more about the Lord than I did. So I trusted her judgment, which was wrong. Before we got married I told her that I was gay. She only said, "God will change that." He didn't.

Donald and Seth first met at a party. Donald was swinging from the water pipes wearing leotard shorts. Apparently that appealed to Seth. During the next week Donald fell in love with Seth, and in large part, according to Donald, it was Seth's education and intelligence that impressed Donald, who viewed himself as uneducated. But Seth's interest in Donald grew more slowly. It was only after a year that they agreed to become lovers. The first year together was very rocky.

> *Seth*: We disagreed about a lot of things. Everything. Especially religion. He decided I shouldn't smoke, and he decided I shouldn't do this and shouldn't do that. That's still a division between us.
> *Donald*: He's intellectual, and he can twist and turn things that you say, and me, I couldn't overcome him. So my only alternative was bang, bang, bang. I got frustrated and blew up. I once bashed Seth with a water

dipper—(Seth interrupts: "I bleed easy.")—and I really think I was trying to kill him.

Seth: He was very jealous, and I'm not the world's paragon of virtue when it comes to fidelity. Donald just assumed that we would be faithful to each other even though we never agreed to it. I knew that if something interesting came along I was going to wander off the track. Incidentally, I don't think he was all that faithful, but he would lie about it.

Donald: Earlier I was faithful. I was faithful to him, and I didn't see any reason why he couldn't be faithful to me. I knew when Seth had sex with someone. I could smell it. He used to like truckdrivers, and he would come home reeking of sex. He never realized how I could tell because he has a problem with smells.

But after a while I learned. I came to the realization, who does he come home to, who does he really want, and who does he really love? When I thought that through, I understood. Something else, too. Sometimes he would come home at three or four in the morning, and he would snuggle up to me and would be real passionate, and I knew what had happened and why he was doing it. Sometimes he only went out talking with people, because he's a tremendous talker. I came to understand that Seth wasn't looking for another lover, just for sex.

It isn't surprising that these two men had a disagreement about outside sex. It is by far the most common source of conflict in every gay male relationship. What is remarkable is the fact that the conflicts continued unabated for eleven years! Seth was pelted periodically with water dippers, sundry vases, lamps, and, occasionally, fists. Both agree that Donald took a long time learning to control his temper. Seth put up with violence but never ceased his forays into the world of macho truckdrivers. The current arrangement is more relaxed. Both have the opportunity for outside sex, and Donald's temper has abated considerably. Currently, after twenty-five years, they have sex once or twice a week, plus whatever other diversions chance to appear. They had their first threesome last year. In general, they live a rather pleasant life now, both employed in occupations they enjoy.

Seth: Other than being a gay couple, I don't think our lives are very different from others in the town. There's no disadvantage here being gay. We've never had any hassles. No one tells their teenage sons to stay away. We go to straight dinner parties together.

Last year we built a wooden bridge across a stream near the house. You can see it out that window. It was just for aesthetic reasons. Then we had a big ribbon-cutting ceremony. The mayor of the town was invited to cut the ribbon, and they had a radio broadcast of it. Hundreds of people came, and we served food and drinks to everyone. It was a wonderful time.

Marlin,* age fifty-nine, has been living with his Puerto Rican lover for fifteen years. Marlin was forty-four when he met twenty-five-year-old *Diego.* He had already come to believe that he would never have another lover. Still, it wasn't love at first sight.

Love at first sight? No, no, no. You don't do that when you're my age.

I've become very close to Diego's family in Puerto Rico. They're like my own parents. They call me "son number two." They have a second son, but they don't like him.

They're country people. They live in a wooden cor-rugated-roof house. They have an outhouse. Very, very poor people. Hardworking all their lives.

They built a stone house for us right next door to them. "Pappy" did, with an old crony. It's really just one room. We use their kitchen, and we share the out-house. When we take a shower we stand under a faucet, like they do.

We've never brought them to New York City for a visit. I don't want them to see this filthy city. I don't want them to see how some Puerto Ricans live here. They've got their dignity there.

Once Diego accused me of showing too much affec-tion toward some friends at a party because I danced with them. I was very angry at that. I shot my mouth off, too, but we kissed and made up. Then I told Diego it's very Puerto Rican to fight and make up, but I said I'm too old to be always fighting and making up. This is a silly idea. Fighting's not an aphrodisiac to me. It just turns me off completely. I said, "I don't want to fight with you, so if you're worried about me dancing with them I won't dance with them. But otherwise you have to trust me, and I have to trust you."

We were together for nine years before we de-cided to have a marriage ceremony. Everyone where I

worked knew I was getting married to Diego because
I told them all, including the president of the company. I always talked about Diego whenever he talked
about his wife and children. [Marlin is an executive.]
So one day there was this conspiracy to keep me out
of the employees' lounge. It was a bitchy, busy day, and
I was getting in a foul mood. All of a sudden I get a
call that I'm wanted in the employees' lounge. "What
the fuck's going on down there? Can't anyone do anything in this goddamned place?" And I go down to the
lounge, and the whole fucking place is there. They've
got a cake there and a shower and presents for Diego
and me.

The *pièce de résistance* was when the UPS man came
over to me. This is hysterical. He grabbed me by the
hand and said, "Oh, Mr. Smith, I want to wish you
and your friend every happiness in the world, many
happy years together." I said, "Well, we've already had
nine, and I'm looking forward to a lifetime, thank you
very much." I was actually getting a little teary, had a
lump in my throat. But I don't believe in crying in
public. It's in poor taste.

When we examine the histories of domestically oriented
couples, one major characteristic immediately separates them
from excitement seekers—the maintenance of a family unit.
Home builders want a sense that they are part of a family,
not just two men living together. While excitement seekers
simply want a *place* to live, home builders want a *home*. Furniture, decorations, even the geographical location of the home
will convey messages that symbolize either transience or permanence. This difference shows. Just as the excitement seeker
doesn't want to be tied down by possessions that hamper his
potential mobility, home builders accumulate possessions in order to insure stability.

The concept of *family* to home builders involves more than
simply the love of another man. As in heterosexual marriage,
they work very hard to keep the lines of communication open
between the generations. Married men want their children to
visit and to feel that the gay lover is a member of the family.
Domestic couples want to remain close to their parents and
siblings; they want respect for their union. Marlin's trips to
Puerto Rico with his lover are an obvious example; his lover's
parents built a house for them so that Marlin and Diego could

visit every year. Diego's parents "adopted" Marlin as their number-two son, and he adopted them as his number-two parents. No doubt there are domestically oriented couples who do not have contact with their families, but this happens generally because of the family's unwillingness to accept the gay union.

Another characteristic of the domestic couple is the importance of time and continuity. Two men may view the present as important but will value more highly the changes that occur in their lives as they move toward the future. They have a strong sense of the future and plan for it. To them, this future planning is as stimulating as is "the hunt" for the excitement seeker. One couple in the South said to me:

> After we were together for a year we started saving for a house. Our living room was filled with plans and layouts and ideas for decorating. We wanted that more than anything. Five years later we had enough money for a down payment. It was the most important day of our lives. I immediately started repainting the outside of the house.

Time and planning for the future anchor both men in the relationship, giving substance to the sentimentality that plays such an important part in domestic relationships.

One man gave this example of sentimentality:

> We had been living together for a couple of years. There were a lot of good things and bad things about our relationship. For one, I'm very sentimental, and he never gave me anything for my birthday or remembered our anniversary. Not even a card or a "Happy whatever, darling." Nothing. I was always furious about this, and I never knew whether I should give him a present on his birthday or ignore it out of spite. If I gave him something I felt resentful because he never gave, but if I didn't give him something, I felt guilty for being hostile. Then one night we were listening to some music, a piece he likes very much. We weren't talking, just sitting on the floor near each other. Then I noticed him look at me, and there were tears in his eyes, and he turned his face away and covered most of it with his hands, and he started talking, very slow and very low. "I want you to know that you're the most important thing that's ever happened in my life. I don't care where we are or what we do. I only care that I'm with you."

Then he cried but tried to hide it. Fat chance! He was crying more than I had ever seen before, even times when he was feeling very low and depressed. I started to move toward him. I wanted to hold him and comfort him and tell him how much his words meant to me, how much he meant to me. But he stuck out his arm and moved his body away from me, obviously distressed that I would comfort him.

It mystified me because he never refused comfort from me when he was feeling depressed. Then he sort of pulled himself together, wiped his eyes, and started talking about something totally irrelevant, as if the tears and the feelings never happened. He refused to discuss it.

I was thinking about it when we turned off the lights to go to sleep, laying in bed wondering what happened and why he was so tender one minute and cool the next. Suddenly I realized what it all meant. The son-of-a-bitch is a hundred times more sentimental than me, and he's embarrassed by the display of emotion. He can't control his sentimentality; he'll always cry if he gave me gifts or remembered things important to us. But he does remember them, and he cares about them. He probably thinks about them more than I do. To me they're just symbols of the relationship, but they're much more central to him. He probably never forgets anything. He's the type.

I turned to him laying next to me and said, "You phony. I'm on to you now. Always telling me how silly it is doing special things on a birthday or anniversary, or giving gifts to each other. I understand what's behind it now. But don't worry. I'll keep your secret."

To sentimental people this experience may seem reminiscent of similar experiences in their own love affairs. Excitement-oriented gay men may be appalled by the story and feel grateful they're not locked into what seems to them to be a depressing scene. Certainly there are feelings of dependence that accompany sentimentality, and no domestically oriented couple can ever escape a large amount of dependency in their relationship. If the lover must be consulted before decisions are made, then the other partner is in a real sense dependent on his wishes. From the point of view of domesticity seekers, there is room for negotiation in dependency; to excitement seekers, even a little dependency may seem too much.

The final characteristic concern of domesticity is the matter of monogamy, which will be explored in the next chapter. However, a brief comment is in order here. Fortunately, gays are generally more honest than straight people; hence there is less hypocrisy in gay life about the desire for outside sex than in heterosexual marriage. For many domestically oriented gays, monogamy, the idea of a primary emotional, sexual, and financial relationship with another man, is a mainstay to stability and reliability. No matter what sexual life-style is developed by these lovers, the maintenance of a domestic relationship is impossible if one partner is perceived as undependable and uncaring.

The sexual relationship between lovers comprising a domestic couple is very different from that between excitement seekers. When excitement seekers develop a love affair, the lover must be competent sexually. It is the single most important requirement of such a relationship. This is not so with domesticity seekers. The relationship is primary, not the sex. There are stable domestic couples who have never had sex or whose sexual interaction vanished long ago; on the other hand, there are those whose sex lives vary from the tedious to the hot and heavy. The lack of emphasis on sexual satisfaction among domestic couples is an indication that sex as such is not the primary criterion used to evaluate the relationship. It takes second place to stability and family organization. James waited years for his lover, Edgar, to reciprocate sexually. Edgar refused to have James's penis in his mouth. James said, "You learn to live with limitations. I had hope and faith in the future." It was twenty years before they had anal intercourse! And they've been together for thirty years. Jonathan never had a high sexual drive, and he's been living with Stephen, who has, for the past thirty-two years. Poor Seth got bashed with water dippers wielded by a jealous lover who insisted that Seth stop molesting truckdrivers, and this went on for eleven years! Nathan was brutally molested as a child; it took two or three years of an eight-year relationship until Nathan relaxed sexually.

This does not mean that any problem between lovers must wait decades for resolution. The point is that domesticity seekers do not immediately reject a lover because of a sexual problem or sexual incompatibility if the important theme of the relationship, the feeling of intimacy and "home," is present. Sexual excitement is clearly less important than trust, and where there is a mutuality of trust, no sexual incompatibility or problem will break up the couple. In every case cited above, some resolution of problems has occurred, and each couple mused on how far they have come from those "early days."

Domesticity seekers are also more likely to get to know each other before they have sex than are excitement seekers. But once again, as in their sexual relationships, they show more variation on this point than excitement seekers. The domesticity seeker may jump into the sack immediately or wait for quite a while; he may judge the man on physical looks only, or he may be conscious of an emotional magnetism. Excitement seekers, however, make their judgments on the basis of physical looks and availability, and they do not wait.

Domestic couples do not like excitement-seeking gays or excitement-seeking couples whose style of life seems foreign. They usually develop a circle of other gay couples whose lives are similar to their own and with whom they share values. In addition, they may socialize with a small number of single gays, mostly of their own sort, who may be just friends or occasional sex partners, or both.

The distinction between home builders and excitement seekers does not appear to be related to age, even when we take into account the greater sexual capacity of the young. Some of the most domestic attitudes expressed in this study came from young men, even teenagers like *Vinny*, age seventeen:

> I want someone to share my life with, someone I can count on. Respect for another person's mind and needs and trying to fulfill them. You may not succeed, but you try. I know I have to compromise. Sex isn't everything. You've heard this expression. It wears off, and it has to be someone who you can wake up with in ten years, you know, and still turn around and say, "I love you." I think it's hard to do.

Long-lasting gay couples are not very visible in the gay community, and the long-lasting relationships are generally, but not always, of the home-builder variety. In fact, it is extraordinary how many gay men refuse to believe that such couples exist. "Where are they?" is the question I heard over and over again from young gay men looking desperately for couples to emulate.

They are seldom seen in crowded gay bars and wouldn't be noticed if they were. They're not likely to be marching in gay liberation demonstrations or signing petitions. Some occasionally go to the baths, but it's dark in there, and socializing is not usually on the agenda. The disco scene? Now that it's become synonymous with drugs, it's not their favorite form of entertainment, although they may go on special occasions or during a vacation to a gay resort.

For the most part, and especially outside large gay cities in areas where nonconformity is frowned upon, domestic-type lovers live the same life-style as do heterosexual couples in the community, except that the gay couples often appear to be a bit more stable. These lovers, especially couples who have been together for a number of years, are seldom discriminated against in a community, no matter what its size or bigotry, simply because they live in accordance with community standards. They even get elected to political office as long as they are discreet. Of course, requiring gay couples to be discreet is a form of discrimination, but the point is that many domestic couples prefer to live in small, quiet communities, not viewing the necessity for discretion as prejudice—they would have been discreet anyway. Since they blend into the rest of the community and avoid the most visible gay rendezvous, they are all but invisible to the younger gay community. This has led to many inaccurate ideas of the longevity of gay couples and the effects of aging on gay men.

The pictures drawn here of excitement seekers and home builders are very generalized portraits. No one fits entirely into one category or the other; every man is multidimensional. Further, the description of the two types is not meant to preclude individual differences between men *within* a category, nor is it to be seen as some kind of life sentence. Past experiences in life shape a kind of program for the future, but the program does change, or at least is capable of being changed, on the basis of new experiences and new goals, and, frequently, with aid and support from a lover.

People alter their motivations in life, perhaps first by interest in sexual variety, typical of an excitement seeker, and then by movement toward a quieter, domestic life. There may be men who start their gay lives domestically oriented, only to discover a world of sexual riches there for the taking. There is no reason to assume that one life-style is actually more mature or rewarding than any other, or that we grow out of one and into the other. We certainly know that our society is more willing to accept home builders than excitement seekers, since the former conform more closely to married heterosexuals. But acceptance by the straight community is hardly a legitimate criterion by which to judge ourselves. If we allow the hetereosexual community the right to approve or disapprove of our life-styles, we also invite them to withdraw that approval at their convenience. Acceptance of variations within gay life must come from us. The heterosexual community will have to follow.

CHAPTER FIVE

The Monogamy Battle and the Demons of Jealousy and Envy

> Instinct tends to amplify indefinitely the number of objects which satisfy it, whereas love tends toward exclusivism.
>
> ORTEGA Y GASSETT

> I know I am but summer to your heart
> And not the full four seasons of the year.
>
> EDNA ST. VINCENT MILLAY

For centuries, the faithfulness of a wife has been crucial to her husband and family. After all, any child she bore had to be the product of her husband for the family name and family inheritance to be transmitted legitimately. In earlier days, people took the idea of "blood" very seriously; mucking up its purity could only lead to disaster. The queens of France gave birth to their children in public, for no one wanted the royal family to substitute an imposter for a legitimate royal infant. Infidelity of women, before reliable birth control measures and medically safe abortions, was therefore not allowed, but this prohibition against wifely philandering was mostly a matter of property and family. In those days, our modern notion of love had nothing to do with marriage.

It was only in the eighteenth century, with the rise of bourgeois sentimentality, that love was married to marriage. Husband and wife were expected to love not only each other, but their children as well—a matter of indifference during the Middle Ages. Love and its sentimentalities were celebrated in songs and poetry, and the official religious doctrines taught that as the people should love God, so they should love one another, husbands and wives especially. While the need to maintain bloodlines continued to be an important reason for fidelity, a second reason was added: sex between husband and wife as an expression of their love and intimacy. No longer was sex for procreation alone; now sex had become an expression of deeper feelings. This was quite revolutionary; previously, most people in the Western world believed that love was something that interfered with the important business of marriage.

In this century, family loyalties have grown less important. We generally find that merit, ability, and competence are more likely to bring success than "good" birth. The increased safety of abortions, the reliability of birth control methods, and the invention of antibiotics have now made "fooling around" a possibility for wives—a possibility always open for husbands. Yet husbands and wives are still wary of outside affairs or keep them quiet because of the relatively new notion that an exclusive sexual relationship between spouses is evidence of their intimacy and loyalty.

Beliefs about heterosexual marriage are the foundations on which gay love relationships have been constructed. Whenever there is discussion about gay relationships, what form they should take and how lovers should act toward one another, talk invariably centers on the similarity or dissimilarity to heterosexual marriage. Gay couples pattern their behavior after that of their parents and other heterosexual couples in their community. Although gays do formulate some new ideas, these arrangements reflect in large part the historical norms of the heterosexual world.

At some point in the life of every gay couple the monogamy battle will be fought. There is no more universal conflict to be found among gay lovers than the question of whether or not to maintain an exclusive sexual relationship. Rural gays who get up to work on the farm at 6 A.M. and city excitement seekers who are just returning home from the disco at the same hour share this issue. Geography, life-style, religious affiliation, age—none of these exempts the men from having to reach some agreement about outside sex, commonly known as "tricking." It is not that the same issue isn't important to heterosexuals, but one of the practices that seems implicit in heterosexual marriage is dishonesty. It is rampant, and few heterosexuals appear willing to change that norm. They prefer deceit to dealing openly with the issue. Gays are much more honest about their sexual needs, and they often express these feelings to a lover. It is this honesty that creates the conflict about exclusive and nonexclusive sexual styles.

Discussions about the possibility of outside sexual experiences reveal many differences of opinion. Some men say to their lovers, "I don't care what you do so long as you don't tell me about it and don't bring it home with you." Other men believe that outside relationships are important—even necessary—but they feel threatened if these relationships aren't discussed. "It's a form of sharing," one man told me.

The range of opinion concerning sexual contact outside the lover relationship is enormous. Clearly, a number of people feel their relationship is the counterpart to heterosexual marriage and want to follow the same rules married people do. Many, though not all, are church-affiliated. Demands for sexual exclusivity are certainly frequent and vehement during the "romantic" phase of a love relationship, the initial period when the two men are still judging one another on the basis of their sexual compatibility or lack of it. Jealousies and spiteful actions are most apt to occur during this getting-to-know-each-other period. But whether a couple will agree to be monogamous depends on many factors.

Following are some of the more common attitudes about fidelity to a lover provided by the gay men interviewed in this study.

Ken, age thirty-eight, has lived with his lover, *Francis*, age twenty-three, for the past two years. Before that, Ken had been married twice. They live in a small southern town.

> I want my lover to be mine and only mine, and I want to be his and only his. He is my life, and I am his life, and that's the way I want it to be.
> I think our situation is similar to the one I had with my wife. We do everything together. It's as though we are a normal married couple, the only difference being that we're two males.

Milton,* age twenty, and *Derreck*,* twenty-seven, have been lovers for three months. They live in a gay beach resort. Their current attitude expresses the popularly believed "domino theory" of tricking.

Milton: If we felt the need for outside tricking, then our relationship is dead. It means we're no longer completely happy with each other.

Derreck: I believe in monogamy, I'm sorry. I believe the joy and benefits you get from having one person in your sex life is worth a little sacrifice. Admittedly, I see people on the streets and in the bars that I would like to have sex with, but I'm not going to because to me the benefit I get from caring, loving him, having him, and being faithful to him are a hell of a lot more. You may think it's stupid, old-fashioned, virtues like faithfulness, but I don't think it's bullshit. I think it's very valuable.

I want to be the number-one man. I want to be the only man. Maybe that's selfish, but it's the only way for me.

Milton: If I say go ahead and trick once, it's going to be easier to trick a second time; then it's going to be a lot easier to trick a third time and a fourth time.

*Marlin,** age fifty-nine, has lived with his lover for fifteen years in New York City.

Outside sex? No, that's a no-no, that's a very bad habit, a very sloppy habit to get into.

You see, I've had all sorts of relationships. I've had love affairs where you do what you want and I do what I want, and we have gruesome threesomes together. The only thing I've found out about gruesome threesomes is that somebody invariably picks up the clap; then you spend the rest of the week arguing about who brought it into the house, and what you're really doing is losing respect for each other.

I disapprove of it morally. I don't think adultery is a very pretty thing. I think you slip into it when you're dissatisfied with your lover. It's a bad habit, just like becoming an alcoholic.

Men with the strongest need for outside sex are generally those who are more experienced in love relationships, having had one or more lovers in the past. The young man is usually thought to want sexual variety, but this is not generally true. What is true is that demands for exclusivity are more common during the early stages of a love relationship, during courtship and the moving-in-together period. But there are also men who shift from demands of more freedom to less as they mature. The most frequent reasons given for wanting outside sexual contact are a need for greater variety of sexual experiences than one lover can provide; a way to avoid feelings of property ownership and possessiveness; and a means of learning new sexual techniques to bring back to the love relationship. Following are examples of men who do not believe in monogamy.

Philip * is thirty-five. After living with *Barry*, thirty-eight, for the past six and a half years, he decided that he wanted to live apart from his lover. The opportunity for more outside sex was one of the reasons.

> I still feel that a commitment to a relationship like this has very little to do with what I choose to do with my body. My commitment is more intellectual and in the heart.
> I differentiate between having sex and making love. There's a great difference. When I feel strongly toward a person, I make love. When I don't, I have sex. And I can enjoy both of them very much.

Richard, age twenty-five, has lived with his lover in New York City for the past three years. At the beginning of their relationship, Richard wanted monogamy.

> My lover believes that you're only young once, and you should maximize your youth by going out and having as many experiences as you can. I said, "Fine, I'll get you when you're old!" But that's something he can't curb, and I accept that.

Jim,* age twenty-six, is a graduate student at a large midwestern university. He recently ended a one-year relationship.

> Gay relationships to me are very exciting because there are no rules. Each relationship has at its disposal an infinite number of rules that it can create. Not like a heterosexual relationship where engagement follows, monogamy emerges, children, the whole trip. But gay relationships set their own parameters. Once you put boundaries on me, like monogamy, there's no way for me to grow. I want rules of the heart, of the spirit.

Phil * is thirty-two. He has lived with *Danny*, twenty-six, in a large midwestern city for the past two years. They both allow threesomes and sex with hustlers, alone or together.

> It's a marvelous thing for me. Danny's very open-minded about it. And it's great for me because one of

the problems I had in a previous relationship was that
I got this terrible quest for sexual adventure, and after
a while I can't continue to get it satisfied with the same
person. The challenge, the hunt, the conquest, the excitement. Maybe it's because I was repressed sexually
for so long.

The monogamy battle is fought both within ourselves as individuals and without between ourselves and our lovers. We
fight our own needs—as we perceive them—and the demands
placed upon us by the lover to conform to his personal needs. It
is this double set of conflicting demands, our own and our lover's,
that makes the issue so central in the lives of gay men; what
makes it a problem that defies solution lies in our conflicting
motivations. While the demand for monogamy or sexual liberal-
ism may seem simple and straightforward, it is not. It is the
motivation behind our request that is the most important de-
terminant in the conflict, and this motivation is often camouflaged
in socially acceptable ways. While various men may express the
same demands to their respective lovers, their motivations may
be very different, and they will judge their lover's response according to a different standard. The rest of this chapter will
consider three separate motivations for demanding monogamy
in a relationship.

Some men believe in a romantic ideal. This is reflected in one
of Plato's theories of the origin of love: two who were split
apart in childhood forever search for each other, hoping to
integrate their souls. "Human nature was originally one and we
were a whole," wrote Plato, "and the desire and pursuit of the
whole is called love." It is the belief that an integration of all
our personal needs with those of a lover is possible. It is a meld-
ing of souls, not a set of compromises.

Since fidelity is an important component of every Western
religion, some men who are religiously inspired believe this romantic ideal has moral value. But not every man who aspires to
the romantic ideal is morally motivated. For many men it is a
personal ideal (even an aesthetic one), regardless of their devotion or lack of devotion to religious doctrine.

In an ironic way, the demand for exclusivity may not be a
romantic request from a man who believes in the moral ac-
ceptability of outside sexual experience. Most often this kind of

person has had a good many of these experiences. Some men, particularly the experienced, have come to believe that "arrangements" interfere with the quality of their love relationship. They maintain that they have worked out any potential problems of jealousy and competition with a lover, that their arrangements are acceptable to both parties, but that the energy required to find third parties and to coordinate them with the relationship destroys the intimacy. They reject outside sex for this reason. For them, it isn't a moral issue but a practical one.

The second motivation for demands of monogamy is jealousy. Regardless of whether a couple decides on exclusivity, they must come to terms with feelings of jealousy. Expressions of pain are common. Feelings of abandonment torment the lover whose partner has spent the night with another man, unless, as is often the case, he has the chance to punish his wayward lover by means of accusations, moodiness, crying, or a physical fight. If jealousy does not appear in the sexual arena, where it occurs most often, then it will surface in financial matters or domestic arrangements. One has to accept the fact that jealousy is a normal part of any relationship, and the maturity of the couple can be measured by its ability to resolve jealous conflicts. Here is a rather hysterical example of jealousy in a relationship.

Lenny, age twenty-four, was living with a lover for a short period of time in New York City.

> I was at Twelve West with my lover and a couple of my friends. Then he insisted that I go outside with him. He insisted that I came to Twelve West to see this boy, but I said that he's just a friend. He wanted us to leave right away. I said I wouldn't. Then he started hitting me, and we got into a fist fight. It was real horrible, and he was the aggressor. We both looked horrible, and we didn't want to go back in looking that way, so it was real bad. We calmed down and decided to go back to his house and go to bed, and we got into this taxi and got into another fight.
>
> It was basically the same thing. He accused me of being after this other boy. I said I wasn't. You know, maybe I was, but so what, because I knew he had gone out with other boys.
>
> When we got out of the cab he said, "We're taking another walk." I started walking with him, and somehow we got entangled in another fight. This one was

worse than the first because he started attacking me
with his fists. He ripped my shirt off. I ran from him
and hailed a cab, and just as I was getting into it he hit
me square on the face and ran away.

I asked how this could happen. I never wanted it to
happen again. I felt like shit because I was beaten up.
Then he called me later that night and apologized on
the phone. He asked me to go to his house, and I
agreed.

A few days later I was doing the dishes, and he said
something that I didn't like, and I flicked water on him.
He just let loose and we had this fight, and he ended
up by getting burned with hot water—the tea kettle
spilled on him. Then he really started hitting me.

We decided to move in together about a month
later, but it all ended very soon after that.

Incidents of violence motivated by jealousy occur in gay relationships, but only a few were reported by gay men in this
study. More often there were direct statements from one lover
to the other about what constituted proper behavior. Almost always the lovers had discussed the potential or actual problem of
jealousy in their relationship, particularly with reference to outside sex. Most gay men who want an exclusive sexual relationship
make their point firmly. *Milton* * said to *Derreck*: *

Do it. And when he came back, his baggage would be
outside the door, a note saying, "Don't knock."

Ramon * said to *Charles*: *

Go and do it. Just know that while you're doing it, I'm
home here by myself, that I love you, and that I should
have been enough for you sexually.

Some lovers appear to confront the issue frequently and occasionally do things guaranteed to cause trouble.

Dan, * age twenty-seven, and *Patrick,* * age thirty-four, tell the
story of "The Monster Affair." They went dancing at the
Monster, a popular Key West disco. Dan started dancing with a
friend.

Patrick: The longer he danced the angrier I got because it looked like he was having a much better time
dancing with our friend than with me. So when they
came back I was in a state of absolute rage. Finally,
after I was silent for a while, he asked if there was any-

thing wrong, and I said no. But finally, when our friend left, I told him, yes, I was angry at him.

And we had a screaming fight in the middle of the Monster, at which point I was about ready to take the plane home.

Anthony, age thirty-one, and *Sheldon*, age twenty-seven, have been lovers for nine years. They live in a midwestern city. It is the first lover relationship for both of them. Sheldon admits that he was extremely possessive and jealous at the beginning of their relationship, particularly during the period when they weren't living together.

> *Sheldon*: Anthony had a friend he used to go to the movies with, or whatever. There was nothing sexual there, but I wouldn't believe it then. So I would sometimes call up my friend who had a car and say, "I want to know where they are and what they're doing." So Joe called me one night, snow on the ground up to your ass, and he said, "Anthony is going out with Mel tonight." I said, "Fine, meet me at the house." So we met, and he went up the front entrance and I went up the back way, and I could see them in the window. Then they drove away, and we tried to follow them.
> *Anthony*: We were just riding around. There was never any sex between us.
> *Sheldon*: I was driving the wrong way on one-way streets. The whole bit, and because there was snow on the ground I was swerving every which way. I could have gotten Joe and I killed in an accident.
>
> I was expecting that they were doing something, and I would find them in a compromising situation. I was going to present this information to them, that I knew what was going on. But the fact is, I didn't know what the hell was coming off.
>
> But to be honest about it, I'll go one step further. At the time I was horrendously whorish. I was going to bed with other men besides Anthony. And because I was, I couldn't understand how he couldn't be.

What is this madness called jealousy? Almost any couple can recount stories of behavior so irrational that one has to wonder what is meant by jealousy. Most of us are familiar with the argument that jealousy is a kind of possessiveness. While this may be true, it helps us little; substituting one word for the other does not explain either of them. A man may feel that a love relationship should be monogamous, and he may feel hurt when a lover tricks out, especially if the tricking is hidden or the lover lies about it. However, frequently we find strange contradictions in the jealousy syndrome, like Sheldon, who describes himself as "horrendously whorish" but demands monogamy from his lover. New lovers, especially young ones who energetically demand that their partners be chaste, later find that they are the first to begin wandering. There are also lovers who occasionally go out of their way to do something that guarantees the other's anger and sometimes provokes revenge. One lover tricks, and the other partner seduces the lover's best friend. Or they have a threesome during which one lover eagerly performs with the third person sexual acts that he has always refused his lover, and they start to quarrel right there in bed. There is no limit to the dimensions of jealousy.

Data from the interviews and my experiences in psychotherapy suggest that jealousy is a complicated emotion that has its roots in many different sources. One man's feelings of jealousy are not the same as another's. For instance, some may try to put the subject completely out of their minds. "Just as long as I don't know about it," is the typical expression of men who want to avoid knowing what they already know. This actually appears to work for some couples, provided the other lover is willing to play his assigned role as the "cheating husband."

Another form of denial is refusing to see the obvious. "I thought my wife started smoking cigars when I found the butts around the house," is a heterosexual joke that summarizes the problem in heterosexual marriage. The same is true in gay love. One lover may refuse to understand the most obvious hints left by the other about a pending or already accomplished affair. "He would never do that," is the slogan of the man who wants to say, "He would never do that to me." But what he really means is, "He better not do that," refusing to acknowledge the possibility that his lover may indeed "want to do that" either now or sometime in the future. Since no discussions are allowed, any transgression is perceived as betrayal.

Some men are more explicit about the rules or demands they make on their lovers concerning outside alliances; hence their jealousy is expressed much more directly. This commonly results in anger, resentment, and sometimes revenge in the form of tit-for-tat sexual exploits. It is among these men that the most color-ful conflicts appear, sometimes in private, but often providing entertainment for passersby. *Bernard* * was standing in a bar when a friend (just a friend) walked in and put his arm around him. The bartender, Bernard's lover, jumped over the bar, bottle in his hand, and smashed it over the intruder's head. Other men, less violent, may become depressed or use the weapon of silence for revenge to create feelings of guilt in the rebellious lover. Whther a jealous lover uses quiet or noisy means to convey an-ger will depend on his past history and the techniques he learned for fighting.

There are also men who, when faced with their failure to maintain their romantic territoriality, "accept" their lot in life and "allow" their lovers to march to a different tune, while main-taining their own purity. They forgive and forget—well, perhaps not forget, perhaps not forgive—and strive to be as chaste as Caesar's wife to counterbalance the beloved's delinquencies.†
Each new affair of the beloved's is experienced as another stab in the back, but the facade of imperturbability is maintained. Both the quiet sufferers and the noisy fighters end by feeling like victims.

While we have many ways to express our jealousy, all are motivated by fear. Our enmity toward our lovers is always a re-sponse to fear. We fear the loss of the beloved and abandonment; we fear desertion and the possibility, perhaps the probability, of being left alone in the world by the one person whose presence saves us from loneliness. For some these feelings are as powerful as the fear of death. The fears that lead to jealousy are not moti-vated by sexual concerns; they are attempts to capture the lover's emotional energy, to keep his "head, heart, and crotch" turned, open and pointed in the same direction—toward us. Even the most jealous man doesn't really object to his lover look-ing while walking down the street. What he does fear is that his lover is looking for someone else. Clearly, those who are most sensitive to feelings of abandonment will be most prone to jealous reactions. Men who believe themselves inferior in some way, men who suffer from low self-esteem, are always ready to believe that

† They subscribe to Schopenhauer's dictum that to forgive and to forget is to throw away valuable experience.

their lovers just "realized the truth" and that desertion will soon follow. Obsessed with their own insecurities and problems, regardless of how much a lover assures them of his love, they cannot believe that they are loved for their imagined or real weaknesses as much as for their strengths. Communication is hardly possible when such damaging forces are at work.

Envy is the third force behind demands for monogamy. It is often confused with jealousy, but there are important distinctions. Jealousy, it may be recalled, is enmity motivated by fear, the fear of being abandoned. Envy is motivated by competitiveness or covetousness. When we are envious, we are resentful of another person's perceived superiority or success. We covet what he has—his good looks, his life-style, his money, or his sex appeal. Envy implies a competition between lovers in which one partner sees himself as second best. Given the opportunity, the envious one would grab whatever he desires that the lover has.

Envy often shows up disguised as jealousy between lovers, since it appears more acceptable socially to be jealous of one's lover than to be envious. The following are reactions prompted by envy.

*Madison,** age twenty-three, and *Walter,** age twenty-three, live together in a hotel room in a large midwestern city. They have been together for a matter of months. Madison is separated from his wife, and Walter has never had a long-lasting relationship before. Walter tricks with other men, and Madison objects.

> *Madison*: I don't mind him going to the baths and things like that.
> *Walter*: Oh, come on!
> *Madison*: Not as much as I used to. I guess I'm jealous. It's so easy to find someone else in the gay world. All those guys that have a new lover each weekend. And I don't want to lose Walter.
> *Walter*: Tricking makes me feel desirable. It gives me an uplifting feeling that someone else finds me attractive, sexy. And then I get satisfaction screwing someone else.
> What happens is that when I tell you about my tricking, you get this look in your eyes. You do, when you think I've had sex with someone else.
> *Madison*: I'm a little envious that Walter can be free with his body. There's envy behind the jealousy. Sex

isn't that easy with me, even with someone I trick with, or even with somebody I know.

If it's a trick, I feel like I have to perform. I don't like the feeling. With a lot of people I feel I'm expected to do this and this sexually, and so it becomes very hard for me. With Walter, it all sounds so easy. He just has sex with them.

I went to the baths one night, and I couldn't do anything. It's very few times that I have good sex, where I feel comfortable.

Irving, age forty, and *Clayton*,* age thirty-nine, have lived together in New York City for twenty-one years. Their attraction was immediate, but they didn't have sex for months; they had problems eluding their respective families. When one of them was able to get the family car, they would often go to a drive-in. "I used to put a kerchief around his head so he would look like a woman." Irving came into the relationship sexually experienced, fully aware and accepting of his homosexuality, but Clayton had battled against his gayness by playing "trade." When they admitted their love for one another, they set up the same sort of role structure they learned in their homes. Their account is interesting since Irving expresses jealousy in the relationship, while Clayton shows envy. How they handled it is even more fascinating.

Irving: I was the woman.
Clayton: And I was the man. I could never get fucked at that point in our relationship. We basically lived our life like a husband and wife because we knew no other way. When I look back on that now, it seems boring.
Irving: We combined our money. We both came home at the end of the week with our salaries, and it all went on the table. Clayton would take charge of everything. It all went into envelopes, and he budgeted everything. That's the way it always was; that's the way it still is. I used to get an allowance.

After sixteen years of monogamous living, Clayton began to be curious about sex between other gay men. They were living a suburban life, taking care of their house and garden—and hearing stories about other couples who led more varied sexual lives.

Irving: Over the years Clayton had been very inquisitive and asking everybody we'd ever met about their

sexual experiences. You have to remember that prior
to me Clayton had no gay life, no running around. I
was leading a very active gay life, and I was all over.
I had been to every gay bar in New York City at the
time, and I danced everywhere. Clayton had never
been anywhere. He felt that he was missing out. He felt
it was a loss to him, and he really wanted to know what
was happening.
Clayton: It was an awful feeling. I didn't even know if
it was right that I should change my clothes in front
of a friend. That's how uptight we were. When I was
straight it was one thing. Now that I was gay and had
a gay friend, I turned away from each other when we
changed clothes. It was terrible.

Their first outside sex occurred on a trip to Rome. It began a
lifelong pattern.

Irving: We went to the Colosseum that night. The
lights went out at midnight, and we noticed the place
empty out—except for some stragglers, who all happened to be men. Imagine, this is at night, and you can
see the lights from the streets through the catacombs.
We noticed that all these men were migrating to one
place, so we followed them. The men were in groups,
and they were having sex, and we stood on the outside
and shivered. We had never seen sex with other people
before—ever witnessed it before. But we got so stimulated that we started to have sex together.
  We were attracting a crowd. This is really a very
strange story. I was on my knees doing Clayton, and
there was another boy doing this man next to us. Clayton became so stimulated that when he started to come
he screamed, "Irving, take me, I'm coming!" And this
guy next to him—you'd never think this was going to
happen in Rome—said, "There's nothing like a New
York blow job, is there?" Ruined the whole fucking
fantasy.

Soon after the trip, Clayton decided to spend an evening at
a gay bath. Irving went to pieces.

Irving: I knew this was a preliminary, and that something else was going to come as a result of it. My own
insecurities were getting the best of me. I thought that
no good would come of it. It was a threat.
  The first time we went to the baths, we sat in front

of the Everard baths for three hours in the car, and I cried for three hours.

Clayton: I said nothing.

Irving: I didn't know what to expect. It was the unknown.

Clayton: One night we finally went in. We made certain restrictions that we respected for a long time. We will have sex with each other. I never wanted to go alone. I wanted to do what we were doing at the Colosseum at the baths. I really wanted to see other men, see what they have. That's ninety percent of the excitement to me.

The first night was a marvelous experience. We looked and walked, and we had a lot of sex with each other, with a lot of people around us, which is what I wanted. I made sure that when we had sex we were right in the middle of the crowd.

I was a little uptight, too. I had more to risk than Irving. I was bringing him back to life, and maybe when he sees it again he'll start to miss it. So I had something to lose. We went slowly. After a while we were allowed to touch someone next to us, but not have sex with anyone else.

Irving: You have to remember that during this time we were having sex about five times a week at home, and we were already together for about fifteen years.

We still have never had sex individually. We're only into a monogamous relationship or groups, and even there we're still having sex with each other.

Clayton: Just a few weeks ago we were on Fire Island, at the Meatrack, and having sex with a lot of people. Irving came off very quickly, and he wasn't into it anymore. He wanted to go home. And I said, "OK, it's not that important to me." He said, "No, I know you're not going to be happy until you come. I know you well enough. I'll be right here. What's going to happen? You'll only be a few trees away. I can see everything." That was the first time we ever did anything like that, but he was right there watching and kind of getting off on it because I saw him playing with himself.

All aspects of sexual role playing have changed, and Clayton makes one very perceptive comment about the "masculine" role he played in their early years.

Clayton: In my mind I may always have wanted to be

fucked, but I may have been afraid of losing my masculinity. And when it started to happen, maybe five
years ago, I was almost ashamed to say to Irving,
"Irving, I'm dying to get fucked—fuck me." I was
afraid I would turn him off. I know that at that time
I would have. Irving was into that macho role playing
too.
Irving: You have to remember that at that time I
hadn't fucked anyone in fifteen years, so all of a sudden there was a little bit of a problem. I couldn't perform the way he wanted me to. But it worked itself
out, thank God.
Clayton: But we're patient with each other, and luckily
we talk a lot. We discuss everything. It may not come
the first night or the second night, but eventually it
does. Irving felt inadequate if I wanted to be fucked
and he couldn't get hard, but I didn't put any pressure
on him. I could take it or leave it.
Irving: Grass helped me a whole lot.

They state that they have done all the back-room bars in New
York City—together. They also have sex together at home almost every day. In an interesting way, they take care of each
other in the back rooms, as well.

Clayton: If I get hold of something that is erotic, or
I know that Irving would be interested, I'll actually
push him away from what he's doing, and he'll get the
message to join us, and vice versa.

It's very interesting that these two very domestic men ("Clayton is not my lover, he is my whole life") did not allow Clayton's
envy of Irving's sexual experience to become catastrophic. Both
had something to lose, and, by talking through every step together, they were able to change their relationship and their
individual roles. Not all couples are so competent. The only
complaint of Irving's is:

Irving: He still gives me the same allowance!
Clayton: Oh, come on . . . !

Julius,* age thirty, and *Chris*,* age twenty-one, were lovers
for a year, when the relationship broke up over mutual feelings
of jealousy and envy. They lived in a small rural area in a
large, sparsely populated midwestern state. Both were feeling
very lonely when they met. In many ways, their relationship

was an obvious misalliance. Chris was very active sexually, liked to be fucked, and frequently arranged to be raped or abused in some other way. Julius was quieter about his sex needs.

> *Julius*: He would come back and he would have been raped on this trip, or something bizarre would happen. I was envious because it didn't happen to me. I have fantasies of being raped, but it was happening to Chris and not to me. I wanted to go to a big city and have adventures, but I never did. I was always tied up with work.
>
> Chris would always tell me stories of his experiences on the road, and I felt he was a very loose person, and I resented how loose he had been and how much he had been around because I wanted to be that loose and be around that much.
>
> Then another time in our area around here, Chris got picked up twice by a man who lives in the mountains. This guy is called "kink man" by several of us. There was basically a rape scene with Chris. I know that I wanted that kind of scene, too.

At the same time, Chris was jealous toward Julius. Julius' early sexual life was with animals. He had sex with a number of animals on his family farm, and he hadn't learned how to be fully sexual with another man. Julius could fuck animals but not his lover. He was anxious about the transmission of disease between humans and about feces on his penis during anal intercourse with men. He had none of these worries with animals.

> *Julius*: I couldn't provide the sex that Chris needed. I felt hurt and depressed about it.
>
> I had sex with my dog a few times when Chris was here, but that was only after our sexual relationship ended. But I didn't do it when he was around. I did it when he was on one of his trips. I think Chris felt that I did it a lot more than I actually did, and he got the impression that the dog meant more to me than he did.
> *Chris*: That's exactly what I felt. There were times when the dog and I would be alone in the house, and I'd want to grab him and throw him, physically throw him out of the house. Yet I knew that was no way to handle the situation, so I sent him outside.
>
> I would say to Julius, "I think you're having sex with the dog, and it bothers me." I came right out and said what I meant. I tried to express how hurt I felt,

how jealous that Julius could do things to the dog that
he couldn't do to me.

The animal experiences may seem strange to many other gays,
especially those who live in large cities, but it's not so unusual
in farm areas. Chris is an excitement seeker and Julius a home
builder, and neither was capable of meeting on mutual ground.
Their physical isolation from most of the gay world also prevented them from learning through other people's experience.

Men who are envious of their lover often attempt to exert
some kind of control over his life, usually as a result of feeling
second best. It's a natural reaction since the lover's every success
is a reminder of failure, and we feel better in preventing his
success. Naturally, the lover resents this attempt to control him,
but the greatest harm is to the envious lover, particularly when
his envy is masquerading as jealousy.

By and large, men sexually envious of their lover's ability to
attract other men want to do exactly the same thing. Instead of
developing their own abilities, they interfere with the lover's
capabilities. In this way, the envious man remains forever convinced of his own incompetence, and it is this reinforcement of
feelings of low self-worth that does the most damage to the
envious man. Of course, not all envy is sexually motivated. One
may be more financially secure than the other, but this doesn't,
of course, imply that the lover with the lower income is poverty-
stricken, incapable of making more money, or that he should
want to. Envious men may also try to restrict the freedom of a
lover or place ever changing rules on their relationship. They
may become angry tyrants or sulkers. While all sorts of methods
may be chosen to express envy, very few will help the relationship, which is presumably what both lovers want.

The three motivating forces of the demand for or against
monogamy are the romantic ideal, feelings of jealousy, and feelings of envy. These are all important issues and by no means
mutually exclusive. One finds a mixture of all three in many
couples: at the beginning of a relationship the romantic ideal
predominates, and with the passage of time, either jealousy or
envy or a combination of both takes the lead. Since individuals
and couples change over time, motivating forces in their lives
change as well. Furthermore, maturity and experience can bring
clarity to the couple. At the beginning of a relationship, lovers

frequently see themselves as pristine and pure; in time they come to look at themselves more honestly, seeing more self-interest than they could admit in the early years. One of the characteristics of maturity is the ability to see motivations more honestly.

There are no quick cures for jealousy and envy. Most men who feel deeply wounded want the pain to go away, but the only way to accomplish this is to experience greater pain and trust again in the person who holds the power to hurt—one's own lover. Only when discussion between lovers is honest, when each can understand the perspective of the other, can there be any real resolution of the conflict. Some lovers try this and it ends in disaster, because they make the discussion a drama of mutual accusation. But if the lovers can express their feelings about the situation and their feelings of vulnerability without demanding anything of the other, then the probability of resolution increases. To achieve it, both need to be willing to change, be ready to relinquish their roles of victimizer and victim and accept responsibility for their actions.

CHAPTER SIX

Two More Demons: Dependence/Independence and Intimacy

Let our hearts break provided they break together.

C. S. LEWIS

The previous chapter dealt with two feelings that threaten love relationships, jealousy and envy. We saw how they influence decisions about monogamy in a relationship and how one man who is jealous or envious can react with scorn or anger, while another may sulk or perhaps embarrass his lover. This chapter will discuss the feelings of dependence or independence and the problem of establishing and maintaining intimacy. In some respects, it is difficult to separate these feelings—jealousy and envy, dependence/independence, and intimacy—since in relationships they are not experienced discretely. What seems first to be a problem of jealousy turns out later to be one of envy and later still of dependence. Then, too, there is a common theme of sexuality running through most of these conflicts, since men typically express their anxieties sexually, judging themselves and their lovers on the basis of sexual compatibility, expressing their rage or resentment through sexual acts.

However, the feelings examined in this chapter differ from those discussed in the previous one because they are more problematic, more covert. For example, since jealousy and envy are directed at a second party, both the jealous or envious man and his lover can take note of and understand the situation. While the resolution may be difficult, perceiving the problem is not; jealousy and envy are easily exposed, while the subjects of this chapter are not. For instance, one partner becomes annoyed at foolish little things, reproving his lover for not squeezing the

toothpaste from the bottom of the tube. The following hypothetical discussion ensues:

> *Annoyed*: Why the hell can't you squeeze this tooth-
> paste right? I keep telling you, and you don't do it.
> Do you do this just to annoy me?
> *Confused*: What's wrong with you? Everything I do
> lately you complain about. I feel like you hate me.
> What's bothering you?
> *Annoyed*: I don't know. I just don't feel right. I keep
> having these battles with you in my head about all the
> things you do that annoy me. I really feel terrible.

Or consider a hypothetical sexual conflict:

> *Betrayed*: I can't believe you did that. It was your
> birthday, and you tricked with some guy while I was
> waiting for you. I spent the whole day cooking, I
> bought wine. I wanted the evening to be special for us.
> I was home cooking my ass off, and you were out giv-
> ing blow jobs! Why did you do that? Didn't you know
> how bad I would feel?
> *Betrayer*: I didn't think about it. I just met this guy,
> and you know, one thing led to another. I didn't no-
> tice what time it was. (Pause; head down as Betrayer
> realizes he is nailed to the wall.) I don't know. I just
> feel uncomfortable about everything. If it makes you
> feel any better, I wasn't really interested in the guy.
> *Betrayed*: Huh! Then why did you do it? (More con-
> fused than ever.)
> *Betrayer*: I don't know. Now leave me alone.

Both the "annoyed" and the "betrayed" say they don't know,
and it's true. It's unreasonable to expect "annoyed" to say, "I'm
having a problem with the individuation process of the depen-
dence/independence continuum of our relationship and therefore need to find a symbolic substitute for the power your
dependency exercises upon me, which in this case is your incompetence as a toothpaste squeezer." It is no more reasonable to
expect "betrayer" to say, "My escapade is motivated by the need
to attack my birthday party, the symbolic representation of our
intimate feelings for one another, because these feelings create a
milieu of psychological vulnerability in which I feel trapped, and
I choose to create a comfortable psychological distance from you
by means of a sexual exploit that shows that I am still attractive

to other men, just in case I get scared to death with you and run out completely."

These feelings begin vaguely, and until they build up in intensity they're most difficult to understand. If the lover is jealous of his beloved, the latter can understand that, but the beloved is always totally confused when the lover is having problems with degrees of closeness. In a mature relationship, there is always a balance between the need for lovers to be dependent upon each other and the need to retain some degree of independence. This delicate balance is often precarious, and from time to time a reappraisal is necessary.

Feelings of dependence can be exceedingly frightening for some men. To them, dependence feels as if the walls are closing in, exhausting the supply of air; they begin to choke. When this happens, almost any excuse furnishes a pretext to rebel against the lover. In many cases, the rebellion is expressed sexually. The following stories illustrate this.

*Dan,** age twenty-seven, and *Patrick,** age thirty-four, have been lovers for less than a year. They live in a large northeastern city.

> *Dan*: We didn't decide to move in with each other until the third month we were together. I wasn't sure at first whether I wanted to commit myself to a relationship, to live with someone. I have more difficulty than Patrick does because he can afford to be independent. I don't have a lot of material things, and he does.
>
> We were living together only one month when a gay group had a beach party, and we went. Patrick was feeling insecure, and I guess that day I wasn't feeling secure myself. I started to drink a lot, and that's always a disaster with me.
>
> I managed to swim off to the island across the inlet with this child—not Patrick. And we had sex on the island, leaving poor Patrick at the picnic, knowing what was happening.
>
> *Patrick*: We had talked about outside sex before but never dealt with it on a practical level. But that day I can just remember picking up a hot dog. The last thing I wanted to do was eat it. I remember people coming up to me, and I didn't want to talk to them. I was just looking out at the water and looking at my watch, thinking, they couldn't have gone there just to talk.

But the funny thing was that during this whole thing, while it was happening, I felt very hurt. I felt very alone. I didn't want to be at the picnic anymore. I wanted to be by myself where I didn't have to deal with other people. But I never felt that the relationship was over.

I didn't want to leave the picnic until Dan got back because I didn't want him to think I was running out on him. It was painful, but I waited for him to come back, and I called him over and I said, "I'm leaving, but I want you to take the keys to the car and I'm going to walk home." It was about ten miles.

An argument ensued that ended with Patrick driving Dan most of the way home and Dan continuing on foot. They argued more that night and slept in separate beds. Both felt hurt and unfairly accused. "The next day was our six-month anniversary," says Patrick, and he wanted to celebrate the day.

Patrick: When I got home from work there was this note from Dan saying that he wouldn't be back for dinner that night. He was sorry that he hurt me, he apologized, but he couldn't get down on his knees and apologize so he thought it would be better if he didn't eat supper at home that night.

I called him at work and asked him to come home. I had prepared a very nice meal, a romantic meal, candlelight and so forth, and he came in. He had a card and a present, too. We both had tears in our eyes. We embraced, had supper, and we talked some more.

Dan: I had talked with a good friend of mine, and I got some insights into why I had done that. I really needed to establish my independence from Patrick again.

Patrick: I was very clinging at that point. As a matter of fact, before we left for the picnic I said, "Promise me you won't leave me at the picnic like a puppy dog on a leash." I was very clingy.

Dan: I couldn't deal with that. To this day I feel badly about this independence thing, but it's much better.

One of the other things that Patrick and I have to deal with in our relationship is my feeling that this is Patrick's house, and I'd be in a bad financial position if he were to decide to terminate the relationship. I don't make a lot of money. So Patrick put three hundred dollars in my bank account which has stayed there, and I would use it if our relationship were to break up, and I wouldn't have to stay just because I was financially tied to him, which I think is a fairly good way of taking care of one neurotic component of my life.

Patrick: In the fall, Dan's going back to graduate school, which will make him more dependent on me financially. That's a problem for me, because I like people to be dependent on me, and maybe sometimes I use it as a weapon. I have to be careful not to use it as a weapon in the future.

Dan: The relationship is sometimes scary, but I would never go back to being single. Being single is like a desert.

Bob, age nineteen, lives in the Southeast. He has never had a lover, but on the day of his interview he had just ended a brief relationship with Joe that shows how dependence/independence problems can undermine any potential relationship. Bob and Joe knew each other for a few days only, and this interview shows how quickly one man can smother another with kindness.

Joe did things to show me that he cared about me, but he did too much. He gave me breakfast in bed on a silver tray, cloth napkin and everything. First of all, I don't like to eat in the morning when I get up anyway, and he made this omelette. He just woke me up, and there it was.

This was the second morning. I told him the third morning that some mornings I don't like to eat, and I said, "This is very nice, what you've done, I really enjoy your apple and cheese omelette." The second morning it was a "heartburn" omelette, mushrooms, peppers, onions, and potatoes—and my stomach just isn't ready for stuff like that in the morning. So I told him that. And I said, "Some mornings I just get up and gobble down a bowl of cereal; other mornings I don't eat anything until six P.M. at night." So he said, "I understand," and every night when we went to bed he asked me if I thought I would want to eat in the morning. I said, "Stop catering to me. I'm capable of getting up and getting my own breakfast if I want something. I appreciate your doing things for me, but please don't overdo it."

I started to wonder whether he was what I wanted because he kept telling me that that was the way he was. I get tired of being catered .o because I'm used to

doing things for myself. My laundry was done, the
house was clean when I got home from work.
C. S.: He cleaned the house?
Oh, yeah! He was a good little housewife. He did
everything, everything I had to do for myself and left
me nothing to do for myself. I had these pants. Part
of the hem was coming out. He took the pin out and
sewed the pants.

A couple of days later, Bob asked Joe to leave. The relationship, not yet a week old, was over. Bob said good night and
went into his bedroom to sleep.

The next morning he wakes me up. Breakfast in bed.
Breakfast in bed! * He apologized again. Breakfast
in bed! I was furious. "What the fuck is wrong with
you?" I didn't say this to him. I said it in my head. I'm
still half asleep. He fixes an omelette for me and him
and brings his omelette and mine up to my bedroom so
we can eat together! And I'm sitting there looking at
it. Last night I tell him that the relationship's over, and
here I'm getting the same treatment as the first day he
got here.

Tom, age twenty-one, lives in a town in a sparsely populated
state in the Midwest. He met his lover at a gay New Year's
Eve party. The affair lasted only a couple of months. Tom's
experience shows how severe dependency upon a lover can drive
the lover away.

At the time I didn't realize how much physical contact
he wanted. I needed personal physical space. I needed
my room. When we'd be sleeping he would roll over
me and maybe hold me, and for a while I needed that
holding, but it continued too long. It was touch, hold,
feel, and it was just more than I could handle to have
this person totally fondling me at every hour, minute,
given second.
　　I felt mauled at that point. I didn't feel OK. There's
just so much space I need for myself, and it came to a
point where his touch was like having electricity in a
negative sort of way. It wasn't an exhilarating experience. It was like *zap*—and I'd look there for a burn
mark or something.
　　I told him I needed my space, and he responded,
"I'll give you your space," and it became a total thing.

* Mushroom and swiss cheese. Bob says it was very good.

He wouldn't touch me at all. There was no happy
medium. It was only, "I'm going to supply all your
needs, you're going to supply all my needs, and we're
going to wear each other out in six months." And that's
it. I have a lot to give but not when it's taken all at one
time. It was too much of a leaning relationship.

*Jim,** age twenty-six, is a black graduate student at a large
midwestern university. His affair of two and a half years with
Lionel illustrates an intriguing but common form of the depen-
dence/independence balance. The relationship was based on a
student/teacher model, not uncommon in gay love affairs. In
this example, Jim, the student, changes in time as he becomes
more experienced sexually, but Lionel refuses to change himself, and the relationship ends.

Lionel lived a whole life where people pandered to his
beauty. In his younger days, he was a hustler. I'll make
allusions. Did you read *After the Fall*, the Arthur Miller
play about his relationship with Marilyn Monroe? Very
similar in the way the two of them interacted. Lionel
was in love with black people but not in love with black
individuals. He had an image that because I was black
I was a stud, and if I didn't continually portray that
image, that would upset him.

At first I was getting a lot from him, in the sense of
the prostitute teaching the junior academic student what
the body means. But once I got that, and I got that after
about four months, I began to see everything else, especially his jealousy.

Sex for me—I've always been into what I've been
reading—I had all these intellectual ideals about love
and sex, you know, Tristan and Isolde, into Wagner
and Tennessee Williams. Sex was everything, but it
never involved me. It involved all these characters, all
these opera people, all these people on the screen, but it
never really involved me because I never knew how to
express my sexuality out of fear.

But it became boring after a while. We did the same
thing every night. We went to bed, and I would screw
him. I could fuck him four or five times a night, and he
would love it. By the end of the relationship I wouldn't
even touch him.

I think that if I had stayed with him I would have
seen the last act of *Carmen*. Some horrible, ugly, sordid
scene where he came at me with a knife.

Lionel wanted pure monogamy, and that wasn't for

me. But it was also that he wanted a black stud. The fact that I had a brain just made it more interesting.

I met some of his lovers from the past, white and black. There was a clear difference between them. His white lovers were nice pleasant people, and his black lovers were like hoodlums off the street. I clearly didn't fit in with the line of his black lovers.

The next two interviews are with men motivated toward developing intimate relationships with lovers. In the first, Thomas attempts this with everyone he meets; in the second, Jim tells us of a particular incident in his life.

Thomas * is forty-five, a graduate student in New York City. He had a lover for ten years; the relationship ended in 1973. He is the kind of person who develops intimacy almost immediately.

If I go to bed with someone one night, or even for a few hours, it's the whole thing. I consider it the complete love thing, complete love and trust. A very tender thing. I can think of people I've slept with or just laid down in a bed with, and the contact was so pure, so sincere, so free, I can remember them fifteen years later.

I'll always ask them to spend the night. I'll ask them to come back. I always try to move toward stability, and even if I don't want to continue the affair, I try to continue as a friendship. I pretty much always succeed.

*Jim,** age twenty-six, has been with his lover for a year. They were vacationing in Miami and decided to drive through the Florida Keys.

We were in the car going down to the Keys. We were on Highway One, listening to the radio. We both liked that song a lot. I was driving along and we left Key Largo, and suddenly the ocean came up on one side and I felt —you know—sort of jolted. Then the ocean came up on both sides, and I had to stop driving the car. That was the first time I cried in front of him, and he got this big smile on his face. I didn't stop for ten minutes.

I had really given up on love because the relationships I had in the past left a bad taste in my mouth. And finally there was a person sitting next to me who I really loved, and I knew that he really loved me. And I was surrounded in my most ideal setting. And we were alone together. Four days later he did the same thing.

In examining the interviews, problems related to establishing intimacy with a lover were far more difficult to identify than problems of dependence/independence—not necessarily more important but more elusive. Intimacy appears to be one of the goals of gay lovers and to some the only criterion of a success-ful relationship. Yet, while this attitude was often obvious, it was rarely stated verbally. It was certainly communicated both to me as the interviewer and to the lover, but the words of the transcript fail to convey these nuances. Psychologists are hard-nosed about information that can't be put into words, ignoring many levels of communication while conducting interviews for research purposes, but clinicians must pay close attention to the ambiguities and conflicting messages sent during interviews. Feelings and problems of intimacy expressed by my respondents were crowded with such ambiguities.

Verbal statements were least often used to express intimacy, and this was true of all the couples, regardless of age, experi-ence, geographical area, or any other factor. Perhaps it's the knowledge that words can be used to conceal, rather than reveal, underlying emotions. It has been said, "The spoken word is a lie," and this reticence with words summarizes the attitude of many of the subjects interviewed. Since intimate feelings are most often conveyed by nonverbal means, the interviews were rich in nonverbal messages. Words were sometimes chosen spe-cifically to hold back tears, but the feelings behind them were apparent in the tone of voice. Often when a man cried, remem-bering either a sad event or a happy one, sympathetic tears ap-peared in the eyes of the lover listening. Lovers sat side by side, moving hands or feet slowly toward each other to bridge the physical gap; it was striking how often during an interview this physical connection was made and how important it became after discussing some crisis in the relationship. How amused they were to find their hands or feet touching, as if to say, "How did this happen?" They would laugh, enjoying the physical contact, occasionally moving closer to me as well—an unselfish gesture of warmth not wasted on someone running from appointment to appointment.

Messages of intimacy were also conveyed by pauses in speech, followed by the strength and tone of voice when the subject began to speak again. Eye contact or the avoidance of it with the lover or with me conveyed either trust or vulnerability. The desire to establish trust with the interviewer, a stranger, was often expressed by divulging very sensitive material, including long-maintained personal secrets, and accepting the stranger's assurance of confidentiality. Because of this, the comments that follow cannot be clearly illustrated with extracts from the interviews. The reader will have to be satisfied with impressions and an analysis of the emotional atmosphere of the interviews.

Clearly, home builders are more sensitized toward intimacy than excitement seekers. Building a nest is not necessarily enough for them. They isolate symbols, certain moments of interaction with their lovers, as proofs of their intimacy; without these, the home, the external accoutrements and financial well-being, are seen as a sham, a substitute for love and a question mark against the value of the relationship. Although there are some home builders who will judge the cost of the house and its furnishings to be just as important as their feelings of intimacy, they are a minority.

Excitement seekers are not as pleased with intimate feelings, especially if they live with a lover who likes to express intimacy and receive it in turn. This attempted exchange usually creates conflicts, with frequent retreats to outside sex by the excitement seeker. It should not, however, be thought that excitement seekers are all devoid of desires for intimacy and its expression; they just prefer to be allowed to experience these feelings without discussing them too often. They appear to be worried that intimacy may become dependency, which they experience as a fetter and hence fear it.

Moments of intimacy between men are not found primarily in events. An anniversary or a birthday is not intimate, nor is buying a house or even a period of enormous sexual satisfaction. Events such as these stand on their own as moments of pleasure and pride. Intimacy is something over and above, an overwhelming experience that may be linked with one of these events or else totally apart. It is experienced not because the lovers have worked hard saving their money to buy a house, but because they feel worthy of each other and of the house, or because they can sit together in front of a fireplace and feel there is nothing else they need or want to complete their happiness. Intimacy is found, therefore, in the simplest events and cannot be bought or planned. It is in a sense uncontrollable, found in moments when the outside world ceases to exist or to have meaning. During these interludes, the couple experiences the bliss of being "we two together."

For this reason, buying things for a lover or presents of any kind, physical or psychological, do not convey intimacy; the act is not simple enough and may actually be too costly for intimacy. Gifts always carry symbolic meaning: at times they convey emotional warmth; at other times they are weapons. For instance, a gift can be an apology for an angry moment in the recent past or a payoff to a lover for not complaining about something. Then, too, it can be an obligation for the recipient to return the favor, or a guilt trip because the giver remembered the anniversary (or whatever) and the recipient forgot. It can even be a form of dependency, especially if the gifts are lavish. There are many possible meanings, all subsumed under the motivation of controlling the lover, the recipient of the gifts. It may be seen why important gifts are seldom expressions of intimacy. Of course, some gifts, even costly ones, are given out of love. There are lovers who sacrifice their own needs to buy something, say a costly stereo or an expensive set of books, for their lovers. These gifts are not likely to elicit feelings of intimacy from the recipient *because they were planned.* Planning a gift always carries with it the possibility of mixed motivation, of trying to prove love and demonstrate it in ways that are visible and recognized by the receiver. It is this premeditation that may interfere with feelings of intimacy tied to the gift giving.

Some objection may be made to the statement that planning and giving of costly gifts do not convey intimacy. A critic might maintain that the gift giver is altruistic in the giving and the gift an important expression of his feelings toward his lover. But this is exactly what the recipient may object to, the reason why he can accept the gift lovingly but not as an expression of intimacy. The gift becomes a symbolic statement of intimacy, a substitute for the real thing—the feelings. The gift needs to be interpreted by the recipient; it is understood to be a substitute for the words and feelings he would prefer to hear and experience. In order for it to be felt as intimate, the recipient would have preferred to have all the emotional energy expended by the lover in thinking about the gift, shopping for it, wrapping it, and presenting it to be delivered plainly in words and actions.

Small, seemingly trivial gifts most often convey intimacy. Un-planned, inexpensive, hardly noticeable items make the most powerful statements about intimacy.* The gift may not even require any expenditure of energy; it may be given without any awareness on the part of a lover that he is giving it. For instance, the following scene is almost universal in the lives of many lovers with intimate relationships. Two lovers are washing dishes to-gether after supper. There is little talk between them. Each is thinking how good it is to be here with "him" and how warm it feels knowing that "he" wants to be here with "me." Each lover "knows" that the other is having the same thoughts and feel-ings. They smile at each other, perhaps saying nothing, or per-haps they make a direct verbal statement like, "I love you, too," or an indirect statement that means the same thing like, "I'll wash them tomorrow night."

A physical gift can also convey feelings of intimacy, but only when the object is reminiscent of feelings from the past. A gift given to Albert is a good example. When Albert was six years old he had a set of puppets, and his favorite was a red one. Albert's father crushed it in his hand because he didn't want Albert to grow up a sissy; this memory is a wound that still bleeds. But one day a couple of years ago, Albert's lover, Gilbert, gave him a present—a little red puppet with a note saying, "I'll never take it away from you." That was a gift experienced as intimate by Albert, and understandably so. On the whole, in-expensive gifts are perceived as more intimate than expensive ones; they imply feelings. Above all, intimacy is a rush of emo-tion that is better conveyed without the overstatement of valu-able objects.

There are sometimes conflicts between lovers over the giving of physical and psychological gifts. These are especially evident when one lover cherishes demonstrations of intimacy, while the other prefers to express it through some form of psychological distance like an expensive gift or a party for the beloved (which can always serve the purpose of having lots of people around so neither of them gets too "mushy"). Since the beloved prefers

---

* I do not mean to suggest that lovers should stop giving each other handsome gifts. Gift giving is an important part of all relationships. I am only suggesting that giving presents and expressing intimacy are not the same thing.

the words and the feelings, there is resentment, accompanied by guilt. The lover, in turn, perceives the resentment toward the gift, feeling his love is being rejected; he, too, becomes confused, caught between love for his beloved and rejection for showing it. This confusion is especially pronounced if one partner grew up believing that gifts express love, the other that only the "small things" in life are important. These different attitudes can lead to vindictive mutual accusations, but only in couples that don't express their feelings openly.

This elusive sense of intimacy is so powerful that it cannot be sustained for long periods of time, although the capacity for it varies. There are a few men who claim to want it most of the time, yet we have no idea what would happen if they were to get their wish. At the other extreme, there are those who want only the slightest beginnings of intimacy and then cut it off, refusing more until they recover, which may not be for quite a while. But most of us want periods of intimacy with our lovers with some frequency and miss these severely when we are deprived. It should be noted, however, that almost everyone at some point wants to lessen the intensities of intimacy. This desire is a perplexing one. Why should something that gives us such great pleasure, something we strive for so desperately in our relationships, be cut off at any point?

There are three possible reasons. The danger of vulnerability is the first. An intimate relationship or a moment of intimacy is, psychologically speaking, highly dangerous. It is a moment when all a person's defenses are down, a time of psychological nakedness when everything is exposed, the joys, the fears, the scars, a moment when personal history fades into oblivion and a perfect blending between two people takes place. It is a moment when both men have lost any capacity to withstand an attack from the other, a moment when misplaced trust can only result in personal devastation and humiliation. No compromises with feelings are possible in moments of intimacy. They are experienced either as total intimacy or as complete betrayal. It is one of the most frightening emotions a man can feel and express, and this inevitably leads to a sense of absolute helplessness. Vulnerability in intimate moments is a danger signal that profound helplessness is on the way, a psychological state akin to infancy.* It is rewarding because of the sense of unity it provides with another man and also impossible to maintain because of the fear of emotional harm.

It is important at this juncture to distinguish between true vulnerability and other similar interactions that lack this quality. For instance, bartenders report that their customers tell them the most "intimate" details of their lives. Bartenders say (and I for one believe them) that they hear things their customers are afraid to tell their lovers, their therapists, or their priests; their customers trust them with this information. But I believe the bartender/drinker relationship is neither trusting nor intimate.

The word "trust" has significance only when it is accompanied by *risk*. Without some degree of risk, some possibility that the person will lose something or be harmed in some way—in this case, emotionally—no trust is involved. Trusting someone doesn't mean putting information into the safekeeping of another as if he were a vault, at least not if we're talking about trust as a characteristic of intimate relationships. The "safekeeping" definition of trust, as with a bartender, has no sense of the future; but in the context of intimate relationships, trust has one eye on the future. *Intimate trust* always implies an expectation of future payment and the possibility that the payer may be reluctant to return trust with his own.

A bartender listens to self-disclosure, not trust. A man, afraid to say something important to a lover, says it to the bartender, disclosing secret and important information about his inner self. He ventilates his feelings, expresses emotions and attitudes rehearsed in his head over and over for days, weeks, perhaps years. And the bartender listens, or pretends to, but he doesn't really care. He has heard the story a hundred times before from the same man and from others just like him. The alcohol is irrelevant, except that it loosens the tongue a bit. The man disclosing all this personal information knows that the bartender doesn't really care, which is precisely why he went to a bartender in the first place! If the bartender listened to him and cared, the inter-

* But also significantly different from infancy because intimacy is a voluntary state of emotion, while the helplessness of infancy is not. No adult, no matter how intimate, ever approaches the state of helplessness of the infant.

action might carry the same potential danger the man would experience by confession to a lover. Since the bartender neither cares nor is about to do or say anything to insult a good tipper, there is no risk, hence no possibility of an intimate relationship in the discussion. In all fairness, bartenders believe that helping men to ventilate feelings—some bartenders are very good at it —is a worthy responsibility and trust, in the safekeeping sense. It is also true that some bartenders help lovers get together to discuss a recent conflict; this probably happens more often in relatively small communities where most gays know one another. But helping customers ventilate feelings or mediating disputes is not part of an intimate relationship since no risk is involved; it is not a situation of vulnerability.

There are two other interactions that are often confused with vulnerability and trust. A certain kind of "tricking" is the first. Let's say your lover says or does something hurtful; let's even suggest that the lover intended to hurt your feelings—pure malevolence on his part. Then, when you take every reasonable step toward reconciliation, he only hurts you more. Wounded severely, you leave the house and find another man for the evening, a warm and understanding person, a model of sensitivity to whom you entrust your body and troubles. Since he is such a model of sensitivity, he recognizes your need for tenderness and support, supplying it joyfully. He holds you, kisses you, assures you of your goodness and of the beauty of your body; he satisfies your tenderest sexual needs, unselfishly so. You confess everything to him. You rely on him, trust him with feelings so profound they would frighten you at any other time. Is this an intimate relationship characterized by trust?

I think not. Admittedly, it comes close. There is interaction between two men who have something to lose during the evening: the lover who is tricking takes the chance of being rejected or laughed at by his companion for the evening; the temporary lover, since he is this model of comfort, takes the chance of feeling incompetent to give solace to the man in his arms. But the scale is not balanced. The self-disclosure is coming from one direction only. The rejected lover is taking all the important risks, while the temporary one takes very few. The situation is not intimate; it only provides a substitute.

The tricking example would change dramatically if the temporary lover for the evening, after listening and consoling, then responded with self-disclosures, his own worries or vulnerabilities aroused by listening to another. If he talks about experiences meaningful to him, he in turn entrusts his partner with potentially dangerous information. Now that's a different story. In this case, we have self-disclosure and risk on both parts and hence an intimate experience.

It makes no difference that this experience is transient. Since feelings of intimacy are tied to the here and now, the experience doesn't imply an intimacy in the future, although some people expect it to. It can stand on its own without either of the parties wanting to repeat it. Indeed, in the very moment of intimacy, they may realize that a future relationship between them is impossible. It's much easier to feel intimate with someone who doesn't know you, to whom you show only your best features and not your least worthy ones, the aspects a long-lasting lover knows well. In this sense, remaining intimate with a lover over time is more complicated and more difficult than establishing a short-lived affair with another man. But, regardless of duration, this new example qualifies as a moment of intimacy because of the vulnerability resulting from the risk taken by both parties.

A final interaction that may or may not be an intimate one occurs between close friends. There is no question that some gay men have as much trust and risk at stake in some of their friendships as others have with their lovers. Some men even maintain that these friendships bring them greater happiness than love relationships. In other situations, friends come closer to the model of the bartender or trick for the night, where little risk is involved or where the friendship is based on shared interests, rather than personal details and conflicts.

Friendship networks can be either an aid or a wedge in the lives of lovers. On the one hand, friends can give validity to the relationship between two lovers; on the other, one lover can use his closeness to a friend as a distraction from intimacy with a lover. In one case the couple is supported, and in the other the friend, while perhaps wanting to help, is placed in the role of preventing closeness between the lovers by hearing things that should be said to the lover.

To repeat, there are three reasons why a man may cut off intense feelings of intimacy, even while he wants to bring them about. The first is vulnerability and helplessness. The second reason is fear of losing one's autonomy as a separate and distinct individual. The hallmark of an intimate moment is the sense of unity between two people; but this, while pleasurable for a while, ultimately leads to some confusion about where one person ends and the other begins. The boundary between the two gets fuzzier, more indistinct. The feeling of uniqueness gets lost. Such a feeling is distressing. It is as if one partner doesn't exist except in union with the other and is particularly threatening to those who fear dependence. They mistake extreme intimacy for extreme dependence. Dependence implies that one partner is in a superior and the other in an inferior position, whereas intimacy implies an egalitarian relationship. They are easily confused by those who fear dependence and who therefore demand autonomy to an extreme. But all of us, including those who work toward an intimate relationship, need to maintain some personal autonomy, and we end intimate moments for that reason.

Finally, no one can survive in the world in a relationship of total intimacy. Since intimacy blocks out all other stimulation, all the necessary responsibilities of life are ignored, like earning money, paying attention to friends and relatives, or even mundane shopping. We need to do many things in order to work toward personal goals in life, quite apart from relationships with our lovers. In addition, we may enjoy other kinds of experiences with our lovers that are not intimate, like sex for physical pleasure only, working around the house, being left alone for periods, holding friendly, warm conversations about shared interests. It would be a terrible mistake to judge the success of any love relationship solely according to the frequency of intimate moments, as if such closeness were the only measure of a successful relationship. All the other moments count as well. Being *capable* of a certain kind of feeling doesn't mean one must demonstrate it constantly.

During the interviews, there were couples who had obviously frightened themselves over the demand for intimacy, especially when it was combined with worries about "commitment" for a lifetime. These couples appeared to view commitment as a penal sentence and were aghast at their responsibility. They were too future-oriented, each lover worrying about whether he "could make it" or if he was worthy of his beloved's love. It is best for couples to maintain their emotional contact in the present and let the future take care of itself.

It should be obvious to the reader that since intimacy is defined as an interaction in the present between two people, it cannot exist in one person only. A person cannot be intimate by himself. He may long for intimacy, he may try to shower it on another, but unless these feelings are returned, intimacy is not present. Once again, vulnerability, hurt, trust, and risk are all key words, and they cannot exist with any meaning unless two people are involved. The interaction definition of intimacy explains why some men are always hurt in relationships; the feelings of one lover toward the other are not reciprocated. Some of our most painful moments spring from what may be called a false intimacy. True intimacy is always mutual since it is a shared emotion, but false intimacy is one-sided and illusory. In these painful situations, a person may find the present reminding him of intimacies in the past to which he responds ardently. For him, the present is only pretext. Hence this overflow, prompted by the intensities of the past and the reality of the present, leads to bewilderment. Since the emotion is not shared, the other party can never be sufficiently responsive; quite literally he doesn't know what's going on. His lack of response is misinterpreted as rejection, and the result is confusion and frustration.

Again, intimacy is not necessarily related to the longevity of a love relationship. Short-lived intimate relationships have already been mentioned. One can also find long-lasting relationships in which no intimacy is ever expressed and, in some cases, never occurred. People stay together for many reasons, some admirable, others not so admirable. Familiarity may keep a couple together; in other cases intimacy increases with the age of the couple. No hard and fast rules exist for judging the quality of a love relationship by the number of years two men have spent together.

Lastly, there is the matter of how feelings of intimacy affect sex between lovers. The subject is highly complicated, because sexual needs and feelings between lovers change with time. The most common pattern at the beginning of a love relationship is frequent, passionate sex with a high degree of intimacy. Much caring and support during sex are usual during the romantic period, with the willingness of each party to modify his own sexual needs to meet those of his lover. At the beginning, lovers are very accommodating toward each other. Since the expression of affection is considered the basis of love, any physical and sexual need on the part of one of the lovers that violates the rule of affection is dismissed as inappropriate and unloving. The affection rule mandates that all sexual activity must express sweetness, consideration, tenderness; it precludes expressions of frank lust, rough stuff, kinkiness, far-out fantasy, and impersonality. Given enough time, the affection rule for some men becomes a burden of unspeakable proportions, a cage that confines sexual needs to an arbitrary standard that has lost all sense and reason in the relationship. They find sexual experiences outside the relationship.

Alan, for instance, has been involved in a long-established love affair complicated by changes in his sexual needs over time. Again, in this case his sexual interests moved from affectionate sex to nonaffectionate sex, and the result created difficulties in his relationship.

*Alan,** thirty, lived an exceedingly domestic life with a lover for twelve years in an eastern suburban community until they broke up two years ago. Alan was only sixteen when he began this relationship. Throughout it, he preferred to be fucked, but his lover became limp whenever they tried. Alan never complained about the problem, nor does he feel that it was important. The final breakup was over their conflict between Alan's desire to remain in their house, for which they had saved for many years, and his lover's wish to return to New York City and a more exciting life. There were other subterranean forces at work, particularly in Alan's changing sexual life. What probably kept them together for so long was a sense of intimacy that was very important.

> Anniversaries were always a big thing for us. It was our day. We would go to a gay restaurant so that we could just sit there and gaze at each other, just admire each other and get off on that. We did that every year, and I loved him more every year. I still do. Sometimes we would read poetry to each other. In the twelve years we were together, I never walked into a gay bar.

We both knew that there was some sex outside, although neither of us was interested in developing any kind of affair. It was a sexual release, and part of the reason I didn't talk about it was that I normally would get fucked when I had sex with somebody else, and he couldn't do it, and I didn't want him to feel bad. So I wouldn't tell him. He didn't tell me about his sexual encounters. I don't know why, maybe because I didn't tell him.

I still love him, and I know that he still loves me. How? It's just like there's air outside, we just love each other.

One night we were driving back from New York, and we drove up West Street. We stopped at this red light near Christopher Street, and it was the first time I had seen all these guys in leather walking between the Ramrod and Badlands. They were just sort of hanging out there. And I said, "That's really cool." It was all so safe because I was in the car and the safety of my relationship.

Then I started having S and M fantasies. I didn't tell my lover about them. I guess I was a little ashamed of being turned on by them. We had just had a really lovely evening and we were going back to the house, and I was shocked by it. I wasn't ready for it. I sort of knew it was there, and it turned me on.

Then one weekend we were in Provincetown, and I told him I thought I was a masochist. He immediately said it wasn't true, and I told him it was. He said he couldn't understand why anyone would want to hurt me, and I said it's not so much hurt as very erotic. I went into my fantasies of surrendering and going into this whole masochist trip.

We had a pretty honest relationship, and that's why I told him everything. I wanted him to understand. I guess in the back of my mind I was hoping we could experiment with it, but he wanted no part of it. So because of the negative reaction he gave me, I never asked him to experiment.

Alan began experimenting with masochism at a New York bar and found it erotic and satisfying. The facts of the breakup are not credible. They had a disagreement at a shopping center, and one said, "Then let's break up," and the other responded, "OK." Clearly, they were unwilling at that time to confront each other with the way their sexual lives had diverged, prob-

ably out of worry one would hurt the other. Alan now lives a
similar domestic life with another man in a well-defined S and M
relationship.

> With my new lover I don't want sex with anyone else.
> He totally satisfies me sexually, and I totally satisfy him.
> I can't even think about having sex with someone else.
> It's not a moral question. Our relationship is a very
> tender thing, a very beautiful thing. I could go on like
> this forever. Some people think I'm confining myself,
> but I don't feel confined. The year after I left my former
> lover I was going to bars, and I never felt more confined
> in my life as I did then. I don't know how people do it,
> I really don't. I couldn't live like that.

Alan's story demonstrates that home builders can maintain
their domestic interests and drive toward intimacy regardless of
their sexual inclinations.

Many people misinterpret the meaning of intimacy in their
relationships. Intimacy, especially with regard to sex, can be
either the cement of a relationship or a millstone around the
necks of the lovers. Presumably, some lovers interpret "dirty
sex" and S and M as outside the bounds of intimate relationships, as would many who subscribe to the sugarcoated doctrine
of sexuality between lovers. All of our early training and the
teachings of our parents and church authorities, to say nothing
of the spate of marriage manuals, have suggested that sexual
expression between lovers is always highly nurturant, with only
the kindest, most endearing words and tenderest of emotions
expressed. But this long-maintained historical interpretation of
lover sex does not perfectly coincide with intimacy. Trust and
risk are the hallmarks of intimacy during sexual activities, not
nurturance, although nurturant feelings may be important at
other times, or most of the time, depending on the couple. What
is important about intimacy during sexual activity is the relationship between the two men, not their particular activities. Therefore, "dirty talk" is not necessarily a handicap to "loving talk"
in the bedroom and has as much possibility as an expression
of intimacy, when trust and risk are involved, as loving talk.

One hears often in gay circles that sex between lovers ends
after a while, and each lover chases after new people. This belief,
which just about approaches the power of a cultural truism, has

not been found valid in this study. There are enough cases of lovers together for years who do not have sex together, but the same is true of some couples who have been together for a very short period and yet choose to remain together. I have also found that most couples together for many years continue their sexual activities with almost as much fervor as before, limited only by the age factor and the interval needed between sexual activities. But where this has been revealed, the couples have allowed new experiences to change their lives; they have incorporated new ways to express themselves sexually. Sex between lovers becomes stale with fear of potential changes in partners and their relationship, fear of the direction that may be taken with the changes, and avoidance of the potential intimacy of working together toward a readjusted relationship.

The position expressed above obviously contradicts the more commonly held belief that intimacy prevents change and leads to dull sex or no sex between lovers. Familiarity, it is claimed, is deadly to sex life in a relationship. C. A. Tripp (*The Homosexual Matrix*) theorized, in a book highly regarded by gays, that some form of psychological tension between lovers is necessary to maintain the passion of a relationship. This tension, which Tripp calls "resistance," creates a motivating force toward sex; without resistance, boredom sets in.

My interpretation, based on the men interviewed, is that "resistance" is analogous to excitement seeking and that Tripp's hypothesis is appropriate for excitement seekers in or out of a relationship. There were certainly enough men who felt that Tripp's concept described them well enough, but it won't do for domestically oriented men, the home builders in this book, whose drive is toward intimacy, not tension. For them, dull sex is not an example of intimacy, but its avoidance. Once again, the definition of intimacy in a couple and the frequency and fashion of its expression are based mainly on the personality characteristics of each of the men in a love relationship.

CHAPTER SEVEN

Cock Rings and Lovers

Allah knows, none has
A member of the size
Of mine; so measure it—come,
Take my prize!

ABU NOWAS

Many of the problems that haunt gay love relationships spring from the difficulties of two men each imbued and trained in the demands of masculinity as defined by our society. In its most extreme form I call it *cult masculinity*, in which the symbols of masculinity exert more influence over behavior than the need for love. Cult masculinity is excitement seeking carried to its most extreme form.

The cock ring is the most prominent symbol of cult masculine excitement and authority. Maintained by the myth that it keeps an erection for long periods of time, it is really little more than an adornment of the penis, a costume for the cock, a special way to exhibit phallic power—it is, in fact, only a fetish.* It may indeed do a great deal for the wearer, but only psychologically. Just as the ancient Greeks kept a *herm* (a statue of a nude man) with his penis erect on their doors, so, too, the macho gay today has transformed himself into the herm. But the Greeks believed in their herms, while the macho gay is only an actor in the theater of the macho gay world. The myth of the cock ring is a modern way of saying that the adornment has magic powers, externally granted.

Cult masculinity has replaced femininity as the social behavior of gay men. Just a hundred years ago the English dandy was all the rage, with Oscar Wilde and a cadre of Cambridge scholars as the role models. In this century people believed that sissylike boys grew up to be effeminate men. Of course, the campy

---

* There are a variety of devices sold for the purpose of helping men achieve and keep an erection. They all have one thing in common. They don't work. But men will continue to buy them anyway.

behavior of femme men was only a way of expressing hostility and deriding the rejection they experienced; whatever the reason, the "queen" stood at the apex of homosexual openness. Now the image has changed completely—"queens" are a dying breed (unfortunately, so are their art and wit), replaced by the "macho man" who ironically has become more macho than his heterosexual model.

The bar scene and the pleasures available at baths and cruising places are integral aspects of the new opportunities gays have to enjoy themselves and sex. Never before in history have such openness and freedom been extended to our persecuted minority. We are savoring every moment—and so we should—in a scene filled with sexual excitement and conquest. For some gay men it's just what the doctor ordered.

As men we are inevitably a combination of two independent life forces. The first is our historic inheritance of masculinity, cult masculinity, partly determined by the traits of aggression, power, and competition. But a second life force is our homosexuality, our love as men for other men, and here history is obscure, more tenuous and less tied to standards and models, which may account for the rapidity with which the homosexual image changes.

Yet cult masculinity and homosexuality are often in opposition to each other. Each has a different set of characteristics and a different relation to self-esteem. Successful cult masculinity may be devastating for one's homosexuality, and an overemphasis on one's homosexuality may make cult masculinity impossible. This conflict between our masculine heritage and our homosexual needs is the major conflict in many gay male love relationships.

In the first place, cult masculinity *demands* sex with another person, while homosexuality is an emotional need for another man to love. It is not merely a difference in emphasis; it is a difference in goals. We have seen in some of the early chapters that heterosexual boys can engage in almost every possible sexual act without calling themselves homosexual. The same is true of adult heterosexual men. In the past as today, heterosexual men have screwed little boys when they were available, sodomized their wives or girl friends, and indulged themselves freely in "circle jerks." The social status in prisons is maintained by rape. This form of male sexuality demands genital pleasure, regardless of the consequences for the other person, male or female. Cult masculinity, therefore, is selfish and self-absorbed, with the display of masculinity symbols and the accumulation of sexual conquests as goals. This rigid form of masculine power is image-making and defensive, closed to negotiation.

Homosexuality is softer in its image. It has taken many years for the Western world to develop homosexuality, which is a new moral system that cannot be defined in sexual terms only. In the present state of the world, it should be viewed as a cultural advance. Homosexuality, like any modern characteristic, is still open to change and fluid in its potential. Its goal is not sexual behavior but the development of love, a compact of companionship and sex with another man or a series of men.

The second difference between cult masculinity and homosexuality is the relationship between sex and aggression. In cult masculinity, sex and aggression are inseparable. It is for this reason that so many lesbians (particularly politicized ones) are outraged by gay men's sexual conduct. Many gay men think it is unremarkable to have sex with another man to orgasm without knowing his name or even what he looks like, which horrifies many women. Seduction, literally luring someone to have sex with you, is an action of aggression proving that the seduced is not as masculine or as strong as the seducer. The man who *never* has sex with someone a second time, no matter how enjoyable it was, is essentially saying that the conquest—the seduction—is more gratifying than the genital experience itself—a position, it seems to me, typical of sexual aggression, rather than of sexual love.

Few men understand the anger of some lesbians toward gay men's sexual interest, or their complaint that gay men objectify other men just as much as straight men have objectified women. This reminds women of the sexual aggression from which they have suffered, and perhaps they fear that the sexually aggressive gay man may one day turn against them. Gay men are perplexed by this attitude. We think of our new opportunities as a way of enjoying each other's bodies. As for objectifying another person, we men rather enjoy it. We know we're doing it, and we know our partner is a voluntary participant.

What is it that frightens lesbians about our sex? I think it has to do with speed. Men are fully capable, physically and psychologically, of functioning sexually in the briefest time. But most lesbians want to get to know potential lovers.

While this is not the appropriate place to theorize whether the sexual response rate of women, which is slower than that of men, is culturally or biologically determined, the differences do seem real. I suspect that to women the speed of male (gay or straight) sexual response and male readiness are symbols of aggression, and this frightens them. To women, men always seem determined to impose their sexual demands, and lesbians view this as an aggressive act. There's also the possibility that male sexual speed is a paradigm of how men attempt to resolve conflict, completely and all at once. The speed with which some lovers, caught in a conflict, try to resolve it may also explain the quick breakups of some gay couples. Lesbians may be right about how some of us express our aggressiveness and domination through sex: by anonymity, by the speed of our response, and even by the frequency of our sexual contact. Not understanding the nature of male sexuality, they feel this aggressiveness of men is concerned only with women, whereas its real purpose is to compete with and win out over other men.

Most people seem to forget that competitors war against each other; they do not war against the object of their competition. In the past, men competed against each other on the battlefield and only secondarily for sex. Now, when the competition for survival no longer exists (at least in this country), the arena is mainly the sexual one; it is here that gay men express their delight in competition. They compete against each other for sex, but it is really more than that; the competitor (another gay man) and the object (they're competing for) are both the same person. Since we no longer allow castration as the right of the winner, cult masculinity demands a symbolic victory over the loser in the competition. It is this symbolic meaning of sex with another man that lesbians may identify as threatening and aggressive. And it is. We see the effects of the competitor-warrior behavior all over the world, and its consequences for the development of gay relationships are nothing short of staggering. Hostility and desire are confounded; the objects of our affections and our anger are the same. Men win victories over one another in bed but leave feeling depressed.

Competition between men appears in almost every gay male relationship, arriving in the guise of jealousy, the arch enemy of permanence in gay life. No matter what the age of the partners in a gay love relationship, no matter where they live, no matter what their politics, jealousy may come to live with them and proves a fertile source of division in matters of sex, finances, and power.

It always happens over sex. A newly formed couple in the early stages of a relationship swears an oath of eternal loyalty and devotion. The partners also swear off all other men for the sake of monogamous union. Sometimes both insist on a "no-tricking" rule, sometimes only one; this is a common rule in gay male relationships, even in large cities. But the rule seldom remains unbroken: it is a rare couple that has stayed together for any length of time without sex outside the relationship; the pages of this book are filled with incidents in which the no-tricking rule was violated.

Jealousy is the usual reaction of someone who learns his lover has spent the night with another man. Expressions of pain and resentment are frequent; the common refrain is, "You don't love me"; "You did it to hurt me"; "You're just like my last lover"; or, better yet, "You're just like all other men." Feelings of abandonment torment the victimized lover, unless, as is often the case, he has the chance to punish his wayward lover by means of accusations, moodiness, crying, or a physical fight.

The current ideology suggests that jealousy is an emotional relic of the long tradition of marital property rights. A man takes a wife, who is defined by law as his property and whose financial value is considered before the wedding. If the wife makes it with some fellow down the road, the aggrieved husband has suffered injury to his property, and the law requires some restitution be made. There were also the possibilities of pregnancy and false heirs, again related to property rights and the necessity of "owning" one's wife. This is essentially the argument of ideological gays who maintain that monogamy among gay couples is an extension of property ownership.

To some extent, this argument is useful. It does explain the anger some gay men feel when a lover tricks out, even if the lover says it's only sex and nothing personal. There is no question that some men destroy their love relationships by making the lover feel as if he is owned and controlled. We see it all the time. However, it doesn't explain the curious fact that some lovers don't treat each other as possessions, yet still turn into raving maniacs when the first reports of tricking come in. There is more to the story.

Those caught in the conflict of cult masculinity, those to whom masculine superiority demands winning the competition, are furious because *they didn't do it first*. No matter how hurt they pretend to be, no matter how they sulk or how loudly they maintain that they have been and always will be faithful, it is merely a facade to hide the shame of losing the competition. It is *envy* that more accurately describes what is so often called jealousy. It is the wish that one had done it first or done it with George, and the fear that by not having done it one becomes second best in the couple.

Gay men, even gay lovers, compete against each other for the hand of some "cocky" fellow down the road or in the bar. This competition is not a pleasant business, since it is inevitably mixed with feelings of love and compassion for one's lover. Yet still another ingredient is added, feelings of self-esteem. In a large number of couples, one member of the pair does not feel as competent sexually as the other. Perhaps he feels shy in the cruising scene, or he feels his body isn't as attractive as his lover's. It could be almost anything; the key is that he believes, rightly or wrongly, that in a head-on competition with his lover for a third person (and it's awesome how often they choose the same guy), he would surely lose. That's enough for him to demand fidelity and to cry foul when the bonds of fidelity are loosened. Behind the tears is the wish that he could be as good at attracting other men or felt the freedom to roam sexually that his lover does.

Loss of the competition and the resultant envy do not explain all the feelings that lovers experience when the fidelity rule is broken. Even if we include the property rights issue, we are still left with other reasons for conflict, often idiosyncratic to that person—like a man who has been abandoned early in life and for whom the outside sex recalls that experience. Most gay couples who experience outside sex conflicts can be explained by these two theories, property rights and competition.

Cult masculinity victimizes many gay men in other ways that

have nothing to do with competition and envy. Indeed, some men wish that their lovers would trick repeatedly. These men are frightened by the possibilities of intimacy, which is a strange phenomenon in conflict with the historic male character. It is synonymous with vulnerability and trust, and, for some men, with weakness. This trusting feeling, this integration of personalities that is so fulfilling for some men and women, is dreaded by others. Since sex is easy for the man who is fearful of intimacy, he'd rather haunt the streets than develop a lover.

Intimacy in a love relationship is quite new historically. It was only in the seventeenth century that people began to think that a man should love his wife, in addition to having children with her. By now this idea is so ingrained that gays have also come to feel that love cannot be sincere without this intimacy, this bond that runs so deep that the two of them are like one in a kind of magical fusion of their egos, a dissolution of boundaries between them. When this occurs with two men in love, they become stronger than each could be separately, or so it is said. Other men believe that love is possible without intimacy.

But the gay man who is still under the sway of cult masculinity cannot buy either argument even if he tries. In his view, intimacy renders him a victim of the other person. His emphasis will always be on sex, which is considerably easier for him to handle, and his evaluation of the other person will always be determined by skill at sexual gymnastics.* It is as if the sexual capacity of the potential lover is the only attraction. Here is a sure sign: a friend tells us of a wonderful night he spent with another man. After the second date he says, "Ah! He wasn't as good the second time." And it's all over. Of course it wasn't "as good" the second time; it rarely is. Our first sexual experience with another man is partly a fantasy that transfigures the sexual component. The second time around, some reality begins to interfere with the fantasy, and we must deal more honestly with who the other person really is, not what we pretend him to be. It is this reality testing, this willingness to see the other person for who he really is (including his liabilities), that intimacy is all about. Our hypothetical friend concentrates on the sex and in a subtly hostile way ignores every other feature of the potential lover's character and personality. We can also add that

* "Better to fuck than feel," is his motto.

only men frightened of themselves and others will act this way. Some of us do have a better time the second time around, but only when we become interested in the other person, quite aside from the genital experience.

The phobia of closeness, the most common one in men, may strike at any stage of a love relationship. One partner in a couple with a good relationship and sexual compatibility may, after two or three years, begin creating a disturbance, arguing over little things, wanting to be with *his* friends more often, but mostly demanding sexual freedom. It makes no difference how much sexual freedom there may already be in the relationship, since this disturbance breaks out in love affairs founded on fidelity as well as in those allowing a wide latitude of outside sexual experience. But outside sex is not the goal, and whatever tricking does occur is seldom rewarding; the goal is psychological distance from the lover, and since men (or most of them) find "getting their rocks off" the easiest thing to do, they fall back on it whenever they are frightened. This hypothetical fellow is scared right down to his boots; he's afraid of the closeness that has developed between him and his lover.

It is ironic that many gay male love affairs break up *because* of the closeness and intimacy that has developed, not because men can't become intimate. Unfortunately, the phobic member of the pair seldom understands what is happening or why he is acting the way he is. Nor does he mean to hurt his lover, though he starts doing it constantly. He feels his discomfort only in the presence of the lover, and he knows that he wants to get away, to do something, to take some action outside the province of his domestic life.*

It is painful for the lover as well. As far as he knew, everything was going along well—and it was—when suddenly conflicts arose over trifles. He soon learns that almost any statement can lead to an argument. If he asks his lover what the problem is, he generally gets a sulky response or an "I don't know," which may be true though hardly enlightening. The only solution is a lot of time spent talking together, which can help only if they agree not to get angry at each other.

A third characteristic of cult masculinity is the representation

* The "doing something" stops the possibility of their talking together, which is his goal exactly.

of another man by only one physical part of him. In general, it springs from an overemphasis on "types." We all have a preference for a certain type of man, say, someone older than we (who presumably likes someone younger than himself); or someone cultured in compatible ways; someone who has certain physical characteristics that are sensuous; or a man whose presence makes us feel alive and energetic. For each one of us there is some magnetic attraction to our "type." One of the advantages of experience is the educated attention we can give to finding another person who will be compatible, instead of the hit-and-miss procedure of the inexperienced. In a sense, the ability to look for a certain type of man is an indicator of sexual experience and personal maturity. When the search for compatibility is formed by knowing one's type, the choosing process aids in the development of love. In this case, it is a positive trait.

But knowledge of types is also used in the name of cult masculinity to reject men as often—no, more often—than it is used to welcome another man. The most frequent form of using a type for rejection purposes occurs when the sex partner is classified on the basis of only one part of his body. In the gay world of today (as it has been in historical cult masculinity), the penis is revered. The big cock is the prize, adorned and adored, the possessor immensely attractive to the hungry hunter who wants to engulf it or be overpowered by it, with minimal regard for other physical characteristics and none whatsoever for social and emotional ones. It is worshiped as a fetish and worn as a symbol of masculine sexual abilities; the bigger the cock the more masculine.* "There are only two things I can't stand," said one man, "size queens and small cocks!" It is as if the tradition of transmitting masculinity current among the Dorian Greeks were still in practice today, with the *arete* (the full force of a man) transmitted through the semen into the boy's anus

---

* It was jock night in a well-known bar in New York City. Everyone's gaze drifted toward one man leaning against a wall with a cocky air so much in demand at that bar. His jock bulged, and he pretended to ignore all the stares drifting his way. Suddenly another man, whose jock did not bulge, walked over and quickly pulled down the winner's jock—and enormous wads of toilet paper came streaming out and fell on the floor. The silence turned to a deafening roar the poor fellow ran out of the bar (jock at his knees), and everyone felt much better.

(the adorer of the big cock). Braggarts beam when telling how they "took" a trick's ten inches straight down to the throat or up the butt, as if the extra length were more masculine or more homosexual than modest amounts.

The reasons for the magnetic appeal of a big cock are probably diverse, but two suggest themselves right away. Feeling more masculine because a big cock is attracted to him is comforting to someone who questions his own masculinity. If he can't be a "real man," then at least he can capture one. Men with low self-worth probably form part of this group. The second motivation is more interesting. If the size of a cock is a measure of the power of a man, then men with big cocks are dangerous and frightening, and by symbolic means the frightened young man must "win" his competition with the man whose cock is all-powerful. But since the defeat needs to be secret and nonthreatening to the powerful man, it must be symbolic. By "taking" ten inches, the small man symbolically castrates the big man, becomes the victor, at least in his own mind, and reestablishes his self-worth. After all, it's almost as good to win the competition against a big man as it is to be a big man oneself. So the two possible explanations of the fetish of the big cock in gay life are low self-worth and hostility. If we could trace the roots of both reactions, we might find that both spring from deep feelings of inadequacy as men, different reactions to the same feelings. The big cock syndrome is not the whole story.

The most difficult question any lover was asked in this study was, "What was it about him that was attractive to you?" Rarely could any man state clearly why he was attracted so quickly to one man in the midst of a room full of other men. A gay man enters the arena of other gay men. Perhaps it is a bar or a bath or a pleasant party given by a friend. His eyes search the room, quickly evaluating the men in view. He notices only one or two, his type, and only then turns his attention to the others. He will be drawn to his type; his manner, tone of voice, and body posture change dramatically when talking with the type with whom he is open, charming, and alluring. With the others he is merely polite and friendly, but not inviting. Men have fallen in love this way—instantly—without a word, without knowing anything (at least consciously) about the other man. The "love at first sight" phenomenon, though most often a sexual experience, has actually led to long-lasting relationships, wonderful affairs where the sparkle and enthusiasm of the first meeting are present twenty years later—but not often.

This "type" business is very complicated, and nowhere is its importance more prominent than in the first gaze. One remarkable characteristic is how quickly it all takes place, most often in a few seconds. For some men, those still obeying the regulations of cult masculinity, the agenda for the night is over and the hunt is on; but there is a second characteristic that is more interesting. If we persist in asking a man why he was attracted to his lover, he begins to list physical characteristics such as the shape of his body or the hair on his chest; generally speaking, it is physical traits that we are concerned with when we speak of a certain type. We are all used to our friends' types. He *must* be "cut" or "uncut"; he *must* have a beard or be hairless; he *must* have hair on his chest or nothing more than a furrow of small blond shoots; he *must* be robustly muscled or long and lithe; he *must* be dressed like a man of distinction or in western garb; he *must* . . . he *must* . . . he *must* . . .

We are accustomed to these social and sexual demands, these conditions in the search for one's type. But it is a more active process than that. We are not merely looking for a certain type of person; we are also actively rejecting others. The glance around the room is not just a searching process; it is a highly complicated evaluation process based on a dimension of acceptance and rejection, and it happens at computer speed. Devotees of cult masculinity spend more time rejecting people and then competing with them for the "treasured" one than they do looking for someone who is compatible. It is another example of "the hunt." Physicality is important and for some of us the only possible beginning of a relationship—and this is not necessarily bad. It all depends on the extent to which the attraction is dependent on rejecting other people, in which case a poor prognosis for a relationship is indicated; the chosen man will be assigned a rigid role to play, rather than allowed to be himself with his unique set of assets and liabilities.

Seeing a person in physical terms is easy, but the acceptance/ rejection dimension operates on a deeper level as well. It is uncanny how accurately a man can choose another who almost always has certain personality characteristics—*that no one else can see.* One look around the room is all it takes, and the searcher has found a man who is depressed, regardless of whether the depressed person is sitting alone in the corner or chatting amiably with the other guests. Another man always finds someone who will reject him after the first date. Then there is the "father type" looking for a "son type" to guide, and the son looking for his father; it is not always a matter of age but of psychological posture.

What happens here? How is it possible that we can walk into a room and choose another man because of his personal characteristics without actually talking to him or knowing anything about him? This frequently happens; we see our friends choosing the same kind of person over and over again, and making the same complaints about the lover after the affair cools down— and they see us doing the same thing.

The process is highlighted in psychotherapy when we examine as many of the cues transmitted by the parties as we can. It is incredible how much information we all send to one another without ever speaking; with experience, we read these cues quite accurately. For instance, a person's clothes tell us quite a bit —not only whether he's a slave to fashion, but what fashion, how well he wears the clothes, and his sense of comfort in them. The posture of the body signifies the state of relaxation or tension, and this is continually conveyed by how a person stands or sits, how he uses his hands and arms, the position of the head indicating interest in his environment or boredom or contempt. The face may be either a mask with a frown or the frozen smile of tension that the wearer tries not to show. A man's mobility in the room is another indicator, the "stay-put" type more like a sphinx than another who greets people openly. All this information is processed by our personal computers and matched with our experiences from the past. Out comes the data, and it is awesome how accurate it is. Age and experience count, which is why the young are more disappointed than the old; more experienced people have a better idea of what they're doing.

We find the people we want—no matter how much we may protest later. For those men who are still motivated by cult masculinity, the choices are made on the criterion of psychological danger, rather than the potentialities of personal fulfillment. They are attracted to men who will not threaten their

self-esteem, men who will not remind them of their personal
liabilities and who cannot be allowed to become a part of their
growth. In a sense the choice was made in the past, since the
chosen one must not upset the personal equilibrium that the
chooser has already created for himself. It is "past" in the sense
that the choice indicates no motivation to change in the future
or to allow the other person to become a part of that growth.
Other men who might see the chooser's liabilities are rejected
outright.

For instance, a man who feels inadequate sexually may seek
another man who is just "coming out" and is sexually inexperienced. In the role of teacher and guide, he is relaxed and comforting. Here he can feel he is master of the situation, whereas
with the sexually experienced his feelings of incompetence rise
to the surface to plague him. A different man may fear loss of
power and control in an egalitarian relationship and seek someone whose financial position is insecure precisely because the
effect of having more money will make the less secure man
grateful and thereby less challenging. At no time need the
chooser mention or hold over the other man his sexual experience or financial security; its presence is enough to maintain
control. Naturally, such a man is seldom aware of what he's
doing. He believes that his sexuality and money are irrelevant
to the relationship, and he protests vigorously any suggestion
that he might be using them to control his lover. Since control
by these means is unconscious for him, he is not lying. But if
his lover changes, the control factors surface with full force, and
the lover soon finds out, if he doesn't already know. The choosers
in these examples are dedicated to maintaining the status quo,
and since sexual experience or occupational success on the part
of the lover is a challenge to the status quo, the sparks begin to
fly. Accusations of ingratitude are made, and possibilities of
growth in the relationship are perceived as challenges to authority. Disaster follows with resentments and bitterness, and finally
the relationship is dissolved. Then the search for a replacement
begins, and the process starts anew.

But a caveat is necessary. Medical students seem always to
suffer from the diseases they studied that week, and people who
read books like this wonder whether the example typifies them.
I did not mean the two examples—helping someone to come

out and being more secure financially—to be a condemnation of people in these situations. There are love affairs in which one man helps another come out and they grow and change together for the rest of their lives; while men who are financially more secure than their lovers at the beginning take pride in the lovers' vocational advancements. *It is only the motivation for the original choice that is the issue here.* There are even examples in the lives of gay male couples in which a lover was chosen "defensively," and the relationship became a success because the chooser was willing to realize how he was controlling the lover and why he needed to do it. When two men can accomplish that, they have resolved the problem and met the demands of intimacy, which again is a condition of vulnerability.

Some people may protest that *defensive choosing,* as I call it, cannot actually occur so quickly, as if there were a computer inside of us processing information in milliseconds. They will maintain that it is only physical traits they notice and respond to, and that only after they get to know the person do they react to his personality. But I think they are wrong, and I think we all do it, though some people do it more consistently and more narrowly. My experience also suggests that the personality characteristics are ultimately more influential than the physical type.

Finally, the issue of sexual roles in cult masculinity. Here there are two components, usually confused. The first is sexual behavior in bed; the second is the day-to-day behavior toward a lover and with friends. The current gay liberation ideology lectures us on the evil consequences of playing "husband and wife" roles, imitating everything that is wrong with heterosexuality. We are told to maintain an egalitarian relationship in bed and to share the responsibilities of the relationship. It is pointed out, accurately, that roles have historically been defined as "masculine" or "feminine"; it is maintained that these socially conditioned roles are unnatural and oppressive.

A large part of the problem is semantic. He who does the fucking is called "masculine" and cast as the one with power and authority; he who likes to get fucked is called "feminine." The same is true of the person who deals with "financial" matters in contrast to the one who likes "domestic" duties. It is a historical plague on our house, and we have not yet invented a new terminology to express personal fulfillment as distinct from historical role. Roles are dehumanizing, but only because we believe that preferring a certain kind of activity over another is necessarily a part of a role, when in fact it may be a genuine preference that should be respected. Nowhere is this seen more clearly than in the sexual sphere.

If it is all right to have a sexual preference (gay or straight), it is also OK to have a further preference (what we each like to do in bed). Gay liberation ideology suggests that we are not sufficiently liberated unless we all participate in the full range of sexual possibilities in bed. What our lover does to us, we should do to him, and only when the sexual relationship, to an outside observer, is egalitarian does it qualify as nonoppressive. My own experience in working with gay couples in sex therapy suggests that the roles may be more important in the mind of the perceiver than in the behavior of the perceived.

"I do it because I like it" is a fine reason to "do it," regardless of how others may interpret it. We all learn to prefer certain sexual acts, and, while experimenting can be fun and sometimes enlightening, we will invariably end up with a preference, which should be encouraged, not discouraged.

But sometimes fulfilling a role is *more important* than the sex. The maintenance of sexual roles is exclusively a problem of trust. "Masculinity" and "femininity" have nothing to do with it, and as gays trying to find new ways of relating in the world we might as well drop this archaic terminology. There is nothing intrinsically masculine or feminine about being on the top or the bottom. But one can be either *trusting* or *controlling* sexually, and trust and control are the end points of this dimension of sexual roles. It is not a matter of acting like a man or a woman. What men do is masculine behavior. Sex is not characterized by its conclusion, the orgasm; rather, it is a complex interaction, a system of communication between two (or more) people. The agenda of communication and the degree of trustfulness or defensiveness in this communication are what we characterize as "sexual roles."

One common form of defensiveness is illustrated by the person who says, "I do the fucking." It is not his focus on a masculine role that is the core of his attitude but his demand for control of the situation. It could just as well describe someone who says, "I want a strong man to fuck me." They are two sides of the same coin; the issue is control of the behavior of the other person. Calling one masculine and the other feminine only obscures it.

Controlling people are frightened of new territory. It is not the new behavior that is scary but the consequences of giving in to another person, which means making a change in defenses, a willingness to be vulnerable. That implies trusting another person. At the heart of the matter is the inability to trust anyone, even a lover. A man who feels good about his body and about himself is unlikely to give any consideration to what his "role" is with his lover or with a trick. But where trust is impossible, power issues become primary, and no matter how talented a sexual partner he may be, he will never be satisfied with his own sexual experience. Inevitably this leads to depression and feelings of worthlessness. It may take a while, especially if the man is attractive and sought after, but as his youth wanes, so will the power of success turn to perceived failure, and then to loneliness.

These then are the traits of cult masculinity: the worship of the phallus, together with the necessity for public displays of masculinity; the confusion between sexual pleasure and aggression; competition with lovers and the fear of intimacy with them; the fetishism of "types"; and finally the need to control another man sexually. This is our masculine heritage in the Western world, and gay men have inherited these characteristics just as fully as straight men. To this extent, gay men are no different from their straight counterparts.

But there are differences within the gay male population. Not every man is controlling in bed. Indeed, many are open and trusting and move toward intimate relationships, reflected in the large number of gay male couples who have lived together for many years in greater happiness than most heterosexual couples. The point here is that the more one subscribes to the cult of masculinity, the less likely one is to develop a long-lasting relationship.

PART THREE

Variations

CHAPTER EIGHT

Love Between the Generations

Blessed is the man who knows how to make love
    as one wrestles in a gym,
and then goes home happy to sleep the day
    with a delicious young boy.

THEOGNIS

When this study of gay couples was first planned, no provision was made for collecting information on sex between men and teenagers—often called by such names as man/boy love, Greek love, pederasty, or intergenerational relationships. While some age difference between adult lovers is common enough in the gay world and the study was designed to include a discussion of its possible effects on lovers, the relationship between a pubertal youngster and an adult man did not seem relevant. However, people are always complicating the neat plans of data-collecting psychologists, upsetting their preconceptions. The histories of many men interviewed showed how often relationships between the generations had profound effects on both partners. There were too many boy/man experiences reported for the issue to be ignored.

At the outset, let us consider an initial bias against pederastic relationships: their transient character. Like the charms of the boys of ancient Greece, they are perceived as "here today, gone tomorrow," a consideration that made their treatment problematic in this study of permanence in gay love. But concentrating on permanent relationships and labeling pederasty as transient turned out to be prejudiced viewpoints. It was remarked earlier that permanence in a relationship may be as oppressive as running from relationship to relationship. The criteria for happiness are subjective: different goals suit different people. Moreover, there are enough accounts of longevity and loyalty in pederastic relationships to suggest that the separation between boy and adult is not inevitable. Indeed, the longest-lived relationship found in this study, lasting for fifty-one years, began when one partner was fourteen and the other twenty-four. Clearly, there is as much diversity in intergenerational relationships as in couples of similar ages. While it may be psychologically convenient for those who disapprove of these relationships to think of them as simple and essentially transient, they are neither. They have the complexity and dynamics of all other relationships.

There is a great deal of prejudice against men who prefer emotional and sexual relationships with teenagers. Even today, when the gay liberation movement is striving so hard for equality and civil and legal rights, the prejudice against boy lovers continues. Not only does the straight world condemn them, but so do many of the recognized gay liberation organizations. There have been many campaigns against these men (and sometimes against the boys as well), which have led to police raids, special laws, and harassment. One has to wonder why the "chicken hawk," the man derided so frequently these days, has become so heinous in a society that prides itself on sexual freedom. Why do gay liberation groups seem all too willing to join the attack?

One might think the desire to be accepted by the heterosexual world is a major component of antipederasty gays. Acceptance means compromise with those responsible for the persecution and legal harassment of gays. It has been the strategy, right or wrong, in the past few years for gay liberation groups to seek redress of their grievances through legislation and courts, which means the collecting of votes and data to support the cause. A major theme throughout this process has been an implicit statement that, "We're just like you," a fine middle-class sentiment and probably more true than untrue, but involving the sacrifice of some of our subgroups along the way.

For instance, the Stonewall riot in 1969 began the modern gay liberation movement. This riot was instigated by "drag queens," transvestites, and effeminate hustlers who frequented the bar; they are no longer represented in the gay liberation movement, except at the very fringes, because movement people want to maintain that gay men are just like straight men and that gay women are just like straight women. The last thing they want is a man in drag speaking to a congressman about gay rights, or a lesbian doing the same in "men's" pants and smoking a cigar. The prejudice against S and M is only now beginning to abate in a few of our large cities. Sado-masochists, too, were considered "weirdos" within the gay world. It's OK to dangle the keys from your left side as long as it's just for the image, the fantasy—but to take it seriously, actually get involved in bondage and humiliation? What the straight world used to say of all gays, many gays now say of some of our own minorities.

Sex with teenagers is even more taboo these days. The epithet "child molester" rings loud. The fantasy of elderly men "recruiting" tender young boys into scarcely imaginable sexual scenes frightens both gays and straights who want to keep the world more orderly, to make everyone contribute toward the goal of winning acceptance for adult gay relationships. By no stretch of the imagination is the straight world ready to accept man/boy love relationships; hence men who participate in them replace other gay men as the "sick" ones, the "immoral" ones, the ones who make it difficult to win the battle for civil rights.

Oddly enough, the most interesting fact that surfaced was the frequency with which the parents of a teenage boy were aware of a sexual relationship between their son and the adult man. Since most of us believe, almost without question, that man/boy sex must be exploitive, it is disquieting to learn that a boy's parents would allow the relationship, at least tacitly. But quite a few instances of this situation were found, even to the point of occasional sex between the boy and the adult in the boy's home. However, it was impossible to interview the parents to get a better perspective, though there is no reason to believe the respondents exaggerated. There is some evidence that such parents tend to be poor and culturally deprived, seeing the influence of the adult gay man as a step up in the world for their son. There is also the possibility that the son is "better behaved" at home, regardless of the economic status of the parents, when he has contact with the gay man and that the parents appreciate the peace, after the previous experience of having their home a war zone. Again, these suggestions are merely tentative.

We need to collect reliable information about the characteristics and diversity of man/boy love affairs. At the moment, ideology in the gay liberation and women's liberation movements interferes with evaluation of these relationships without prejudice. Man/boy love and sex appear to contradict so much that ideologies harangue us with. For instance, the puritans among us demand that all aspects of a relationship be egalitarian, especially sexual roles—that we not use each other as sexual objects. They fantasize man/boy sex as a scene where a young, reticent boy with tears in his eyes lies on his stomach, acquiescent to the demands of the exploiting man forcing entry at the rear. It is viewed as a classic case of adult exploitation. Hustling is also condemned as exploitative. The lack of long-lasting relationships between men and boys, assumed rather than demonstrated, is perceived to mean that contact between the generations lacks depth and character.

Naturally, not everyone agrees that exploitation is the main ingredient of man/boy relationships. These attitudes are mainly, but not exclusively, the result of the influence of the women's movement on the gay movement, and the number of these attitudes appearing in any particular gay rights platform is often directly proportional to the influence, degree of politicization, and outspokenness of the women involved in the organization that produced the platform.

The intention in this chapter is to examine, without prejudice, the kinds of relationships that develop between men and boys and to begin to identify the various forms these relationships take. It is no more than a small start, meant more as a call for further research than a comprehensive view of this kind of relationship. It has been very difficult to gather information because these men justifiably fear exposure. Some of the information I collected cannot be included here; a few men interviewed refused to allow use of the information in this book. They expressed their mistrust of my intentions, the only ones who did so in all the interviewing over the year and a half of research. My own view is that I had come to symbolize in their eyes all the sanctions against their romantic desires.

Sex Between Teenagers and Adults

The first group of men who as teenagers had relationships with older men are now adults. They now have or have had long-lasting relationships in their adult lives with other gay men.

Alan,* age thirty, left home when he was fourteen, leaving behind his parents and a childhood lover. He went directly to New York City and had sex with a truckdriver along the way. "Everybody knows Forty-second Street," says Alan, and Forty-second Street, the subways, and the Port Authority Bus Terminal were his homes for the next four months.

> I discovered that you could meet other gay people, and of course I had no money and no place to stay, and if you went home with people you had a place to stay and breakfast the next day.
> I went home with the first person who offered in the tearooms. I was relieved that he wanted to go home. I thought that was real nice, so I went home with him. I knew he was gay and interested in sex, and I was interested in him and sex.
> It was really a matter of survival, but I was also having a good time. I was getting a place to stay, wasn't working, wasn't going to school. I didn't have to report to anyone. I was enjoying every minute of it. I didn't look at myself as a prostitute. Sometimes I stayed with someone for just a day, sometimes for a month. After New York I did the same thing in Washington.
> These men weren't molesting me. I never viewed it as that. I felt really grateful that these men felt the same way I did. We were doing it, and it just felt so natural, so wonderful. I never questioned it. I have nothing but the highest respect for those men. They were really nice to me. There were a lot of gay people on one campus, and they looked out for me. They didn't abuse me at all. I feel really fortunate that I fell into that group.

One of the most frequent statements made by men who have been sexually and emotionally interested in boys, and by boys who have been cared for by gay men, attests to the sense of loyalty and appreciation the boys have had for the men. This has been remarkably consistent in all the stories. In two cases, men were accused by the police of having sex with boys, and neither boy—even though great pressure was applied by parents, clergy, and police—would testify against the men. Exploitation does not lead to such protectiveness and loyalty. According to the accounts given, this loyalty did not result from payoffs, giving the boy large sums of money or overwhelming him with presents. In only a few cases was money involved at all. Alan, for instance, was given only two or three dollars daily for spending money while the man with whom he was living was at work.

Some boys are unquestionably escaping a horrible home and looking for a father replacement. By and large, these are homes where the fathers are psychologically absent, or where physical brutality is the only form of contact between father and son. Alcoholism sometimes plays a part, especially when both parents are alcoholic, and the child has no adult to whom he can turn for support. The hordes of runaway children in every large city are testimony to how often the horrors of family conflict impel a child to leave. Many parents hardly bother to find their runaway children. Some simply abandon them.

*Thomas,** age forty-five, has an extraordinary story. He was born into a military family in which rank had its privileges and used them. His family is filled with generals, colonels, and majors. Even his stepmother was a high-ranking officer. As Thomas tells it, his father was not one to "spare the rod."

> My father was sort of like a sex maniac, all out for sex. He didn't really care what anybody thought. He did exactly what he pleased. I've never known anyone so free from external controls as him. He was terrible. He was sort of violent and had lots of love affairs. There was always anger between my parents. And he wasn't interested in his children at all.
>
> For instance, when my brother was a child, he had a teddy bear he was very fond of. One day my father decided the teddy bear was dirty, so he threw it into the garbage. My brother started crying and he wouldn't stop, and my father started beating him until he was unconscious, and that stopped the crying.

When Thomas was fifteen his parents divorced. Neither of them wanted their two sons (the older brother was nineteen). Thomas went to live with his brother in Fort Lauderdale.

> My brother was gay and ran in gay circles. They drank a lot, and I got into that circle of friends. And I started having love affairs with men who were thirty years older than I was. They were very happy affairs in terms of giving and receiving love and affection. I thought it was absolutely marvelous.
>
> At age fifteen I thought of myself as a homosexual, and all my friends were homosexual, and we go to sleep with each other and suck each other's cocks, and we were queers and the world hates us, and that's it.

These men made me feel secure, their strength, their experience, their savoir faire, worldliness, and maturity. They were also role models. I chose people I wanted to be like. People I thought were grown-up, fully formed, fully developed, and I wanted to be a complete person.

It was almost like a ranking system, like the way I grew up in the army. A premium was placed on people aged twenty-five, but the people who were older, people in their forties and fifties, were like the high-ranking officers. They were like my uncle the general, my father the colonel. These were like the big guys with all the medals and brass. I never thought about it then, but if I think about it now, it has to do with a system like that. The premium is not on the young men; the premium is on the ranking men, the ones who are older.

This military thing was ridiculous in my family. When I was in the army my uncle was the commanding general and then I got sent as a PFC to Germany where my father was the commanding officer and my step-mother was a colonel, all on the same base.

I've always had good experiences with older men. It's interesting. You read about chicken hawks and child abuse. The only people who ever abused me were straight people, like my parents abused me, like my teachers abused me. But gay men never abused me. They gave me love, warmth, and affection I was one of them, I belonged to them, and the straight people were the bad guys. You hid from them because they were crazy and ugly.

I was always the aggressor. I wanted them more than they wanted me. Older men tend to be shy of a young kid. I learned I had to make the first move because they were afraid to. In every case, and there were hundreds of them, I would go after the man. I can't remember being pursued.

Those guys were so unbelievably sensitive about where I was at, developmentally, emotionally. I can't remember a single incident of anyone coercing me or suggesting I do something I didn't want. I'd say these guys were extremely responsible and aware they had a young life in their hands. I can only remember incidents of tremendous patience and openness on their part.

In that respect I feel deeply grateful to these men, a lot of them. I think they saved my life. I think they took a terribly lonely, confused, unhappy kid and really saved him. And they gave me a beautiful thing. I needed it, and they gave it to me.

> I owe everything to those guys. I owe them the fact
> that I'm a human being at all.

Thomas began a ten-year relationship with an older man, a
scholar, who took good care of him. After the relationship ended,
Thomas fell apart, became a recluse and an alcoholic. For four
years, Thomas never made a friend or cared for himself. His
reliance on other men had been so complete that he never
learned how to take care of himself. He is putting his life in
order now.

> You know the story, the riddle, about the man who has
> the wolf, the sheep, and the cabbage, and he has to get
> them across the stream in a rowboat? The idea is that he
> has to do one thing at a time. He can't leave the wolf
> with the sheep or the sheep with the cabbage, so he has
> to make several trips. So I see my development in the
> past few years like that. I had to get some stuff across
> the river. I had to learn how to take care of myself.
> While I was doing that I was neglecting human relation-
> ships. Then I went back to getting human relationships
> again. I think I have it all across the river now, feel
> I have it complete now. For the first time in my life I
> feel like I'm able to love somebody without being de-
> pendent on them. I can take care of myself.

Many boys attach themselves to adult gay men because of the
need for guidance and support, which is not the same as looking
for a substitute father. They learn about preparation for the
adult world in ways different from those they have experienced
at home. The intellectual level of the man, his cultural pursuits,
his political involvement may be attractive to the boy because
these qualities are lacking in his own home. He tries to understand and appropriate these attributes. He finds a man who is
willing to spend the time, and it can be considerable, to discuss
his grievances, complaints, and frustrations, a man who is willing to put up with the impulsiveness that teenagers call "spon-
taneity."

Of course, there are also boys who prefer having sex with
older men. They like both learning about sex and expressing
affection, preferring a mature body to an immature one. Setting
aside the prejudices of the majority, there is nothing illogical
about such a preference.

When *Ronald* was fifteen (he's now thirty-four), he began a six-year relationship with *Basil*, a man in his thirties. Basil was married and had a young son.

> It was a memorable experience. It's very hard to remember everything. I'm so overwhelmed by it even now. I still think about him almost daily, even though I've been living with someone else for the past six years. Basil is still very much a part of my life.
>
> My life totally revolved around him. We were very compatible sexually. We never went to bed without having several orgasms. I remember in the beginning I used to love to get screwed, and Basil sort of believed in it intellectually, but he had never been screwed. I taught him how to, and when he got into it he began to love it. Sometimes we would get some food, and he would buy a bunch of flowers, and we would hole up in the hotel room for a few hours, just screwing constantly and being together. It was very intense.
>
> I wanted to go back to Harvard, and Basil kept reassuring me that he would wait for me. We were sitting downstairs in the car, a lot of our life took place in the car, and I remember I was very depressed and withdrawn. And Basil wanted to prove that he would be faithful and true to me, and he took a match and he burned his hand. He had that scar for the rest of the time I knew him. He just took the match and burned himself as a sign that he would be true to me.

The relationship ended when Basil decided to divorce his wife and marry a female student in his class. Basil wanted Ronald to participate with him and his new wife in a three-way relationship, but Ronald refused.

> I remember Basil and I spent the night together before his wedding. And it was important to me. I guess I knew in my heart that he wasn't there at all, that he was somewhere else. That I was taking a back seat.
>
> A funny corny word that keeps popping up in my mind is that we were like brothers, though I was never as close to my brothers as I was to Basil. It was like some fantasy of what it would be like to be practically in someone else's skin.
>
> I just stopped the tape for a minute. I couldn't even bring myself to replay what I've already made. Somehow just talking about this relationship is making me feel sad and tearful. What I'm beginning to feel in the pit of my stomach was the sense of union we had, and the sense of being one, which I guess was also one of the

reasons why Basil tried to get out of the relationship. I guess it was claustrophobic, but I couldn't see any other way to live. I really idealized him.

I thought he was the most handsome man I had ever seen, and everything he did was nearly perfect. But I couldn't follow him into that second marriage. I couldn't expand. I wanted to hold tighter.

A few teenage boys who have gay sex are not certain that they are truly gay. *Johnny* is sixteen years old and for the past two years has had a sexual relationship with *Arthur*, age twenty-nine. They both live in a northeastern suburb. Johnny's first sex, at age seven, was with an uncle. Oral sex with the uncle continues to this day. At thirteen, Johnny began hustling on Forty-second Street, but only as trade. He met Arthur while hustling, and they became friends.

One thing I've noticed about other men that I meet that are interested in the same type of thing, teenagers. They don't get along with each other. I've seen that happen time and time again. It's like there's competition or something.

As far as sex goes, I look at it this way. It's the least I can do for them [Arthur and other adult men]. Not that I've ever said it to them. Arthur does a lot of stuff for me, and he really enjoys that. So this is one way I can please somebody who likes me. They're like big brothers to me. I figured sooner or later I would find a big brother on the street, and I did.

It seems to me the men I meet or Arthur get so serious about sex. They make it sound so important. When Arthur sees a kid, that's all he thinks about right away. Most of the guys I meet think of the kid as a sex object instead of thinking of you for other stuff, for a good time, or going to a game. Like, if a guy blows me I don't even think of that as sex. It's just that it feels good, just messing around.

I don't know if I'm gay. I'm confused about it a lot. When I see other kids in school in the shower I don't think, "Oh, I want to mess around with that kid." The only time it comes up is when I'm with Arthur, and he notices it all the time. "That kid's a nine, that kid's an eight." As far as messing around with my friends goes, I don't think that's gay because they do it all the time. If I could fuck a girl, then maybe I'd know.

There are also boys who simply enjoy having sex. They attach no premium to emotional involvement, don't think there is anything homosexual about it. They prefer learning from older men, rather than bumbling age mates. For these boys, it's as simple as that. Some boys often have sex with both girl friends and men during the same period and experience no conflict. It is also interesting to note that some are willing to express affection as well as to have sex. Again, they don't necessarily view this as homosexual. Some of them start as hoodlums on the street and turn into "teddy bears" in the arms of a trusted adult man. There is even some indication that heterosexual boys are more likely to fool around sexually with men and boys than are gay boys. Straight boys, even after gay sex, do not question their masculinity; gay boys, by contrast, fear being exposed as homosexuals. Ironically, straight teenagers often participate in more homosexual activity than those adolescents who are destined to become gay adults.

There are a number of men who consider themselves a part of the man/boy movement. These men see their role as helping the boy free himself from the sexual and moral restraints imposed by our society. They don't see their relationship to the youngster in sexual terms, although sexual contact is a part of it; much larger are issues of redefining social and gender behavior such as male and female, homosexual and heterosexual.

As in any social movement, there are differences in approach and style. Some men and some of the boys are more politically oriented, seeing sex between a man and a boy as a representation of a political/social revolution; others are more inspired by romantic notions of love, using the Athenian model of pederasty as their guide. Pat is an example of the political adherents to the man/boy movement, while Nicholas is a romantic.

*Pat,** age forty, is a firm supporter of the man/boy life-style. Pat had two age-mate lovers when he was a teenager, but his first sexual experience with a boy occurred when he was an adult. He was sitting in a restaurant, and a thirteen-year-old boy asked him to buy his papers. "If you buy all my papers, I'll go home with you." Pat was engaged to a woman at the time but responded to the offer. This boy taught Pat about sex; he in turn practiced his lessons on the woman. It has been twenty years since their affair began, and Pat and the "boy" still see each other, occasionally having sex. At the moment Pat has lived with his lover, who himself is a boy lover, for several years.

> A teenager has not yet become a man. He hasn't accepted all the shit that adult males in our society accept. He's still free, still has options. He's not gay, he's not straight, not any of the things we've all become. And that's really exciting, physically, emotionally, and intellectually exciting. When I'm with Joe I enjoy it terrifically for the intellectual stimulation because there's a rebelliousness there. He's not a child. He can choose, but he hasn't been zeroed into one of those nice channels that we have.
>
> In our society, at least, early adolescence is the last time you can really afford to defy immoral authority. That's what attracts me to boys, politically speaking. I don't think boy love is revolutionary, but for me boy love is an act of revolution. It's part of my refusal to accept the family as the norm, part of my hope that the boys I relate to will also refuse to grow up in the bad sense of that word, to accepting all the parts of the society and the patriarchal family and the sex roles they are supposed to accept.
>
> It's not radical and revolutionary to want to get away from intimacy, or even get away from lifelong relationships. Lifelong relationships are not reactionary. But relationships in which either or both parties dominate or limit the other in a relationship are reactionary.
>
> The boys I have sex with are not looking for their fathers. They're looking for passionate and compassionate friends, an older friend who will guide them and be easy with them and not need them in certain ways as much as they need him. The boy lover has a certain responsibility. He doesn't need the boy, and any time he feels a psychological need for the boy—like you are falling in love in some fantasized way—then I think you have to draw back. To possess another person, rather than relate to them, is harmful, and you can't relate without a certain distance, I think. If you don't have the ability to put a distance between yourself and another person, you haven't got your own identity, and you're still in the stage of relating to people as if they were an extension of yourself.

Nicholas has been a boy lover for most of his life. He's now in his fifties. He's a romantic, identifying strongly with the model of pederasty prevalent in ancient Greece, and, like the ancient model, he is married himself. He shows pictures of the boys he has loved over the years and keeps in touch with many of them. Some are married with children of their own; a few others are gay. None of them rejected their early experiences with Nicholas.

> An adolescent's sex drive, stronger than it ever will be again, includes an urge to branch out, to try this and that, to see what feels good and what feels better. And so we have a partial explanation of why some boys go from the Greek love experience to women, or other boys, or other men. The key to the homophobe view is, of course, that their own earlier sexual experiences were most often so heavily laden with guilt as to inhibit experimentation, or they learned from anxiety-ridden elders to believe that experimentation would make them effeminate. People don't want boys to make up their own minds about sexual preferences.
>
> Homophobia, and specifically the aversion to anything like the Greek love experience, is at the root an unwillingness to allow a boy to make up his own mind about sexual preferences, any more than about religion. The implication is that a boy might find out that gay sex can be more fun for him than straight and that if everybody did so, the human race would die out. Put that way, it sounds silly, and it is. Yet I am convinced that some archaic fear is at the basis of homophobia, reinforced by theological objections which call such fun and games an offense to God. But this is to characterize the Creator of the Galaxies as a bedroom snoop, more easily offended than Mrs. Grundy or even Anita Bryant herself, and I find that concept of God offensive to the point of blasphemy. The "early seduction" theory is the American gospel, but it is time people stopped believing it to be inspired by God.

One reservation should be mentioned. The discussion above has been limited to instances of man/boy sex and affection in situations of benevolent contact, in which the adult is as concerned about the emotional well-being of the boy as with his sexual gratification. There is no exploitation by either the man or the boy. But there are other instances of exploitation that have not been investigated in this study. What has been shown here is that age has no necessary relationship to exploitation. Exploitation exists in the characters of certain types of people, some of whom are adults and some teenagers. Some adults do exploit teenagers, and some teenagers do exploit adults. Some are gay, and some are straight. The point is that the capacity for exploitation is a personal one, not a trait of a class of people. Regardless of what sort of person turns a man on, how he treats that person will be determined only by his character.

Generation Gaps in Adult Lovers

Worry about the difference in age between adult lovers is socially conditioned and in just about every couple interviewed was a problem for the older partner, not the younger. The elder of the pair invariably feels insecure, and will, no matter how often the lover assures him of love. It appears to be a way the older man punishes himself and must exasperate the younger lover. There is no indication that an age difference has any bearing on the success or longevity of a relationship, unless one partner makes it a problem. If there is insecurity on the part of the older lover, it seems to pass in time. It has in every case interviewed in this study. Perhaps with changes in our social mores, this worry will diminish. The fact is, there appear to be no special problems or unique traits among adult gay couples in which ten or more years separate the two partners.

The following adult gay men are considerably older or younger than their adult lovers. They are included in this chapter because of the generation differences, but the inclusion does not imply any similarity to man/boy lovers. There is simply not enough of an issue about generational differences to make a complete chapter, yet the topic is important enough to discuss.

*Nathan,** age forty-two, is fifteen years older than *Loran*, age twenty-seven. They have lived together for eight years.

> *Nathan*: The age difference is the only problem I ever felt. I felt there was a self-destruct element there. I felt that Loran was young enough, attractive enough, and he was in the service. I thought it was stupid to believe we could stand the separation of the service. I believed there was too much working against us, no matter how much we wanted it.
>
> Under no circumstances have I ever sensed that Loran has an awareness of the age difference. He has never exploited it or been apologetic. To the same ex-

tent, I don't think I've ever felt it to be an approbation on my part that having a young lover was a feather in my cap. I only saw it as a negative thing, that Loran would be attracted to someone his own age, rather than myself.

Loran: I think he was afraid to lose me. He feels there are limits built into the relationship, where we'll break up over age.

Nathan: Yes. But also this point. I was not certain at the outset, I guess two or three years of being together, that Loran really understood that I was not going to be his father. That I was not going to be one because of "greater experience," would lead him, make demands on him, and tell him what to do. We went through a period where Loran would say, "What should I do?" I would back off; I wasn't going to play that role. I remember saying it several times. "I don't want you to view me as an authority."

I worry about what's going to happen to Loran when I go. We never talk about it, but I think about it.

Steve,* age fifty-four, is nineteen years older than *Mark*, age thirty-five. Both were previously married, both have children, and both are recovered alcoholics. They have lived together for almost four years.

Steve: The age difference was a real problem for me for a long time. I guess I've grown up thinking that it's an impossible situation. I spent a lot of time worrying about it, which Mark didn't seem to do. It took me a long time to realize that it wasn't an issue for him, only for me.

Until very recently I came up with the "right answer." When somebody asked me about the difference in age between me and Mark, I finally said, "Well, I suppose the youth that attracted me to him in the first place is going to be gone, because he's going to get older." Now I think I'm mature enough to handle that. And that felt all right.

Mark: When Steve got worried about it, it was like he was trying to get me worried about it. It never occurred to me until he started worrying about it. Steve doesn't seem a different age to me.

Steve: I think about our retirement. We both want to retire to Hawaii. But by the time Mark retires, I may already be dead, and that saddens me. It's one of the realistic things we have to consider.

The following forty-year-old gay man has lived with his twenty-two-year-old lover for two years in New York City.

I'm eighteen years older than my lover, and not at all considered attractive in the gay world, and he's very attractive. Whenever we're in the street, men cruise him constantly. I doubt they even notice me. There have been times when we're at a dance or a bar and some gay man will come over and push his way between us and proposition my lover.

These things used to drive me up a wall, and you wouldn't believe how jealous I got, how angry at him if he even so much as recognized the physical existence of another man. We had violent quarrels about it, with me accusing him of actions he never even contemplated. I couldn't believe, not for years, that his interest in me was anything but temporary. Here he was, he could get anyone he wanted, and all I could get was him. But that's all he wanted. He wanted us to have each other. I refused to believe that a handsome young guy would want me.

You see, I thought about the difference between our ages a lot. I wondered what other people would think about me loving a guy much younger. But my lover never even asked me how old I was. He never cared. He doesn't have any hang-up about age, and he was always confused that it worried me so much.

He's right. I don't worry about it very much anymore. We are contemporary to each other in our relationship, and that's what love should be about. He's more mature than me in some ways, and I'm more mature than him in other ways. So the hell with what anyone else thinks. Once you accept being queer, you're a renegade already, so you might as well drop the rest of your conditioning. We're both a lot happier that way.

There is no reason to believe that large age gaps between lovers are any more or less problematical than difficulties between lovers of the same age. Generally, one or the other lover (usually the older) may worry about the reaction of friends, that they think of the older one as "stealing from the cradle," but there is no reason why any lover should be influenced by reactions or potential reactions of friends. If the lover does worry, it suggests that he hasn't yet resolved his own feelings about age gaps.

One frequently asked question is whether age gaps between gay lovers may signal a substitute father/son relationship. Father/son relationships in the guise of compatible lovers are certainly found in the gay world, but a difference in years between lovers is not necessarily an indication of father/son dynamics. People are more complicated than that. For instance, a man may be chosen by another man because of a symbolic resemblance to a father. This resemblance may be a certain physical trait. A good example of this process of physical symbolization was Fred, who chose men with particular hair patterns—especially the hair from the navel to the crotch— regardless of age. At other times, a personality feature of the father is symbolized, and the gay man seeks out men who have this special feature. Albert, who always sought what he perceived to be strong men, is an example of personality symbolization, and once again age was not relevant to the search.

It is also true that some men use age as the symbol of the father, enjoying as well the beloved's status and financial success. And there are relationships, some with age gaps and others with no generational differences, that are present-day dramas written in childhood, recapitulations of complicated father/son relationships. But age differences alone are not suggestive of this complicated process.

CHAPTER NINE

Religion and Gay Love

The more I study religions the more I am convinced
that man never studied anything but himself.

RICHARD BURTON

Some gay men believe religion to be nothing more than a pernicious influence in their lives; others feel that their religion has
cemented their homosexual love. Certainly, the Western religions
have not looked kindly on gay love. Religious morality has always condemned the physical acts of homosexuals without consideration of the emotional context.

Many of the men I interviewed reported the devastating effects
of a strident religious doctrine on their lives, particularly in
early childhood. This is especially true of fundamentalist groups,
where almost any physical need is interpreted as sexual and
therefore perverse. There were many stories told by the respondents of childhoods filled with injunctions against all forms of
sexual thought or play. The more humorous examples included
parents who cut out advertisements for sanitary napkins from
magazines so that the children wouldn't see them, or not allowing any book in the house in which the word "sex" appeared.
More serious were parents who never touched each other in front
of the children or kissed, as if touching and kissing were sexual
stimuli to their children, rather than acts of love. Most serious
were the examples where children were taught that sex before
marriage, in both thought and deed, was sinful, perverse, and a
giant step forward toward hell. Homosexual stirrings in some
children only further reinforced the conviction that they were
tainted and corrupt. Surely those who believed themselves to
be corrupt and sinful came to believe that other gay men were
also corrupt—and loveless. Even those who rejected much of the
orthodox doctrine of sex were left in conflict, wanting to believe
in the power of love as a religious force but rejecting the arbitrary regulation about who was acceptable to love.

Feelings of guilt are very prominent in the lives of gay boys from religiously oriented families. Just being taught that something like sex or masturbation is wrong is not of itself successful in creating guilt in a young boy; it merely teaches him that he needs to be careful not to do these things within sight of the prying eyes of parents and other adults. To experience guilt, the boy must learn to punish himself—it is self-punishment for violating the rules, whether in thought or deed, that defines guilt. Unquestionably there are many gay men who learned to punish themselves for sexual feelings; their guilt only increased as they turned toward homosexual rather than heterosexual interests.

Inevitably, the concept of God the Father has its parallel implications for the boy's real father and hence his family. The worship of God carries with it an obligation, and violation of the accepted rules of religion often creates a feeling in a boy that he has transgressed doubly, sinning against not only his Heavenly Father, but his earthly one as well. The boy perceives himself as a profound disappointment to his father, his family, and his God. He feels guilt and shame on many planes.

There are some men who are very close to their religions: they are clergymen or children from the families of clergymen. Quite a few were interviewed for this study. In many ways their backgrounds are more telling than the experiences of ordinary churchgoers because of their sophisticated training in theology and because the penalties for transgressing the doctrine of acceptable sexuality are greater. The emphasis in this chapter, therefore, is on the religious experience of gay clergymen, all of whom have fought long-standing personal conflicts about their gayness, and on the success they have enjoyed in finding love inside or outside the church.

The transcripts in this chapter are much longer than in any other in the book. They could have been shortened by summing up or paraphrasing the language, but when I read and reread the actual interviews I realized how often these men had thought about their presence in their respective religious orders and for how many years they had mulled over their lives and their goals. I felt that their statements contained an integrity that would be violated if shortened or summarized. For this reason, some of the men who speak in the next few pages are quoted at great length. They express far more eloquently than I could how significant changes in the search for love can occur at any time in life.

For the record, no examples of gay rabbis were found, although I know they exist. Perhaps Jewish clergymen are not yet as open about their homosexuality as members of most of the Christian denominations.

Gene is twenty-four. He was born and raised in a farming suburb in Texas and is a graduate of a Bible college. He is an example of someone who still hates his homosexuality. He now works for a fundamentalist religious foundation in the South. His mother is a member of the United Methodist Church and is an orthodox observer of religious doctrine; his alcoholic father has only recently come to religion. Gene believes that his homosexual feelings result from being afraid of girls, a substitute for "genuine love." His first sexual experience, mutual masturbation, was with an eighth-grade friend.

> I was ashamed of the act itself, not just masturbating. I was ashamed I had done it with someone else, even in the presence of someone else. I felt it was very downgrading. Of course, it's not the thing you're going to stand out on the sidewalk and say, "Here I am."
>
> I was very active in the church from the age of thirteen. When I was fifteen I became a born-again Christian. I accepted Jesus as my personal savior. I felt an emptiness in my life, not really knowing a purpose, and I felt kind of friendless. There was just something there that was missing. From what I had been taught, I felt this would be an answer, something to fill the void. That's why I became a Christian, to see this void filled.
>
> At that time it was very simple. I just followed the instructions in the Bible. All you need to do is ask forgiveness of your sins and repentance. Truly give up the past life and ask Christ to come into your heart.
>
> I know of a lot of religious water drinkers. The difference is that when you become a Christian, it's trying to follow the steps of Christ, be more like him. You can belong to a church and not be a Christian.

Gene had one sexual experience with another boy when he was seventeen. He felt extremely guilty about it and never saw him again. His next sexual experience was at Bible college where he slept with another student.

It was mild petting, and we masturbated each other.

Then we went to sleep in each other's arms. The next hour I woke up, and I was feeling very bad. I felt sick to my stomach, but it was more from guilt, sorry for what I had done. I thought, "Oh, no! I've done this here at school."

Gene discussed the experience first with a married friend and then with the campus chaplain, who told Gene to stay away from the other student. A few nights later the student invited Gene to his room once again; though protesting, Gene followed him to his room but refused sex. Somehow both events became known to the dean of students (exactly who told him remains a mystery), and the student was expelled from college. Gene was suspended for six months.

When Gene returned to the college he had sex with another student, this time in a motel room. Once again, sex was mainly mutual masturbation ("Do it and get it over with"). Oral-genital contact was avoided because "It was too gross for me. I tried it once, and I immediately threw up."

Gene has recently broken up with a woman he had been seeing for two years; they never had sex together.

It's the old cliché that I respected her. This other girl I had no respect for whatsoever. She was a good lay, and that's why.

With men I'm chauvinistic; nobody is going to touch me, nobody is going to fuck me. I don't like it. I have to play the male. I have to be the male in the action, I'm not the female.

I don't know that I'm a homosexual. I could state it two ways. I'm a straight who is having problems, or I'm a gay frustrated with my life-style. I want to believe I'm a straight who is having problems. I guess what I'm looking for is some way to bridge this. I think it is going to come down to the fact of giving up one or the other. Giving up Christianity or giving up homosexuality. I prefer to give up the homosexuality.

I can't buy the thing with the gay church. I guess I'm fundamental; I believe what the Bible says. I believe that when it says virgin birth, it was the Holy Spirit implanted. When it says Jesus healed the leper, it was a man who actually had leprosy, and the leprosy was gone.

Jesus Christ is the son of God. He died to save us all from our sins. I don't want it to sound too cliché-ish. I really feel that He didn't just do it for a bunch of people. I can actually feel like He did it for me. It's hard for some people to grasp, but I feel like I can sit and talk to Him just as easily as I can sit and talk to you. He's just that real to me, even though I can't see Him physically like I can see you. He's a comfort to me—and yet my psychological—I look at it—He's not there, tangible all the time. Sometimes I reach out for something, for a physical comfort, and I reach out for people, someone to lean on, someone to kick me in the butt when I need it.

The following three men were all ordained in the church. The first man, Nathan, is a Baptist minister; Matthew and Leo are priests of the Catholic Church. All of them give us a rare view of their experiences while studying for the clergy, experiences in their ministries, and personal conflicts they've experienced as each has proclaimed his gay love. All three have experienced overwhelming personal conflict because not one rejects his faith, but all reject the orthodox doctrine that condemns them for loving other men. Nathan and Leo have found deep commitment with a male lover, while Matthew has not.

Nathan * is forty-two. He has lived with his lover, *Loran*,* for the past eight years. His background has enabled him to sense both what is right and what is wrong with the practice of religion in the United States. Like most religious gay men, he has had to come to terms with his attitude about gay love and his feelings of devotion. He is a minister of the Baptist Church, but he is no longer attached to a congregation.

> Whatever drew my mother and father together is beyond my comprehension—or theirs, at this point. My childhood was tumultuous and frequently violent. For instance, my father was very upset by reading material, and if he would find Mother or me reading, the material would be confiscated or destroyed. He didn't want a "bookworm, fairy son." He was very conscious of what was sissy and what was not, to the point where he had no understanding of the physical limitations of a child. My father pitched on a baseball team, and he was insistent before I was five that I learn how to throw and catch a ball. But it was beyond my interest and beyond my capabilities.
>
> My father used to beat my mother and throw it in her face that he was having affairs with other women.

Mother decided to get a divorce and needed to prove a rumor that Dad was having an affair with a particular married woman, and I was placed in the car—the back seat of a car with a blanket thrown over me [age five]. Dad was expecting to take a woman out for the evening, but he discovered me and took me home, and I was beaten very severely, and my mother was beaten. He took the children in the car and told my mother that she would never see them again. And my father sped away with my mother still holding onto the running board of the car. My father swerved and stopped and swerved, purposely to throw her off the car, and she was badly injured. We were placed in a foster home.

It's important for you to know that at the age of eleven the Baptist Church became the overriding force in my life. I found in the church friends who cared about me as an individual and for my ability to read, speak, and learn. I couldn't compete in athletics in school, but I was the darling of the Sunday school.

I became very convinced in the fundamentalistic way that Jesus was very present, that Jesus was calling me to do something, and that my temporary situation of being without mother and father in the long run was going to be taken care of.

In the context of the Baptist Church a great deal of attention was given to "negativisms"—one does not dance, play cards, etc. It was only when I reached college age that I perceived the absence of affirmations, of saying, "This is what a Christian is, this is what a Christian loves." And that stand within the church was in opposition to what I saw in Jesus as a loving, outgoing person Who kept stressing that the law was not everything, that I come to fulfill the law and put it aside, as it were. That He transcended the legalism of the Judaic faith.

During my childhood, in the context of the church, at least, sex was never mentioned. The closest thing I can recall was the woman taken in adultery and the harlot where Jesus Himself interfered. I wasn't aware until I was in college, at nineteen, that that episode with Jesus would matter to me. Let me explain it this way.

These two verses from First Corinthians when Paul wrote, "Do you not know that your body is a temple of the holy spirit which is within you, which you have in God. You are not your own. You are bought with a price, so glorify God in your body." A great deal of attention

was given in the church to your body as a holy temple—
don't stain it, don't make it unholy—and I perceived
sex initially as a violation of the holy temple. Even
with masturbation, for a long time I thought that every
time I did it I was doing something that was displeasing
to God, shameful about it. And I felt hypocritical because I was perceived by the Christian community as a
person of very high standards. I thought, if they only
knew what I did in private they would condemn me.

It kept me from reaching out to another male. I would
have feared that I had been party to corrupting someone
else. That I had led someone astray, that I had sinned
all the more because I had taken someone to hell with
me.

The few sexual experiences I had, starting at twenty,
I perceived as a need for affection, rather than sex.
There was something right about one person loving another, and I relished the fondling, the cuddling, and I
was repelled by the quicky sex.

Nathan entered a Baptist college to study for the ministry.
During that time he divulged to a minister at the college that he
had had gay sex. Nathan was told to report to the health service
doctor who asked him to draw a picture of a person. Nathan
drew a woman with an evening gown, a grand piano, and a
circular staircase. The psychiatrist said, "You're an incurable
homosexual." Nathan was asked no further questions, the fact
was reported to the dean, and Nathan was expelled. He was
placed in a hospital and aversion therapy was planned, but he
refused it.

My father came, unannounced as it were, and at first
refused to see me. He only spoke to the doctor. Then
my father said to me, "Well, I want you to know that if
I were in a similar situation, and if I discovered that
I was gay, there could only be one recourse, and that
would be suicide. And I want you to know that as far
as I'm concerned, you are dead."

When Nathan was released from the hospital, he decided to
become a medical missionary. He now admits that his career
choice was partially determined by his negative view of sex. The
association between male aggression and sex was stamped in his
head so fiercely that he viewed all sex as domination. Whatever
sexual needs he experienced from his own body must have been

very confusing. But Nathan rationalized his gay sexual needs in a way common to many gay clergymen.

I rationalized affection for a man. It was not the same thing as affection for a woman because it would not end in pregnancy, which loomed so large in my mind. In the absence of anything being said about homosexual relationships I felt a little freer kissing a man because there would be no pregnancy. It seems so naive looking back on it now, but as a teenager it opened me up to male-to-male feelings.

I didn't know about sodomy because the word was never mentioned. It was "licentiousness" that was the crime of the people of Sodom.

In the church I felt I mattered, like the sparrow. And through my teenage years I wanted to help other people. I threw myself into every project. I was hurt very much in terms of returning to Virginia at the age of twelve and seeing how blacks were treated in that southern community. I couldn't believe it. I couldn't understand what it meant to have "colored" drinking fountains. Their schools were dilapidated and substandard. My father couldn't understand why I would concern myself with "niggers." And that shaped a desire on my part to go to Africa as a missionary.

When I was in the South I was an assistant minister of a Baptist church. In the Baptist church, like some of the other fundamentalist churches, the requirement for a minister used to be extremely low. Ministers frequently didn't go through college, no less through a seminary. For years the Baptists and Methodists had a technique of licensing, and when one was given a license as a minister, one could do everything except perform a marriage. And one should refrain from giving communion except in an emergency. There were also ordained ministers. I was licensed as a Baptist minister one month before I left for college. Therefore, when Billy Graham came to Richmond for his campaign, I was named to be in charge of college and youth recruitment for counseling and getting workers for the crusade.

We met weekly, up to five hundred ministers, to prepare for the crusade and went through counseling sessions with the Billy Graham staff as to how to persuade people to accept Christ, how to listen to their problems, how to take advantage of the moment of religious fervor, how one can enroll them for Christ, to persuade them to be led to a life commitment includ-

ing a financial commitment toward making a tithe to
the Lord—at least ten percent of one's income. That
was always stressed, that there was not just concern
for one's soul. If one could persuade a person to tithe,
the person would have an investment in his or her
church and participate more fully.

Every night for two weeks Billy and his staff would
meet with us for prayer sessions before the service
began, and then afterward we would counsel people in
the tent. They told us what to wear, what to talk
about. We were told that we were a chosen people; we
were set apart as God's holy people, God's ambassadors; we were "ambassadors for Christ." We were the
bridge, the conduit to Christ.

Sometimes it was impossible to separate what was
being done for Jesus and what was being done for
Billy Graham. The requirements for Billy seemed
higher. I felt that way at the time. I was stunned. I felt
it was all so calculated that there was no concern for a
person, only for numbers. I felt that I had been en-
meshed in a machinery that wouldn't turn off, that Billy
Graham was caught on a treadmill, and he reached
out and grabbed me and put me on it with him. And I
really resented that.

He used huge buckets to collect money. My father
owned a restaurant, and we would get hamburger meat
from the butcher in five-pound buckets, and it was that
identical bucket that Billy used. There were no collection plates; they didn't hold enough money. You couldn't
slip money out of it as easily as a plate, either. When it
went in, it went in. I was on scholarship, and I tithed
every bit of it. I more than tithed. You were taught that
a tithe was an obligation to the Lord. But I also gave a
gift to the Lord. That's what you give out of joy. I gave
a ten percent tithe and a five percent offering of my
money. Some people just wrote out a check as if to
pay up for what they hadn't paid in the past. I also
know some people who had sex with Billy Graham's
staff, gay and straight. It's not unusual. I know of some
evangelists who are antigay and sleep with men and
women.

I decided not to seek ordination because I felt it
would be hypocritical of me to be a preacher behind the
pulpit and never to affirm my sexuality, to keep that in
the dark recesses of secrecy from my constituents, and
I chose instead to go to the classroom.

I went to a Presbyterian seminary. There were nine

classmates of mine who were gay, and all married within
their last year. I had sex with most of them. We dealt
with the double standard. On the seminary level they
felt that their sexual identity should never be exposed,
so the closet was tight, even tighter than the military.
We didn't have sex on the seminary grounds, as if the
seminary ground was holy and the eyes of God were
bigger there.

Out of four hundred in the seminary probably more
than thirty-five were gay. I think most of them shared
my idea that sex with a man wasn't as dangerous as
with a woman. I think there's only one person I've met
in the ministry or the seminary that ever felt good
about himself or herself—because I knew four lesbians
at the seminary. They were not free as lovers. They
would have sex as a release and then not feel good
about it. I found that our relationships were altered
negatively after we had sex. They hated themselves,
would not talk to me; the downcast eyes, the distance—
really was so threatening that I came to the point of
not wanting to have sex with them. I knew it would be
the last communication between us.

The quote is again from First Corinthians, Seven:
Seven. Paul is writing to the church at Corinth, and he
says, "I wish that all were as I myself am," meaning
single, "but each has his own special gift from God,
one of one kind, and one of another." And he then
says, "Nevertheless if your passion burns, then go ahead
and marry. It's better to marry than to burn." It was
in the seminary that some of my classmates came to
the realization that they would never be ministers successfully if they didn't marry. That the wife was a com-
modity, that when he went to an interview, he had to
take the wife. That the wife was going to be as important
to the board of a given church in making their determi-
nation as to whether they would call him, because
they were going to pay for one, but they wanted two
workers. They wanted a man and a wife. They wanted
a family to come to that community. So of those
men I had sex with, all but one married. Knowing that
they were gay, not one perceived themselves as bisexual, but they knew that as a single male they would
be under suspicion, and they needed a wife on the arm,
high heels and a beautiful smile. It became career enhancement, and it was perceived as that.

I would challenge them as to how they were jeopard-
izing both their marriage and indeed turning the

woman into a thing, an enhancement, their meal ticket. But there was a working knowledge about how the church functions that was so great that that took priority over the personal.

One of the things that meant a great deal to me was this verse, that each one has his own special gift from God; slowly, and far too slowly, I began to perceive myself as gay, not condemned. I began to see that perhaps there was a special gift about being gay.

In First John, not the Gospel John, it says that God is love, and those who love receive their love from God, and that love is of God, and there is no love that is not of God, and he's very clear about that. And that love is the property of God, and that you cannot have it or express it without its generating from God. That became a liberating, celebrating awareness that I was loving another man because God had placed within me the capacity to love, to share, to receive.

Matthew is forty-two years old. He was born and raised in a large eastern city. His family was Irish Catholic; he attended Catholic schools. It was in the service that he had his first homosexual experience. Matthew has never had a long-lasting gay relationship, and he is a little bitter about his religious training, even though he prides himself on his faith.

I was always interested in the priesthood, from the age of six. I think the early seeds were not intellectual but more romantic, growing up on a lot of history, martyrs and saints, and religious orders, the things the church has had in two thousand years. But it wasn't theological.

My first relationship was with a soldier. I was eighteen, and he was twenty-six. We were together for a year. I would go to Mass in the morning, and sometimes I would come back upset. During the Mass I was always thinking about my homosexuality. I would come back a little bit down, and he would say, "Well, if it bothers you, why do you go?" But I was a Catholic and a strong one, and I couldn't buy that. He once told me that he knew a gay priest, and at the age of eighteen I couldn't believe that. This all sounds so naive now.

At twenty-six I entered the seminary. I think that even at twenty-six at a very deep level I didn't believe I was gay. I felt there is nothing wrong with feeling something as long as I didn't do anything.

There was a metamorphosis coming about in my second year. I was starting to develop a healthy skepticism, not about the essentials of the faith, but about some of the bullshit. I think I confessed my sexual feelings once more, and then I said this is ridiculous and stopped confessing.

I would guess that sixty percent of the seminary was gay. That's a conservative estimate. I don't know how many were acting on their sexuality, but there was a lot of camping going on, a tremendous amount. For instance, three days a week we had maid service, and you had to roll up your carpets and sit them outside your room so that the maid could scrub the floors. Some of your personal objects would be outside the door. Across the hall was another student who had a pair of fuzzy bedroom slippers, and they looked like rabbit's feet. As we were arriving at our rooms one of the other students saw the slippers and said, "Oh! My dear, those are an occasion of sin. What have you been doing with those?" I mean, you got the message loud and clear. I can remember another time a student had an argument with the rector and called him "an old queen." It wasn't unusual. But I never slept with anyone at the seminary, and I've only heard from hearsay afterward about students sleeping with one another. Two advances were made toward me, but I stayed clear of it.

The student across from me, the one with the slippers, he just about told me he was gay. He had lived in San Francisco, and he would talk about the gay places there, and he would joke about the fleet coming in and things like that. I mean you'd have to have had a lobotomy not to know what he was talking about. He said once, "I'm becoming a priest because I believe in it and because I can make people's lives a little easier in terms of homosexuality in the confessional."

I was very friendly with another student who was an external student, and I had a crush on him. We were always together. He was a Roman Catholic of the Eastern Rites, so he wore the Eastern Rite garb and had a little beard and mustache. Very handsome boy. Some of my classmates would say, "Well, is it going to be a Latin Rite wedding ceremony or a Byzantine Rite ceremony?"

After his third year in seminary, Matthew took a leave of absence to study in a secular university; he then transferred to a second seminary to complete his training for the priesthood. Once again he states that about sixty percent of the five hundred students must have been gay, although he says he never had sex with any of them. He did have infrequent sex with people outside the seminary. He was ordained in 1973 and assigned to a pastor who he later learned was gay. He spent a year in that parish.

> I have never been laicized. I'm on leave of absence. I was struggling with my sexuality and also having serious questions about church policy. My faith today is different than it was when I first entered the seminary. My faith is much less magical, much more human. I see my relationship to my Creator and also to my neighbor as sort of a triangle, as opposed to the vertical of man and God alone, like we were taught. Much more communal. I'm less of an institutional Catholic and more of a communal one.
>
> Some gay priests are struggling like me, trying to integrate their ideals with their commitment in life. Others repress that part of their psyche. Many of the priests in the church, because of their own psychic struggles, are homophobic. But there are also many other courageous people in the church who have come out, because they are saying this is who I am, and it's God-given, and it should be an asset to society.

The last clergyman is *Leo*, a Catholic priest of middle age, who was interviewed with his lover, *Jeremy*. They have been lovers for thirteen years, though they decided to live together only recently. This particular interview gives us a look at homosexuality within the church and also provides us with a seldom-expressed experience of a priest's lover.

> *Leo*: I'm from a very strict Irish Catholic family. I was in the army during the Second World War, and I saw death all around me. Then I came back and went to college and had a strong feeling of Providence—why did I escape death? So right after college I entered the church.
>
> For sixteen years I was successfully celibate. I felt a call to religious life, feeling that God wanted me to serve. During my army experience I had to think seriously about religious life. I felt there were fundamental religious values that were necessary for happiness. What kept me alive during the war were those values, and if I could cultivate them for myself I could share them with others.
>
> But at the end of those sixteen years I began to wonder what God wanted of me. I started to find that my religious sublimation broke down, and I started acting

out. I went through hell because I felt my whole life was going down the drain. There I was, hanging around toilets looking for men. I came close to suicide. But then I wondered—I had asked God what He wanted, and this is where I am, so this must have something to do with it. Somehow or other, this is the experience He wants me to go through. So I had a sense that this had meaning.

Shortly thereafter I met a man who was bisexual, and we became friends. He fully accepted his sexuality, and through this relationship of three years I learned to feel comfortable about mine. It put sexuality in a human perspective. The sex was no longer something you do in a tearoom but part of a relationship.

Today I'm not being celibate. At the same time, I'm doing better work as a priest since I met Jeremy, better work than ever before.

Jeremy: There's tension sometimes because I would like to have a more expanded social life than we do now. I'm finding it more and more important that we have friends who are gay and who know who we are so that we can be totally ourselves. There's tension keeping track of who knows what about us. It can be a strain at times, and it limits our social life. There were certain bars we used to enjoy going to, but we can't anymore. Sometimes a person will come up and say, "Hello, Father." People get uptight as if he just came out of an egg.

Sometimes, when other gay priests want to talk to Leo, I feel isolated. One day they were all coming in on him like vultures because they all had personal problems. They all had problems with their priests or bishops, and they wanted him to come up with nice easy answers. And I was just out in the cold. We couldn't be there as a couple; I could only be around as a friend, and they don't even want to acknowledge my presence. I'm there, but I'm not.

Leo: From my own personal experience there was very little homosexuality in my seminary. I've been to a number of different seminaries, and I never saw any camping or innuendo. I've heard the stories, but I'm inclined to be skeptical. A lot of the times it comes from people who were either put off seminaries or by those who left for various reasons, being angry about the seminary experience. If anyone had a sexual experience, they would have to confess it. They couldn't conceal it. And if they did confess it, they would be told they had to discontinue or leave.

I am aware of a lot of Catholic men and women who grow up homosexual, who do not know how to deal with their sexuality except to renounce it and enter into religious life. They try to live a totally asexual life, and I think that's behind a good percentage of vocations. There's no way to know how high a percentage, but it could go as high as twenty or thirty percent of vocations come from gay men and women. They probably couldn't get married but don't want to lead a totally single life, and they are attracted to religious life precisely because it does make the claim that it will help you to live a celibate life where you don't have to deal with your sexuality. And it's a perfectly acceptable social position; you can escape the consequences of having to deal with your homosexuality.

I don't think these people enter the priesthood primarily to escape their sexuality. Very frequently they are sensitive to spiritual values—what God means to them, the idea of a life of dedication—and deeply committed to those values. It strikes me that homosexuals are more dedicated to these values than heterosexuals. Among the deepest spiritual leaders I have met in the Catholic and Protestant communities over the past twenty years, many were homosexuals.

There are a number of ways of interpreting celibacy. The church's basic idea of celibacy is that it is an extraordinary gift, that the ordinary person needs sexual fulfillment, and that it's a spiritual grace to be able to be celibate successfully. It's sort of a gift from God.

There's also a strong position in the church that celibacy doesn't get you to heaven, that it's only warmth and love that gets you there. If your celibacy means that you're incapable of warmth and intimate love with other people, then it's an impediment in your spiritual development, not a help.

Saint Augustine once interpreted the scriptural passage about the wise and foolish virgins. The wise ones had oil for their lamps and were allowed into the wedding feast. The foolish ones didn't have any oil. He interpreted that as the oil lamps symbolize warmth and love. They were all virgins; none of them had had any sexual activity. But some were frigid virgins who weren't capable of any warmth and love and therefore were not admitted into the kingdom. Only those in their virginity who were capable of outgoing love were to be admitted into the kingdom. So there is a strong tradition that celibacy is not an ultimate value.

Many of the people who look at religion as repressive have their religious beliefs frozen at a childlike level. But others mature and develop; their image of God ceases to be a parental extrinsic figure. It's almost like God is a superego to some people.

The body as the temple of the holy spirit has been interpreted by some people to mean that the body should not be touched. To me this is heresy. If you say the body is the temple of the holy spirit, my interpretation is that the holy spirit is the link between father and son, the holy spirit is a relator and exists only where there are loving relations. The holy spirit cannot be contained in an isolated person, only where there is genuine love in a community, and that would necessarily involve touching and embracing.

The final history is an example of a church believer who is not a clergyman. Many of the men interviewed believe that a gay union should have the same church blessing as a heterosexual marriage, and many of these gay unions are performed each year, mostly by the Metropolitan Community Church (MCC), the gay church founded by Reverend Troy Perry. The historical church demands two things: accept Christ and obey the church rules. The gay churches (like MCC) that have sprung up accept the first but deny the second. In essence, the gay churches believe it is all right to accept one's sexual feelings, that these feelings are not inconsistent with the teaching of Jesus. The gay churches are communal rather than hierarchal, a fact which is bound to lead to conflict with church authorities who have never been known for their leniency toward deviations of any kind.

The rise, within recent years, of gay religious organizations and houses of worship shows quite clearly the importance of religion in the lives of many gay people around the country. In a sense, the interest in practicing one's religion within the confines of gay love is an expression of conservatism within gay life. Couples who participate in holy unions are asking for the same rights and privileges as heterosexuals. They are quite different from other gay men who, like Karl Marx, believe that religion is the opiate of the masses and whose goals are to change, not to integrate with, contemporary society.

*Marlin,** a middle-aged Englishman, insisted on a traditional marriage ceremony for himself and his lover, *Diego*. Marlin had very definite ideas as to what should and should not be included in a marriage ceremony between two men.

> There really isn't a tuppence worth of difference between a straight marriage and a faggot marriage. There's no difference at all. The only difference is you don't breed—thank God.
>
> Diego and I had our marriage in church, and most of the people who came to the wedding were straight married couples. It's the church we go to now. About the service, I wouldn't have the words changed. These gay marriages are very tacky. They change the vows to, "Do you take this lover, will you love and be with him until you both fall out of love with each other," which is just a cop-out where they don't make a commitment.
>
> The marriage vows are very explicit, very simple. "To love, honor and obey, cherish in sickness and health, for richer or poorer, till death do you part." Very easy, very simple. There's no allowance for having a blow job on the side with somebody else because they suck you better. You don't marry for that reason. Marriage is not built on sex; marriage is a friendship in which sex plays a part. It has to be taken care of like a plant, and if you foul your soil you're going to have a withered plot, as far as I'm concerned.
>
> It wasn't at MCC. God forbid. I'm a vestryman at an Episcopal church. But first let me tell you about seeing a gay marriage. It was when I first went to a gay church. I had heard from a friend of mine that two faggots were going to get married here in New York. And I said, "*That* I have to see." Two demented queens getting up to the altar, this I've got to see.
>
> I wanted to laugh, the idea was so amusing. Well, the service was very beautiful. It goes back to the Abbey of Paris. The vows were exactly the regular marriage vows, except they changed the words "husband and wife" to "lover," but the vows were quite explicit. And they were two perfectly average young men tying the knot. They were very beautiful. No one arrived down the aisle in drag; there were no fucking bridesmaids (which I was terrified of). I said, "If I see one queen dressed in drag I'm going to be pissed as hell." I thought it was going to be a circus, but it wasn't. Actually, it was quite a beautiful service. It was very touching. One could feel that there was something

very nice going on with the two young men, and I also felt like an old man watching some son get married.

But Diego and I decided that we would get married in a regular church. The ceremony was very important to me. I realized that I hadn't committed myself to anybody. I'd always come first, but then I also realized that God had been very good to me. I hadn't gone to a church in a hundred years, couldn't get me near one. It was very simple. The church wouldn't accept my homosexuality, so I wouldn't accept the church. You don't talk to me, I don't talk to you. And I was too busy leading a thoroughly selfish life, indulging myself, promoting my career. I was greedy for money and other things. I didn't believe that God cared about me at all. Then all of a sudden I realized that here were my latter years. I was getting old, and after the kind of life I'd led, that God had been good to me, had taken care of me, and I figured I owed it to him to make a commitment in His house.

The wedding cake was something. I was determined to have a beautiful wedding cake, and I ordered one at a wonderful German baker. I was telling him what kind of cake I wanted, and then I came to the decoration on the top. So I said, "By the way, the bride has got to go. I want two grooms." So this old German said, "You want what?" I said, "I want two grooms. I'm marrying my boyfriend, I'm not marrying a bloody woman." And so the poor boy almost dropped his teeth. He said, "I can't do that." I said, "Forget the cake." He said, "No, no!" He started pulling the plastic dresses apart and showed me that the dolls were one mold. I said, "Take the bloody bride and bridegroom off and put two lovebirds on top," and so the cake was delivered to church.

I don't believe you're put in this world to care for yourself. If you never actually share your life, it's pointless. I had all the money in the world, and I spent it all on myself in my youth. You get all your jewels, and you put them all on the table sometimes and look at them, look at your medals, badges of achievement; then one fine day you look in the mirror and you don't like that face at all, not a very nice person. You know what's going on behind that face. You have a terrible suspicion that face is going to come right back and go *rrrrrr* to you, and I decided to mature. It was worth waiting for. It's been fifteen years together, and it's the best part of my life.

People have strong opinions about the influence of religion in their lives. Some offer testimonials on how belief in a superior being changed their lives and saved their souls and bodies; others recount stories of the suffering religion has caused them. A portion of our society believes that all morality will be destroyed if religious beliefs erode any further, while another segment maintains that the historical religions constitute the main barrier to the development of a human morality. What everyone agrees on is that religion and its power to shape community and family values has had an enormous influence on the lives and happiness of the people. This power is particularly obvious in the lives of gays whose behavior has been consistently condemned by all Western religious groups. It is apparent in the early experiences of gay men, and it even exerts its influence in later love affairs.

Ironically, there are similarities between the Christian church and homosexual male behavior. Both are antiwoman; the church defeats women by excluding them, while homosexual men direct their sexual energies away from them. Both have been considered to have criminal elements and have faced attacks on their morality by established religions. Both maintain that their primary interest is the development of love and sentimentality, and both claim to be uniquely different from those around them. But the most significant similarity is the fact that both the church and gay men represent homosocial institutions; the monastery and the priesthood are even more withdrawn from the influence of women than the gay ghettos of our largest cities. It is hardly surprising then that homosexuality, or at least male-to-male sexual conduct, is an obsession within the church.

What the church has taught us is that sexual feelings have their source in a higher power than oneself, that sex is meaningless if unaccompanied by a spiritual relation that we now call "intimacy." Hedonism, sexual pleasure for pleasure's sake, is condemned in the same way, and probably for the same reasons, as the early fertility cults in which bizarre sexual practices constituted a significant part of the religious rites. The morality of the church insists that sex between people (that is, a man and his wife) should represent the love a man feels for God and His church; consequently, one's sexual responses are conditioned by compassion, love, and generosity to the exclusion of sexual needs. The emotional component of sexuality becomes more important than the sexual marriage; it becomes a way of reproducing the power of the male God in the person of the father of the family. Just as the wife and children look up to the father, they all look up to the Father of all, God. What exists in heaven is symbolized on earth in the hierarchy of the church and the family. This is not a system which encourages the enjoyment of "hot sex."

Sex begins in childhood with games of touching between children. The extent to which men vividly remember these games testifies to how exciting and memorable they were. Of course, masturbation is the first step in the process of defining a boy's sexuality and educating him in the pleasures of satisfying desire, so it is here that religious morality sets to work. Masturbation is condemned earlier than any other sexual practice, and its control underlies the ultimate success of religious doctrine's rule of a person's sexual behavior. If masturbation can be brought under control (and that means stopping it or imparting guilt feelings about it), then authority can short-circuit a boy's opportunity to learn about himself through self-discovery.

Self-discovery is dangerous because if a boy is allowed the psychological feedback provided by masturbation, he may begin to obey a different master, the one within, rather than the principles set forth by the church. This can lead beyond masturbation to all forms of reproductive and nonreproductive sex and a host of variations that lie outside the realm of intimate sexual communication. A boy may also begin believing that his own pleasure is just as important as giving pleasure to another.

What is ultimately condemned, however, is not masturbation per se but all sexual feelings and behavior. It is impossible to teach a young boy that one type of sexual expression is taboo without contributing to a generalized negative attitude toward all sexual feelings. A guilty masturbator will be affected in other aspects of his sexuality; if he is guilty about masturbation he will probably be emotionally tense about sex with a partner. If a boy feels uncomfortable with his own body and guilt-ridden about his masturbation experiences, all other aspects of sexual expression will be colored by this guilt.

Guilt feelings are themselves motivators. When one feels guilty about sex, he is motivated to obey the rules more carefully, creating still more guilt the next time so that a vicious cycle is maintained, and the man feels he is out of control. Out of such cycles of behavior and guilt self-hatred is born.

Part of the reason for this generalized negativity is the vague terms in which most religions speak of sexual behavior. The lack of specificity adds greatly to the guilt, since almost anything that one does sexually might be condemned. For young boys, engaging in prohibited sex makes the act more exciting, but eventually the insistent condemnation of sexuality becomes internalized.

Religion teaches a boy that his actions have implications and that if he behaves in a certain way others will apply a label to him; it might be masturbator, thumb sucker, or fag. It is this tendency to typify a personality on the basis of a label that impels the boy toward a life of guilt and hatred of those who are like himself.

The messages are usually the same: Jews in New York, Pentecostals in Missouri, and Catholics in Chicago are taught a generalized negative attitude about almost all sexual feelings and actions. Most gay men who came from religious backgrounds remembered being taught not to touch their own bodies and that any form of sexuality before marriage was sinful and prohibited. But even more stringent was the requirement to remain clean in thought as well as in action, making a sexual idea, as in Orwell's *1984*, a "thought crime." Thought crimes in the lives of orthodox people and children taught by the orthodox become identical to the actions themselves. It is a unique system of self-control that demands a rigid policing of one's own ideas and feelings.

Many gay men from religious backgrounds accept and believe in God and the teachings of sin and guilt, but they make an exception of the gender of the loved one. They believe that all the old rules are essentially correct but apply them to loving another man. They make sex wholesome by integrating intimacy and permanence in a gay couple relationship. They dwell on the love of Jesus rather than on the anger of Paul, and their moral standard is based on the extent to which they are capable of love, both in a personal and religious sense, rather than on conformity to the historical interpretations of the church. These men have found a way out of their dilemma, and whether one considers their life pattern valid or not, for them it is the only way their religious beliefs can coexist with their sexuality. The power of this integration is shown by that widespread institution, the gay church.

If we were to count the gay organizations in the United States, we would find that gay churches comprise the largest category. They include the Metropolitan Community Church, a variety of other Christian denominational churches, and the gay synagogues. There are hundreds of them, and they contrast strikingly with the gay liberation organizations which are politically oriented. These churches are visible mainly to their members and the religiously defined. They are everywhere, from the centers of the largest gay populations to the smallest rural areas, and the gay atheists are disheartened by the large numbers of people who attend the services. While the gay liberation groups find it difficult to attract enough members to make their organizations politically useful, gay churches often number hundreds of men and women participating in their activities.

Gay clergymen, priests, ministers, and rabbis, have been invisible for a long time. Not that they didn't exist. The history of the church illustrates how sex between members of the clergy has been a problem. The antisodomy laws of the Middle Ages were directed more toward the clergy than the laity. The attack on the Templars included accusations of homosexuality. What is new is the willingness of some clergymen to talk about their experiences, their desire to reject hypocrisy and lead a humanizing life.

One can only imagine how conflicted are the lives of gay clergymen, especially those who reject celibacy. It is unimportant how many gay men join the clergy, and the argument over percentages of seminary students blinds us to the fact that enough are gay to make it a significant problem in their lives and the lives of churchgoers. It is saddening to learn that some of the most vociferous attacks against homosexuality come from clergymen who are themselves homosexual; how agonized they must be by their own feelings and behavior. These men, who have become obsessed by the sexual aspects of homosexuality, are totally unaware that love and affection between gays are possible. Guilty about their inescapable sexual desires, they attack those who are more accepting of sexuality. This situation makes it all the more impressive when gay clergymen come out publicly by

joining organizations like Dignity and Integrity, in an attempt
to convince the church that its obsession with sex obscures the
love that is possible between gay men.

A word should be said about the differences between religions;
no religious group prohibits every possible diversity or all dissent
within its ranks. Perhaps the bias of the author will appear here,
but the Catholic and major Protestant groups seem to differ
from the fundamentalist religions such as the Pentecostal Church
or the Church of God, groups which call themselves "Gospel"
(meaning that they rely solely on the Gospels for teaching and
reject the works of the church fathers). The fundamentalist religions are colored by an anti-intellectual air, a rejection of
scholarship and historical information and a reliance on testimony (often indistinguishable from hysteria) as proof of their
beliefs. Fundamentalism is strongest among rural and economi-
cally deprived groups, and the recitation of miracles and magical
transformations is prominent in their services. Its power over
the minds of growing gay boys is greater than that of the establishment religions; that is amply demonstrated by the men who
comprise the subject of this book. The possibilities for diversity,
the respect for intellectual rigor, and the brilliance of church
writers throughout the centuries have provided a greater opportunity for Catholics and some Protestants and Jews to find
variety within their religions.

Anyone who has talked in depth about sexuality with repre-
sentatives of the major religions and the fundamentalist groups
has to be impressed by the differences between them. Whatever
the doctrinal requirements of the religion, the clergy of the
major groups allow a diversity of thought and show respect for
historical documentation; by contrast, the fundamentalists em-
ploy a "turn or burn" method of saving souls that makes intelligent discussion impossible. More than one person has observed
that the "love" so frequently claimed by the fundamentalists (the
most recent popular example is Anita Bryant) toward the homosexual is offered within a context laden with hate and anger, and
the only coming out they will ever accept is "coming out for
Jesus." Gay men with a fundamentalist background are likely
to be more bitter about early church experience than those who
grew up in the major religions.

Stringent religious doctrine is most powerful in certain geographical areas. There are still communities in the United States where almost the entire town belongs to the same denominational church and where very little diversity of life-style is represented. It is in those communities that religious beliefs have been most successful in delaying the recognition of homosexuality in a gay boy or man. Of course, such communities cannot ultimately prevent awareness, but they can hold back the surge of sexual energies for a while and leave to the self-policing of the man the responsibility for punishment.

CHAPTER TEN

Rural America:
Gay Life in Mountain Rock

"Come back to the raft ag'in, Huck, honey."

MARK TWAIN

To most gays living in big cities, homosexuality seems a product of urban life. The anonymity of its congested and motley collections of people permits deviations from social norms and provides gay men and women with opportunities to find like-minded companions. But these urban gays have little knowledge of the kinds of gay life that exist in rural areas, on the farms and in the villages of the United States. City gays think of rural America as the stronghold of prejudice, the center of conservatism, and the bulwark of oppressive religion; they see it as a place of tight-knit families, devoid of culture and sophistication, a place where teenage boys prove their masculinity by drinking themselves into a stupor, "souping" their cars, and "scoring with chicks." None of this is viewed as propitious for homosexual love.

But the myth of life in rural America has a positive side. City gays imagine the boys on the farm as somehow more wholesome than themselves. Soaking up the sun while pitching a bale of hay, their bodies taking on a bronze glow, these promising young men develop tight muscles from manual labor and hardiness; the lines in their faces and the callouses on their hands are the results of wind, rain, and the warming sun.

In short, they are pictured as country bumpkins with rosy cheeks, ready to be plucked if they venture into the big city.

The truth, as usual, is more complicated. Gay love in rural America encompasses both the depression of closet life and the celebration of long-lasting gay relationships. Sex between men may or may not be more open or widespread than in the past, but gay love and gay couples are retreating to farm areas in unusually large numbers. Even more exciting to learn is that they have always existed in the country.

While city gays have been entrapped by police, beaten in the streets, or fired by employers for their homosexuality, some rural gay couples have often lived in serenity in the countryside.

Gay in Mountain Rock

In one mountainous area of the United States live a number of gay couples, both lesbians and gay men. I've called it "Mountain Rock," though that isn't its real name. It is a well-known mountain area with a history, a geography, and a native population of unusual interest. It is a clannish place where a family name indicates status, though the region has always been poverty-stricken.

Most of the native families of Mountain Rock arrived after the Civil War, having suffered financially during Reconstruction. Though Mountain Rock covers many counties and hundreds of square miles, its soil is thin and poor (the result of erosion and unscientific agricultural practices), and farming is marginal. Families are large and houses small; even today, conveniences are few or nonexistent. In fact, the mountain itself acts as a natural barrier, preventing outsiders from changing or influencing local customs and culture. Since the farmland at the foot of the hills is more fertile than the soil on the mountain, the "people on the bottom look down on the people on the top."

Though poor, the natives are proud. They know their family genealogy, and any one of them is ready to tell you the history of the family from its arrival in Mountain Rock to the present (as well as gossip about other families). They don't think of themselves as migrants but as people of the land, and they are suspicious of city dwellers and outsiders. They are so insulated that even a native who returns from a few years in a big city is considered an outsider. The label sticks, no matter how long the stranger lives among them or how much he may be liked.

Winters are hard in Mountain Rock. It is lovely in the spring, but by November snow covers the farms and woods in a great white mass. There is no snow-removal equipment! All transportation stops, and the farmers spend their time protecting their animals from frosts (and hungry "critters"). Every family has long since stocked its pantry with food, much of it home-canned, because the supply must last for as long as the two months between visits to the local general store, which could be ten miles away. Older people who can't get out at all sometimes suffer from "cabin fever." During these long winters, wood stoves are still the primary sources of heat and the means for cooking (a pan of water is usually placed on the stove to add humidity to the otherwise dry air). Oil trucks can't get through the unplowed roads.

If there are some who object to this annual isolation, they keep it to themselves. Most take it as a matter of course. Even those with "ordinary" jobs in business assume that they won't be able to go to work very often during the winter, and no one expects them to.

But there is no pollution in Mountain Rock. The streams are crystal clear, and every pebble and rock on the bottom is visible, no matter how deep the water. You can drink from the streams and swim in them; they teem with healthy fish. Some of the best trout streams in the country are found here. There are no factories to cloud the air, and the smells of the forests fill the little towns with a fresh, clean fragrance. Of course, this absence of factories means no jobs, which explains why most of the young people are leaving Mountain Rock to seek employment in the cities.

There is no crime to speak of in Mountain Rock, either, except for the occasional adolescent drunken driver. No one locks a door; many houses don't have locks at all. One fellow left his ignition key in his car so long that it rusted, and he had to go to the city to have it removed!

Here in the mountains, people will tell you that geese are the best watchdogs a man can have, and when offering a guest some fresh eggs, they apologize if they were laid yesterday! At one time natives never sold their land to outsiders, even if they had to take a lower price from another native. But modern times have changed all that; family ties are looser, and land values have soared. Oddly enough, there are families who are wealthy in terms of the value of their land but who don't have a cent in the bank. Some of them are now selling to outsiders and moving to other parts of the country.

There are gays in Mountain Rock, although it is impossible to get a rough estimate of their number because of the secrecy surrounding their homosexual lives. Though aesthetically the area is a dream, natives are hostile to most new ideas and not accommodating toward homosexuality. Currently there are two different groups of gays in the area: natives of the land whose families have lived there for many generations and "outsiders," gay couples who have migrated from, in this case, the West Coast. Both groups must surely be amused that the call letters of the local television station are "KY." Only one native gay man in Mountain Rock was willing to be interviewed.

Leonard Rogers, a native of Mountain Rock, is now in his early thirties. The youngest of seventeen children, Leonard is about to leave the mountains for good to settle with his lover in another state. His account of growing up in the mountains is filled with the splendors of the tall tale. For instance, Leonard believes that mountain men, and especially his family, have larger cocks than city men.

> My father was very well hung, so to speak. I know women, one in particular, she had an affair with my father. She said, "Your dad was hung as a horse." Other people told me that Dad was really hung. They said he could have a pair of waistpants, and he could reach down and take his cock and hang it over the top of his pants and take a piss.
>
> When my brother got married, my mother and his fiancée were in the kitchen the night before the marriage, and my mother told her, "Now I don't know if he's like his father, but if he's a typical Rogers then he's hung like a horse." The next morning I asked my sister-in-law if it was true. She said, "Damn well right! He sure is!" So I asked my brother, and he said, "Ye-ah." He said he had eleven and a half inches. And I said I didn't believe him. I said I would have to see. So he got it out—it was hard—and I took a wooden yardstick and laid it right against his stomach, and it damn well came out to eleven and a half inches. So Mother was right, the Rogers are well endowed.

Leonard feigns shame when he mentions that the genes must have "been all wore out" by the time they reached him, the youngest boy. "I only got ten inches," he says. Incidentally, his father had seventeen children with Leonard's mother, two more with his mother's sister, and a disputed number by some other women in the vicinity—or so Leonard claims.

The Rogers family was one of the first to settle in Mountain Rock, emigrating from Tennessee in 1818. Leonard's great-great-grandmother rode eighty-five miles carrying a child on the back of a mule. When she arrived, she took out a patent deed.

> A patent deed is something you take out on your land that you are going to prove up on, stating that you're going to live there five years and gonna build a house there and settle there and improve the land. This was before the Homesteader Act. But they didn't send off the patent until the Civil War, and Abraham Lincoln signed it. I still have that deed. Quite a document, his signature and flowers and everything.

The Civil War created discord among the brothers in the family. Some fought for the North, others for the South, and memories of the horrors of the war lasted in Mountain Rock long after 1865.

> I have two great-grandfathers who were brothers. One fought for the North, one fought for the South. Both of them came back and settled on adjoining farms and never spoke to each other as long as they lived. And their houses were in easy eyeshot of each other. In fact, they would work in their fields, and if one was working in the field, let's say here, the other wouldn't work on that side of his place—he would go to the other side and work. So it was quite unique. Their families had family gatherings, big get-togethers, but the two old men would never see each other. Neither one would go.
>
> They both fought at Gettysburg, and both fought at Shiloh. They fought against each other. And they seen each other at Shiloh. It was at night. One was on guard duty—no, they were both guards—and he seen this Confederate soldier, and in the campfire light in the distance he could see it was his brother. So they both got together and had a visit at the Battle of Shiloh. One of them died in 1918 and the other in 1924. The Rogers are long-livers.

For all Leonard's stories about his dad, the fact is that he died when Leonard was four; then his mother married a man who insisted Leonard call him "Father." Leonard refused and was beaten.

So I went to my grandad's and told him what happened. Well, my grandad at that time was about eighty-eight years old, and this guy [the new father] was about thirty-seven. And my grandad went over there with a horsewhip and beat him—because he even so much as touched a Rogers. My grandad did not approve of outsiders, no way, shape, form, or fashion.

From then on, Leonard lived with his grandad. A few years later, at the age of ten, Leonard had his first sexual experience with another boy, a cousin of fifteen (he has eighty-three first cousins). In those days, there weren't any spare beds for guests, and visiting relatives had to share one with a family member.

So my cousin and I slept together, and I remember waking up in the middle of the night in terrible pain, and he was having sex with me, not only once but twice in the same night. He was fucking me. I don't remember exactly what I did. I do know I didn't like it, but he told me to shut up. So the next morning, I told my granddad—who was then ninety-four. I told him what happened. He laughed and said, "Boys will be boys!"

Mountain Rock allows more sexual experimentation in early life than city people realize. Distances are great, and children have to travel, escaping their parents' supervision for extended periods of time. Throughout his early adolescence, Leonard played the usual "touch me" games and took part in mutual masturbation with just about every boy in the community. The mere presence of another boy seems to have been justification enough for sex. For instance, in school:

When I went to grade school, the last year there, there were only eight students. This was in the whole school. Eight students, and we were all boys, and we were all in the same class. And all eight of us would get out at noon and fuck each other. We were all thirteen and fourteen years old. But I just watched. Sometimes they would fuck in the outhouse. They would suck each other till they got it really lubricated; then they would spit on their cock—and fuck. I remember the first time I opened the outhouse door, and there they were. It went on every day. Sometimes there were two people who would raise their hands to go to the bathroom at the same time. You could see they already had hard-ons.

We had a real, real old teacher who was almost blind, and it even got so bad that the boys in the schoolroom would ask to sit with each other in the back of the schoolroom in big wide seats. And they would sit there and play with each other under the desk. The teacher in the front couldn't hardly see the kids at all, let alone what was happening. They'd sit back there and actually suck each other off in class. Today every one of them is happily married, but country boys do not go without sex—not by a long shot.

In high school Leonard came across his first adult gay man, the high school athletic coach, though Leonard never had an affair with him.

C.S.: How did you know he was gay?
Because he almost got fired over fucking one of the kids when the principal walked in, and he had a fourteen-year-old boy spread over his desk with his cock up the kid's ass. Yeah, that's generally a pretty good sign a guy is gay!

When Leonard was fifteen, he fell in love with an eighteen-year-old cousin. It started innocently enough.

He came over, wanted to know if I wanted to go fishing, go out to the crick. You people say "creek," we always call it crick. So we took off over the ridge and went down through the holla' and the fields to the crick. We swum in the nude and fished and cooked our supper there at the crick. It was a hot summer, and when we got ready to go to bed we started tickling each other, and one thing led to another, and he remarked that for being fifteen years old, what a big cock I had. He flattered me, and then he wanted to know if he could see it. One thing led to another, and then he touched it. It was like an electric charge went through me. I had never had sex with anyone. I just recently learned masturbation, so it was quite an experience. He did fuck me. Then I fucked him, and we sucked each other.

The two cousins met as often as possible for four years. Each time they had sex, and, as Leonard tells it, they were both hung up on each other; but there was no emotion expressed, none of the kisses or endearments that commonly mark intimacy. Though unexpressed, the emotion was there, at least for Leonard who loved his cousin. Suddenly the cousin announced his forthcoming marriage.

> I felt hurt, felt like I'd been used. See, I didn't even know he was getting married until a week before he got married. It was kept pretty quiet. He knocked a girl up. And he came out to my place and stayed a couple of nights with me. And we had a glorious time of sex. In fact, that's all we done. I didn't do a thing on the farm while he was there. We fucked fifty times in two days. Then he's up and married. It really hurt me, it really did.

The shock threw Leonard into a five-year depression. He stopped masturbating. He refused anyone who propositioned him, man or woman. He brooded constantly. It was only at twenty-four that he had sex again with a man who was putting up hay on Leonard's farm. That ended the depression.

Leonard sees his cousin from time to time, but they never talk about the early days. His cousin is still married and has five children. Leonard has continued the affair, at least in a vicarious way.

> I know his son can be had. The reason I know is because I had an affair with his son. His son is sixteen. I asked him, "Where did you learn gay sex so well?" And, well, he was drunk, and he said, "Well, my dad taught me."

Sexual experimentation among boys has always been permitted, if not encouraged, in Mountain Rock. Even the farm animals get their share.

> When a boy's a boy and he has a stiff cock, any hole will do—as long as it's hot. Almost every one of them have fucked cattle, too. I do know one boy, though. His dad caught him fucking a hog. Now that would be low —the hog might squeal!

But boyhood games must come to an end, even in remote Mountain Rock. "Boys will be boys," but men are required to be heterosexual, married, and religious; deviation is not tolerated. In adulthood, Leonard's life changed dramatically. The boyhood sex play was suppressed, and former sexual companions married local women and started their own families. "You don't try to feel someone out to see if they'll go to bed with you. You just don't do it, or you'll be run out of the community." So for a number of years Leonard had very few sexual experiences in his mountain town. Later, he started driving to a gay bar eighty-five miles away in another state. It was the closest gay meeting place, and in the five years he's been driving there he's never met anyone from his neck of the woods. What do the native gays do for sexual release? They either get married and feign interest in their wives while dreaming of some friend down the road, or "they go nuts."

One would think that such a stifling atmosphere would result in a stampede to the big cities, but the local gays remain and stay in the closet, even to this day.

> They stay out of fear. I stayed out of fear for a long time. In this area you get the impression you can't survive out in the big world. It's like stepping forty years back in time around here. Because literally you get the feeling you can't survive in the big old cruel world. That's why most of them do stay. They'd rather stay here with family ties—they're very clannish—rather than leave their family they'll just closet their homosexuality. But a lot of them marry and have homosexual affairs on the side when they can.

But the cat's out of the bag for Leonard. At least some people know that he's gay, and in the long run it may be the best chance he'll have to live an openly gay life with a man he loves. Recently, a teller at the local bank (these towns rarely have more than one) told the bank president that Leonard was gay.

> He told me he would just as soon I withdraw my money from his bank. I told him no. Since then whenever I go into the bank I wink at the bank president. It don't make him any too happy—but it does a lot for me!

Leonard's family shuns him as well. They have become angry at his homosexuality, often refusing to invite him to family gatherings. But Leonard couldn't care less. Leonard inherited a rather large estate when his grandfather died—in fact, Leonard was the sole heir, which didn't improve his popularity with the other folks in the family. But it's given him complete independence.

Leonard has just left Mountain Rock, his family, and all his friends to live with another man a thousand miles away. "I'd do anything that guy asked. I'd walk on water or fire if he told me to." He still cherishes the memories of flowers blooming in the spring, the smell of freshly cut grass, the evenings when the men competed at telling outrageous stories to whittle away the time, and the games played by a dozen children in a cabin during the winter snows. But he has traded it all for polluted water, smelly air, and the din of the city—and life with a man he loves.

The Outsiders

While the native gays of Mountain Rock view their community as a prison surrounded by a threatening world, some gay outsiders view it as a Garden of Eden. The outsiders come from the big cities of America. They almost always arrive in couples, motivated by a desire to exchange sophistication and the complexities of cities for the simplicity and tranquillity of rural life. The natives and the newcomers are both looking for the same thing—personal freedom and independence from their past. Paradoxically, each finds it in the very place the other is fleeing.

In every case, the gay male couples who have migrated to Mountain Rock came from large cities, mostly in California, though many were born and raised in small towns and rural places. They have experienced the high life of gay ghettos, the sexual opportunities that abound in the cities with their young, transient populations, and the economic possibilities of professional or business life—and couldn't wait to get out.

Robert and *Eugene* have been lovers for six years and residents of Mountain Rock for three. Robert, fifty-two, was an only child. Although he was born in a small town, he knows what gay city life is like, having participated in all aspects of the scene during his early years. Eugene, forty-one, is black. Raised on a small farm, he was eighteen when his family moved to New Orleans.

Robert and Eugene followed a lesbian couple—colleagues in the same business in California—to Mountain Rock. The lesbians moved to the area after retirement and invited Robert and Eugene for a visit.

It was summertime, and the terrain was beautiful. It was glorious. So on the way home we got to talking. Well, we're going to retire some day, so let's buy some property now, while it's still cheap. So by the time we arrived back in California, we decided to buy some land in Mountain Rock.

From California, Robert and Eugene wrote their lesbian friends, asking them to find a piece of property they might buy, but the lesbians protested that the men should see it first. How did they know they'd like the parcel of land? Robert, however, insisted.

The land (eighty acres) was bought, and Robert and Eugene decided to pack up and move immediately. They had no jobs, just a little money, and Robert's mother as a permanent house-guest.

We were tired of the rat race. I mean *tired* of it. Fighting all that crap all day long. I got to work at seven o'clock in the morning, and I had six thousand problems waiting for me that I was supposed to solve—and I didn't even know what happened.

I had had enough of gay life. I don't give a damn for it now. We felt we didn't need that input anymore, because we had it here with each other. We relate to each other extremely well.

Robert was more concerned that Mountain Rock is all white, and Eugene is black. He need not have worried. While Eugene might have been tarred and feathered forty miles away (it still happens there), there have been no problems in Mountain Rock over race, except for a humorous one.

It was their first year in the mountains. Robert was shopping in town; Eugene stayed home to trim some bushes when an eighty-year-old neighbor appeared. "Where's the boss?" inquired the neighbor. Eugene just assumed the man meant Robert and told the old man that he had gone shopping. So the two of them sat and talked for a while, and the neighbor began to tell Eugene about the history of the area.

Then all of a sudden he stopped in the middle of the conversation and stared at me, and he said, "What do you do?" And he caught me off guard, so I said, "I'm the cook." So he spread it all over the town that there was a white man there with a black cook.

Eugene and Robert later decided (since the old man had already spread the word) that there was no reason to change the story. For all they know, people still believe that Eugene is Robert's cook.

Eugene's acceptance by the natives was facilitated when he joined the local church and became their leading musician; the church has never had a competent musical director before. It's a strange thing about church membership in a rural area like Mountain Rock: if you belong, you can do no wrong, and if you don't, you can do no right. Church membership becomes a substitute for moral behavior. But do the locals know that Eugene and Robert are gay? Robert says:

> I don't think so. I don't think they think about these things. For instance, there is a fellow around here; he's about seventeen, and he looks like a flaming sissy. If this were a big city, everyone would know, but he gets away with it in a small place like this. It's a riot. You see him walking down the hall, and you know he's a flaming faggot—there isn't a more flaming faggot on Hollywood Boulevard. But he's a native. And they think he's hot for some secretary in the place. Well, if I were back in California talking with a friend I'd say, "Well, who's going to put their legs in the air?" But they don't even think of that.

Robert and Eugene don't spend much time with the natives, anyway. They have no interest in blending into the local scene and socializing with the old-timers. Their socializing is limited to the lesbian couple and another black/white gay couple. They like the isolation of their eighty-acre place. They are amused when people are frightened by their long, precipitous road which is snowbound in winter. While another couple might feel isolated, socially and sexually, Robert and Eugene find their situation refreshing. They are delighted to live in a strictly monogamous relationship.

Again, this is a reaction to their lives in California's big cities. Robert says:

> I went through that crap of having an affair going while living with a lover, but you're only making yourself miserable because the affair becomes more important than your lover. After a while you and your lover get

used to each other, and all of the little things that made you feel good, you take for granted.

I can remember other lovers I've had. Everything would go along fine until one or the other would start an affair outside the home. It doesn't mean you really want an affair, but if someone is wining and dining you, they are going to make things more pleasant—more than your lover does at home. They're flattering you. Well, the male ego and all that sort of stuff. I can relate to this because I've done it. And that's why I don't want to do it anymore.

I used to say, "A home life is fine." Then all of a sudden I ran into some little trick that enticed me and did all the little things that I had forgotten were important—but they weren't—and then I'd sit home wanting to be with him.

For me it's a selfish reason; playing around makes me so miserable because I want to be here and I want to be there. You know you can't have both. And I just don't want to go through that scene anymore. It makes me just too miserable.

I'm sure that even in the boonies here you can find a closet queen somewhere and do what you like. I'm not interested. Right now I'm happier than ever before in my life.

Eugene puts it all more succinctly: "I've always been a one-person person."

Like most who come to Mountain Rock, they've taken up farming. Robert can't wait until he can quit his job to farm professionally. As with all city dwellers who come to the country, they had to decide which animals to raise (crops are poor in this land because of the thin soil). At first they were going to raise chickens but finally settled on rabbits because they are quieter and easier to breed. Robert had other motives as well.

I don't want cows—they're too big. Pigs are horrible. But rabbits are fun. I can lift them and carry on with them. I could take care of the rabbits if Eugene got sick. But the big reason I really pushed rabbits is that I'm ten years older than Eugene, and I'll probably die before him. Of course he might go before me, but that's beside the point. If I go, I want him to be able to stay here forever and enjoy it as long as he wants to, and the rabbits will take care of him. That's the most important reason.

They have constructed a huge new rabbit warren with temperature and humidity controls for the best and healthiest rabbits. In two years Eugene, who does most of the rabbit raising while Robert is at his job, expects the rabbits to support them, allowing Robert to retire from work.

James and *Eddie* have lived in Mountain Rock for the last five years of their thirty-seven-year relationship. James is sixty-nine years old, from a large city, an only child who "came out" at thirty-five. Eddie is eighty-two, was raised in a small town, and worked on a farm in his youth. One of fourteen children, Eddie came out at twenty-seven. Eddie was clearly the sexier in his young days. Ironically, he was brought out by a Pentecostal minister.

> I knew I liked men a whole lot, but I didn't know what it was all about. This preacher, he made me find out. He got me in a back room, and he started a-kissin'. And at first I resented it, and every time he got a chance he would put his hands on me. Pretty soon, when I calmed down a bit, I found out I kind of liked it.
>
> I never thought anything about it. He said to me, and I thought just as he did, he said, "The Lord knows our hearts, and there's no harm in it." So I thought the same thing—then I branched out into other people.

Eddie and the preacher got together every week for two years. It was almost exclusively an oral affair.

Eddie says he can remember liking men better than women from the age of five and can still recall how much more he enjoyed sitting on a male teacher's lap than a female teacher's. In those early years, Eddie never had sex because of the religious convictions of his parents and his fear of getting caught. Besides, he didn't know what to do. He had no idea what a homosexual was, and he certainly didn't know any, but growing up on the farm did provide him with a rudimentary knowledge of sex.

> Mother was very religious. I remember now one time when we had a hired man on the farm, and we had horses there, of course. I went down to the barn, and he was having intercourse with one of the mares. So I run up to the house, and I told Mom. "He's putting his pee wee up Ol' Bess!" So Mother, when Dad came in, said,

"You get rid of him, right away." And that was all I knew.

Sometimes I would see kids on the farm playing around. One time on the farm the boys was acting like they was cows, and the girls was milking them! But I didn't say anything that time.

At fourteen, Eddie fell in love with his sister's fiancé.

I just loved him. I wanted her to marry him so bad I did everything on earth to convince her. I just wanted him in my family so much. But she decided not to.

At seventeen, Eddie joined the army (World War I) and was assigned to work in a hospital. There were plenty of men. He used to "pat them on the cheek whenever I could," but there was never any sex. It was later, from sailors, not soldiers, that Eddie learned the ways of gay life.

James came from a familiar religious background.

I come from a good Christian home. My foster mother raised me, and she raised me strict [Full Gospel order]. She used to go to Aimee McPherson's temple, and I used to be a character actor in Aimee McPherson's illustrated sermons.

But, drafted into the army, James came under different influences—sex, drinking, and cursing. He seems to have had misgivings about them.

When I went into the army I went backwards, you know. I sure backslid. I got in with the soldiers. That was my downfall. I got out into the world, and I got mixed up with, well, I'd say the wrong class. I'd say it now, but you know how it is when you're a soldier. You go out and drink and you mess around—you do this and then something else.

The exact meaning of terms like "messing around" and "something else" was not clarified. With Eddie smiling quietly in the background, James refused to be more specific. When the war broke out in 1945, James was thirty-five years old and finally came out. His mother couldn't control him in the army.

My mother was living, see, and she was real strict, and I never dared get away from her. I couldn't get away long enough to be with someone. I wasn't allowed on the streets after nine o'clock at night. She was real domineering, all right. So when I got into the army, I kind of went wild.

James was a postman in the war. During the Battle of the Bulge:

> I used to drive a jeep at night without lights through towns that were bombed out, going to headquarters to get the mail and bring it back. Sometimes when I took various roads I didn't know if I was going to drive right into the hands of the enemy. It was a frightening experience, but I got the Bronze Star for meritorious service.

James and Eddie began living together while James's mother was still alive. After her death they moved to California, but Eddie always dreamed of going back to a farm and never adjusted to city life.

> We lived in an apartment house in California. And I tell you, there were people next door, you could hear everything. They would go on, and you could hear through the walls. There was a man and his wife, and our bed was right against their wall. And I could hear everything they did—everything. When they was having sex you could hear her hollering and carrying on. I told a friend about the way she carried on—why, it was terrible.

James and Eddie lived an isolated life in California, at least in regard to contact with other gays. They only socialized with one other gay couple, Peter and Walter. Other couples they knew were into husband/wife roles. It was a style they couldn't identify with, since they thought of themselves as brothers. They continue to do so in Mountain Rock.

> They think we're half-brothers. Of course, we tell them that. There would be talk otherwise. Here in a small town—because they wonder about two guys. Everybody says, "Are you married?" They think you ought to be married—to a woman!

It was Eddie who wanted to move to Mountain Rock.

> I like the hills. I wanted to get away from the humbug of the city, all those crowds and everything. I like all sorts of animals and birds and flowers and things. And this is the nearest you can get to it.

Finances were another important reason for moving. Since James and Eddie are living on fixed incomes, the inflation rate has hurt them very badly. It costs much less to live in Mountain Rock ʌhere the economic level of the population is low.

They've also rejoined the church in their town and are now members in good standing of the local Pentecostal church, with Eddie fixing dinners every week for many of the church meetings.

On Sundays they attend church twice and sometimes on weekdays as well. The contradiction between their homosexuality and the teachings of the Pentecostal church doesn't seem to perplex them.

In recent years they have abandoned sex and seem to believe that they are, in fact, brothers. They have also come to the conclusion that homosexuality is inborn, which to them means it's less sinful. James says:

> That's all past us now. I don't hate the homosexuals; I've got no need to. It's like Jeff Baker [an evangelical preacher popular on the radio]—I don't know if you've ever heard of him—on "Praise the Lord"—"I love the homosexual." He says the Lord says we should love the homosexual.
> I don't know, you take a family and make it have seven kids, and one will be a homosexual and the others will just be butch.
> *Eddie*: I just think the Lord has his hands out. He knows. Like that preacher said to me. The Lord knows what we was doing.

At the moment, Eddie and James are trying to sell the antiques they have collected over the past thirty-five years in order to finance buying a small farm. Eddie complains the town has grown too large and that he keeps bumping into people all the time. The population is now barely two thousand.

> I don't like big towns. I want to be a hermit and live out in nature.

They frequently visit friends Peter and Walter, and Eddie walks among the animals ("God made things to walk free") and climbs the hills around the farm, dreaming of the days when he and James can have their own place.

Peter and *Walter* have been lovers for fifteen years and business partners for ten. They arrived in Mountain Rock three years ago, following their friends James and Eddie. Peter and Walter are both forty-four. Walter still spends most of the year in California, taking care of their business, while Peter works the farm, but they expect to sell their California business within the year and become full-time farmers.

Peter was raised in a very small community in the Midwest. Sex play began at twelve, and at fifteen Peter and a cousin had a passionate love affair that lasted two years. Besides the usual mutual masturbation and sucking, there was heavy kissing as well, but Peter's religious indoctrination caught up with him.

> I had deep religious convictions at that time. I was a
> Southern Baptist. I believed all that stuff about being
> a sinner.

Like other teenagers who are denied useful information about the nature of homosexuality (to say nothing of information about heterosexuality), Peter adopted the common view that loving another boy was an indication of defective masculinity. He was less a man for kissing his cousin and a sinner in the eyes of his church. A way of proving his masculinity was required, and Peter chose two of the more popular methods, joining the navy and getting married.

Peter and his wife had three children, but Peter was dissatisfied. He wanted men, and when he was at home he wanted to go out and meet them. Finally he came out to his wife, and although they tried to make the marriage work it ended in divorce. They are the best of friends today.

One result of Peter's married life is the possibility that one of his sons, age twenty, is gay. Peter does not feel comfortable about it.

> He tries to talk to me about it, but I don't feel com-
> fortable talking with him about it. I don't want to influ-
> ence him one way or another. I don't want to discourage
> it. I don't want him to go through what I did, but if I
> talk to him freely I think he might pick it up that I am
> trying to encourage it. And at this age and with his par-
> ticular type of personality, I think he needs to find
> himself.

Peter's reluctance to discuss homosexuality with his son might be an indication that he hasn't quite resolved his own misgivings about homosexuality, since other gay men have gay sons, and recognition of this has always made their relationships richer and closer. Perhaps Peter will talk with his son one day, though it seems more likely the son will have to initiate the discussion.

It was while Peter was still married that he met Walter, his first and only lover.

> Without a doubt a complete and total love at first sight.
> I met him in a gay bar. We went home that night, and
> right then and there I knew this was the person I
> wanted to spend my whole life with.

Nevertheless, it was two years before they decided to live together, neither wanting to make the commitment until they were sure. Peter was loath to jump from a heterosexual marriage to a full-time lover until he knew that they would spend their entire lives together. In the fifteen years of their relationship they have never had an argument. "We're funny turned," Peter muses, using a local expression that implies something strange.

> Every year we live together is more beautiful and fan-
> tastic than the year before.

The California business is a complication because it takes Walter away more than half the year. They have agreed that each of them can have outside sex during these separations, but they tell each other about the experiences. They don't view it as cheating. "It's reassuring to know that he's not doing anything that I'm not aware of," is the way Peter explains it. When they're together in Mountain Rock, however, monogamy is the rule, except for a rare threesome.

Like all the other couples in Mountain Rock, Peter and Walter came partly to escape the city and partly to return to the lifestyle of their youth.

> I wanted to get away from it all, from the city. We love
> the country. I was raised in the country, and so was
> Walter. I've seen all the glamour of the city. I don't
> want to see another freeway. I don't want to see the
> smog in L.A. again. I was so glad to get away from
> that. And I was tired of dealing with the public in my
> business, even though I made lots of money there. So
> I wanted a real early retirement down here. I wanted a
> hobby farm more than anything else. I didn't intend to
> make money at it. So we bought enough acreage so we
> could have our privacy and our home and our little

> hobby farm and do the things we want to do.
> The type of gay life we want for ourselves would work right into this redneck country. We don't care anything about socializing with faggot-type people.

Peter and Walter socialize with the natives, and they love doing so. It's partly a predilection for people who live close to the land and partly a rejection of the kind of gay life they saw in California.

> We have been in this gay bar scene, the socializing, the partying in town, putting on a front and all that. I don't want to do that anymore. It is quite a comfort to me to come down here to these beautiful straight people, and I'm enjoying right now socializing with them. And I've gotten a world of education from them. I'm just enjoying it.
> I could have a much better time and a better evening by going up to some of my redneck neighbors up here and visiting with them than I could with some screaming faggots in Long Beach.

Peter says he doesn't know if the neighbors think that he and Walter are gay, nor does he care. They neither hide it nor flaunt it.

> I don't think it would make any difference if they found out because I am pretty well respected in the neighborhood. I think hostility is a thing of the past.

Occasionally some of the gay couples in Mountain Rock will get together for dinner, but Peter and Walter don't usually attend. "That's what I just left," is Peter's reaction. Although they have a few friends, gay and straight, they spend most of their time and energies on the farm, which has become more than just a hobby.

Peter wants to build a small herd of angora goats so that he can market the mohair. He got into it quite by chance. His property is filled with fields covered with thorny brush that makes it impossible to farm or raise animals, but goats prefer just this kind of bush, and they eat it, thorns and all. So the goats are clearing his property without feed expenses. "Goats are brush hogs," is the local expression for the process. By planning the birth of kids carefully, he needn't provide any heat during the winter (angora wool is warm, remember), and he shears them twice a year. It's all profit. When he is not busy with the animals, Peter is preserving and canning food, using an all-wood-burning stove (the microwave is hidden in a corner).

> If ever in life there is a time when you feel you want
> to slow down your pace of living, this is the place to
> do it, because there is nothing to do. There is just
> nothing happening here.
>   The most exciting thing you can do on a Saturday
> afternoon is to go up to one of the country stores around
> here and join several of the other locals—the natives—
> sitting around the bench talking. That's the big activity!

Larry and *Frank* have lived in Mountain Rock for twelve of the thirteen years that they have been together. Both in their thirties, they emigrated from one of the big California cities. Frank had been married for three years, and his wife was aware of his homosexuality. In fact, she suggested to Frank that he find a male lover, so that they could all live together. A short time later Frank met Larry in a local gay bar. When Larry moved into the house, things appeared to go along without conflict. Even though Larry was accustomed to having many sexual partners (and Frank insisted on fidelity to one man), a compromise was reached when they agreed to have threesomes.

It soon became clear that Larry and Frank wanted to live together as lovers, without a third party. They got their own apartment, and the next year they were in Mountain Rock. There were two unrelated reasons for the move. They, too, were tired of big-city life, like the previous couples; a second reason was Frank's jealousy, his desire to eliminate some of the potential competition.

> We were living in an area where I felt a constant threat
> from other men. Because, you see, Larry is a very
> beautiful man and a very talented person. It was very
> threatening to me.

Larry was not upset about Frank's insecurity in the relationship. They had often discussed the problem, and Larry wanted to leave California for his own reasons.

> Among my goals in life I wanted to be a teacher, but I
> had never finished up even a bachelor's degree, so how
> could I have a teaching certificate? I wanted to be a

farmer, but how could I ever have enough money to
buy land? But, you see, Mountain Rock is a backwater
place. There aren't any educated people, and the competition is far less stern. I was able to teach here because it was a rural place, and you can take a test to
become a teacher, and then you get a county certificate.
And we bought this farm. So it's kind of funny in a way
—around here we're big frogs in a little pond, instead
of being little frogs in a big pond. That's what I wanted.

They arrived in Mountain Rock with very little money, all of
which went as a down payment on a small farm (which has
grown to 500 acres). Frank got work almost immediately, but
Larry had to wait for some time before his teaching certificate
was approved. They almost starved at first. Living in a century-
old tar-paper shack (they still do, to the chagrin of some of
their friends and relatives) with no toilet (they'll put one in next
year), no insulation, and no stove, they realized they would
freeze their first winter. Since they had no money to buy a
furnace or a new stove, they went to a local junkyard where
they found an old rusty potboiler, paid seven dollars and fifty
cents for it, hauled it back to the shack, and connected it. Due
to the current fad for antique stoves, it's worth a fortune now,
but they'll never sell it; it's too much a part of their lives. Besides, they still need it to keep the house warm.
  Cutting wood for the stove is part of a recurrent sexual fantasy they share. Larry originally came from a farm area and
enjoys the exercise he gets cutting many ricks (a stack) of wood.
Frank is fond of watching.

When Larry's cutting wood I like to watch the sweat
running down his body. Then I come over and rub the
sweat on him, and I make like I'm seducing him, and
then we have sex on the leaves. It's a real turn-on for
both of us.

With mountain streams for swimming, waterfalls to play in,
and hundreds of acres of privacy, sex outdoors has been a habit
for the past dozen years. It gives them a sense of freedom and
a safe distance from the hostile outside world. For them, it is
liberating.
  They don't miss the city. They were never "bar people" in

California, and life in Mountain Rock has all the adventure and
excitement they want or need. Perhaps Frank overstates it, but
it appears to be what they want.

> We have no locks on our doors, we have no problems,
> we've got things to do. You can always go fishing or
> walk in the woods or look at the wild flowers. And there
> is nothing to do in the cities. It's so boring there, you
> know. You can go to the theater in New York or the
> movies, and after about a week of that it gets tiresome
> as hell. But there is just so much to do in a rural area.

How typical is Mountain Rock of other rural areas with gay
people? It is difficult to know, since every region has its own
characteristics. Further research will answer the question. But
we can make a conclusion about life in this rural area. Children
have every opportunity in the world to "play around" with each
other. They have more freedom than city children, since the
large farms allow for a greater degree of privacy. Sexual experimentation with other children and animals continues today much
as it did in the past, and no one cares, for most natives still
believe that "boys will be boys."

There are so many ironies. For instance, sex between older
teenagers and even married men may continue without the oner-
ous label of homosexuality. One fellow from a different rural
area gave an excellent example of this. He lived with his family on a large farm where there were four farmhands. The
"hands" and the family ate meals together, and generally after
supper the men would go off to the barn and have sex together.
The man who told me this story rarely participated himself,
since he was much younger and afraid. While the men never
kissed or expressed any affection, they sucked and fucked at will.
Then, as Peter put it, "They went home and fucked their girl
friends to death!"

Some might say the "hands" were really in the closet, but I
think not. It's just another example of how same-sex behavior
can be assimilated into the definition of heterosexuality as long
as certain proprieties are respected. It is striking how often the
gay boy refrains from what heterosexual boys are doing habitu-
ally. It is as if he fears that his participation has a more serious
meaning (which it does) and that everyone will know about him
if he joins in.

It is the same in Mountain Rock. No one grows up gay. As they get older, childhood lovers acquire girl friends, and for the abandoned rural gay boy rejection and separation become major themes. Most of these boys feel forced to marry; a few have good marriages, even though their thoughts are elsewhere. But it is a deprived and lonely life; its chief pleasure is masturbation, in which happy dreams are relived and aided by hidden stacks of pornography. An army of closeted gay men lives in these backwater areas. Too afraid to talk with investigators or outsiders of any kind, they have rarely if ever had their homosexuality affirmed as a life-force. It has never been anything but a liability. For these men, life is as horrible as any city gay imagines.

In terms of interviewing the natives of the area, my three or four days in Mountain Rock had little to show for my efforts and the efforts of gay couples who assisted my search. Only one native, Leonard Rogers, consented to the interview, and he had already packed his bags to leave the area. Leonard agreed to ask a few friends to meet me (probably because I enjoyed his tall tales so much), but none would accept. When visiting Peter, I noted the occasional single man "just dropping in" for a cup of coffee, and my impression was that they were having a look at me, perhaps thinking about the possibility of an interview. Apparently I failed the test. In any event, one person interviewed is hardly a comfortable sample of an area. But it does give us an idea of how dangerous it must be to reveal homosexuality in Mountain Rock—at least for natives. I wonder how many local gays actually leave?

More exciting than the exodus is the movement *to* rural areas. Each year more gay couples escape the excitement of the cities for the quiet of rural life. In Mountain Rock five male gay couples were interviewed, but twice that many lesbian couples are living there (lesbians moved there first). I later learned of other male gay couples living nearby, who were unknown to those interviewed. Most rural gays become farmers, sometimes leaving sophisticated city professions behind. Others take up less lucrative but more congenial occupations. Almost all feel better for the change.

This relocation is found everywhere I have traveled. There is a significant migration of gay couples to small towns and rural areas. It is an alternative for gay men who have faith in themselves and in their lovers. They don't look forward to opening a rural disco, molesting the natives, or dealing in drugs. They don't anticipate or experience any problem from the local population, in part because they adopt the ethos of the area, but also because they take pride in their relationships, and no one is going to interfere with that. The natives must sense this. To a large extent, financial considerations have influenced the move from city to country living. The cost of city life has become unbearable for some gays. Houses are too expensive and property unthinkable. But land is cheaper in the country, and so is living, and a gay couple of modest means can buy property and live their lives with as much privacy as they like. To *some* gay couples, it is indeed the Garden of Eden.

CHAPTER ELEVEN

Till Death Do Us Part

> This is the hour of lead
> Remembered if outlived,
> As freezing persons recollect the snow—
> First chill, then stupor, then the letting go.
>
> EMILY DICKINSON

Gay men don't die. That isn't what gay life is about. The tragedy of illness or sudden death, the slow torture of mental deterioration, and the myriad physical disorders that accumulate with advancing years—what have these to do with gay men in "hot" cities like New York or San Francisco who disco the night away or cruise the streets, or with midwesterners who wonder if their wives know they're gay or whether they'll find a new face in town? Gay men don't die. The word "death" never appears in gay newspapers or magazines unless it is related to the assassination of a civil rights leader. Fashionable bodies, lately adorned with beards and a narrow piece of studded leather around the wrist, fill the slick magazines that fuel our ever-present fantasies of seduction and sex. No room for death here.

Lovers don't die. They break up, to be sure, as we hear endlessly from those who are unable to establish long-lasting relationships and from psychiatrists who hope to cure us. Young lovers look for the mythical "Mr. Right," the man who will sweep them off their feet and feed their needs with the competence, strength, and physical attributes of a Greek god. The popular gay magazines and newspapers have begun to write about the contemporary needs and problems of lovers. Should we have threesomes? How do we "come out" to our parents? What do we do if our lovers hurt our feelings? Strange how unimportant these problems of living become when serious illness or death appears. I am reminded of a letter to one of the advice columns in a newspaper, a letter written by a woman who complained bitterly that her husband's snoring kept her up at night. A week later a response came from another woman whose husband also snored—but had died the year before. "Now," the widow wrote, "it's very quiet at night, and I cry myself to sleep. I would give anything to hear him snore just once more."

In certain ways, gay life reflects the fears of the straight world. What they fear, we fear—but we fear it even more. For instance, old age and death. We do not see evidence of the advancing years of gay men because we don't wish to. We don't want to be presented with a reminder of our own mortality, a warning that our smooth, lustrous skin will dry and wrinkle, or that a sagging behind will develop one day, or the fearful potbelly never seen in gay newspapers will appear. Growing old is unmentionable to many gay men who believe their lives will be over at forty; this is a sorry indication of low self-esteem, for it equates sexual idealization with human worth. The gay world, or at least a part of it, celebrates couples who have been together for endless numbers of years, then hopes just as fervently that they will go right back into their homes lest one get sick and die—die in public, disturbing *our* equilibrium.

You and I will die. It could happen suddenly or after a long, sustained, and draining illness. The long-saved-for trip to Europe could be interrupted by a heart attack; the down payment for a new house might be needed to pay hospital bills for terminal cancer. At such moments in the lives of lovers, the little treasure chest of resentments, filled with the angry feelings of the past and constructed out of the lives of two men reaching for love and compassion, disappears magically. The self-concern for feelings and status is turned around. The energy of one lover is directed toward the other, toward what he can give, rather than what he can take.

It is uncanny how often this reversal of energy occurs. Regardless of who gets sick, each thinks of the other. The healthy lover consults with doctors, pays bills, communicates with family members, works and takes care of the house, consoles and tries to cheer his lover. In turn, the dying man consoles his lover. Each worries about the other. The dying man wants to do one last thing for the man he loves; the healthy man wants to do one last thing for his dying lover. Perhaps it is only when death is imminent that real feelings of love emerge; whatever problems of intimacy have plagued the lovers are faced head-on. The prospect of living without a man who has shared a life and a bed for one year or forty is devastating. What will he do after his lover's death?

Jesse faced that problem after living with his lover *Harvey* for thirty years. Harvey died at the age of seventy-four. They met in 1948, when Jesse was twenty-five and Harvey forty-five, a difference of twenty years. Although it took them only three weeks to declare themselves lovers, they did not live together for quite some time, and then only after an amusing incident. On a weekend visit to his family, Harvey had a talk with his older brother, who suggested that since Harvey wasn't getting any younger, he should consider a roommate. It's good to have someone around just in case, was the idea. Harvey had just the person in mind, his "friend" Jesse.

> Later that evening Harvey said that he was driving back to his mother's apartment with her, and she brought the subject up. He thought, "Oh, dear! What's this coming?" What she said was, "You told me that Jesse was moving in with you." He said, "Yes," wondering what was coming next. Then she said, "I know that you two are very good friends." Harvey said, "Yes." And she said, "I also know that it's one thing to be good friends and another to live together. I just hope that after he moves in you continue to be good friends, and that it doesn't end up breaking up your relationship." Harvey said that he heaved an internal sigh of relief. He assured his mother that he had no qualms and didn't think it would be a problem.

The couple lived together until February 10, 1977, when Harvey died of cancer. The illness began only a few months earlier, when Harvey complained of a pain in his shoulder. The X-ray revealed some shadows, and the doctor recommended a biopsy, which was taken on December 21, after which Harvey and Jesse went to Florida for a week's stay. On the third of January they were told that the test was positive, and Harvey entered the hospital four days later.

> I was calm. My feeling about it was whatever will be, will be. We will do it. We will go through it together. Whatever has to be, has to be.

The tests revealed cancer in one shoulder, spreading to the other and the hip. Cobalt treatments and chemotherapy reduced the pain, and Harvey felt better. But then February 10 arrived.

I got up at seven o'clock as I usually do. I went into the
kitchen to start making my breakfast. Harvey did not
usually wake up until eight. I heard him call to me.
I immediately went into the bedroom. He had wakened.
He said he felt very dizzy and nauseated and couldn't
get up, and would I please help him out of bed. He
wanted to go to the john. I said, "Certainly." I tried to
help him out of bed. He could not stand on his feet.
He fell on the bed at an odd angle. After some struggle I
got him back in bed and under the covers. I immediately
started trying to call the doctor, because he said he had
the most awful headache he'd ever had in his life.

I finally reached the doctor about nine o'clock in
the morning. He said it sounded as if it could be serious,
and we had to get him to the hospital. He said they
couldn't get him into the hospital until eleven, because
they wouldn't be ready for him, but to call an ambulance and make arrangements, and he would call the
hospital and tell them what to do.

I did so. Made Harvey as comfortable as I could.
The ambulance arrived at about a quarter to eleven.
Got him to Doctors Hospital, where they immediately
took him in for X rays. I got him registered and went up
to wait for him. We got him into the room about one
o'clock.

At that time he was semiconscious. Within the next
hour he was unconscious. Then they moved him to a
private room and tended him very carefully. The doctor
appeared in the middle of the afternoon and said that
he thought that what had happened was the cancer had
suddenly metastasized, and that his lungs were absolutely riddled with it. He thought it had started in on
the brain. And that was why he was having these reactions. It was just a matter of hours.

I was rather dumb. Trying to keep control over myself. I broke down and cried with the doctor when he
was there in the afternoon. Aside from that I was
fairly calm and composed. Tried to be. There was no
point in creating any great scene. It certainly wouldn't
help Harvey and at that point wouldn't help me. I had
to try to keep my wits about me and do whatever I
could.

At eight o'clock that night I sensed that he seemed
not to be breathing. I called the nurse, who came in
and immediately called the resident doctor. Harvey died
quietly. And I took a deep breath, and then I turned
and cried a little bit.

Then I made inquiries about taking care of things. I had to make arrangements as we had both agreed for both of us; he wanted his body left to science and his eyes to the eye bank. These things I did. But then the numbness started, and I was numb for months.

There was no funeral or memorial service. That was the way Harvey wanted it, and their friends understood. But they all called, wrote, or visited and made certain that Jesse wasn't alone. For months, friends entertained Jesse almost every night of the week, and during the day Jesse threw all his energies into his work. "Life continued. Not as happily. Not as joyfully." And then a young man came into Jesse's life, someone destined to change it dramatically. To understand the importance of this meeting, we need to go back in time.

When Jesse and Harvey met, Jesse was still a full-time college student and Harvey an established businessman. To all intents and purposes Jesse was kept—for thirty years! Until the day Harvey died he refused to allow Jesse to pay any bills. "He said that he wanted me to save my money and build up as much of an estate as I could." The impression is that Harvey was painfully aware of the difference in their ages and the probability that he would die much earlier than Jesse. He wanted Jesse to have money on which to survive after he died. He supported Jesse in school and afterward paid all the expenses.

Now the parallel affair was about to begin. "Thirty years of bliss" are not forgotten so quickly. A man's psyche searches for ways to keep alive the energy of the dead beloved, a psychological means of resurrection to avoid the final good-byes. Jesse found his way in a young man who was the same age Jesse had been when he met Harvey. By coincidence, the young man was also preparing for the profession Jesse had been preparing for —and studying at Jesse's alma mater. It seemed as if Jesse was about to relive his own early years with Harvey, but this time Jesse would befriend Clyde, the young student.

He was a raving, tearing beauty. He claimed that he preferred older gentlemen, which was my position at that point. Here he was about the same spread in ages as Harvey and I when we started. Here he was starting the same school. I was starting into the same thing when I met Harvey. I found many resonances in a reverse way of our situation. I hoped it could work.

It didn't. Though Jesse provided many financial advantages for Clyde, including some Clyde never asked for, Jesse found his new friend emotionally stunted and not at all willing to complete his academic requirements. Clyde couldn't climax during sex; whether this was just a reaction to Jesse or a more general problem is not clear. Apparently Clyde sought sexual outlets during his many nights out which annoyed Jesse, who would dutifully buy food for supper each night, prepare it, and wait for Clyde to arrive. Clyde seldom called to let Jesse know he would be late; the conflicts over arriving on time for supper may have symbolized the battle between Jesse's insistence on domestic stability and Clyde's presumed refusal to be domesticated. The final break came within a year of their first meeting when Clyde didn't arrive home one night. He called the next morning.

> About eleven o'clock in the morning the phone rang. It was Clyde. "Hello, Jesse?" "Yes." "This is Clyde. I did it again." My response was, "Yes, the whore of New York checks in." "You shouldn't have said that." And then he hung up. That day Clyde decided to leave the apartment.

Perhaps Jesse had to make this misalliance with Clyde. Of course, it had to fail. The life lived with one man cannot be reproduced with another. When Clyde left the house, Harvey died symbolically, just as he had died physically a year before; Jesse now makes his way alone in the world, content with memories of the past and willing to face the future realistically.

> I miss Harvey terribly. No one will ever replace him. However, I don't know if I can call it grief for him. I feel that I am one of the luckiest people in the world. I had thirty years of absolute bliss. But I recognized from the beginning that with the difference in our ages, in the normal course of events he would have to go before I did. There were times, particularly near the end of our relationship, when Harvey would bring this up and say, "I'm so much older than you. This isn't fair to you." My response was always, "I am so happy with you that whatever time I have with you is marvelous, and I will let the future take care of the future. The crystal ball is cloudy, and how do we know that you will go before me?"
>
> People ask me if being alone in the apartment where

Harvey and I were together makes me feel sad and lonely, and my answer from the very beginning was, "Absolutely not." If there are ghosts in the apartment, they are very happy ghosts. It's a place that we worked on together, and everywhere I look there are memories of him, and they are happy memories. I am the person that I am today because of the care and love and tenderness he gave me.

For what reason should I mourn?

George was thirty-four years old when he met *Malcolm*, his elder by three years. They lived together for ten years, until Malcolm died. It was a relationship of great compatibility, at least most of the time.

We were like one person. We used to dress alike. We were known out here as the twins. We didn't dress alike in business, but strangely enough, even though he was much taller than I was, we wore the exact same size of everything. The only difference was, his trousers were longer.

Sex was a problem. Neither man could be fucked, and Malcolm was very concerned about this. He had anal warts, and the doctors were constantly examining his rectum. To George he used to say, "They can stick all that stuff up my ass, I don't know why I can't take you." Because George liked to fuck very much, they began to pick up people at a local bar for threesomes (though I get the impression that Malcolm acquiesced to George's demands but didn't really like these adventures). Malcolm objected to George's fucking the trick even when Malcolm was there.

He used to say he wished I wouldn't fuck, because to him that was the ultimate intimacy with two people, and since we didn't fuck he was very upset that I was sharing with somebody else what he wasn't participating in. He was a very sensitive person.

In fact, Malcolm was in psychotherapy for chronic depression and heavy drinking. It got much worse after they had been together for six years and Terry entered the picture. Terry was "a magnificent piece of manhood" whom they picked up at the beach one day. Terry took a particular liking to Malcolm. George encouraged this development, hoping that the affair would help Malcolm's depression. George was worried that their lives had become too encapsulated; he felt that Malcolm had become totally dependent on him. "He was very sensitive, and he needed me around all the time. I thought maybe he was being smothered by this relationship, maybe he should get out a little bit."

George's generosity may not have been so altruistic, since Malcolm's dependence was becoming increasingly burdensome. Depression and dependence are traits that walk hand in hand. An affair between Malcolm and Terry would have given George the opportunity for a greater amount of outside sex than he otherwise had. Whatever George's motivation, things got out of hand, and one day Malcolm said that Terry wanted him to leave George and live with him.

> I said to Malcolm, "Go right ahead, but just remember one thing. Don't ever come back to me. I won't be waiting for you." So that was the end of Terry.

A bit later George had sex with someone, and Malcolm found out. His jealousy took an unusual form.

> He wanted to meet him. He wanted to see who I was messing around with. And he called the guy and told him that if he didn't have a threesome with us he would call the guy's lover and tell him that he tricked. So the guy did it, against his will, but he did it.

Malcolm never forgot these incidents and stored them up in his memory. He became obsessed with the prospect of his own death. All the men in his family had died at an early age, and Malcolm was sure that his turn was not far off. Then his mother had a stroke, and Malcolm brought her into the house with him and George. George welcomed her without reservation, and she still lived with George many years after Malcolm's death. "I probably still love him a lot. That's why I have his mother." Malcolm and his mother were very close, but after she came into the house Malcolm began to drink to excess, and his depression worsened. Psychiatric treatment could not allay his fears of impending death.

He was drunk while swimming one day and almost drowned. When he awoke in the hospital, George was in the room beside him. "Why didn't you let me drown?" were his only words.

He used to upset our friends, saying that he would never see the shrubs grow big. It got to me. I knew he was obsessed with a death wish. I knew he would die. It was only a matter of time.

Malcolm would sleep all day and thrash around in the bed and scream all night. It was impossible for George to sleep, and he told Malcolm that he wanted to move to their spare bedroom. "I'm going away, and I'm never coming back," was all that Malcolm said, and he left the house. Perhaps Malcolm interpreted George's sleeping in another room as an insult; maybe he simply used it as an excuse. There is no way to understand what lay at the center of his depression. After twenty-four hours, George became extremely worried and began driving around the area, looking for Malcolm's car. He found it at a local motel. When George entered the room, he found Malcolm lying on the bed, dead, a vial of pills near him.

> I went home and told his mother. Then I went into . . .
> I was totally stone cold . . . literally turned to stone. I
> wasn't hysterical when I found him. The only thing
> I said was, "Oh, my God." I think for the next six
> months I was in a total state of shock because there are
> a lot of things I don't remember. I wasn't hysterical. I
> guess I expected it.

The next week George remembered that they had been invited to a party, and he decided to go. As he walked the long driveway, he realized how alone he felt. But at the party he met a tall man.

> I ended up going to bed with this guy. I didn't feel guilty
> at all. It was the best thing that ever happened to me.
> I thought I had to be discreet and think of the dead, but
> I realized that what I needed was love and affection to
> make up for the love and affection I wasn't getting. So
> from that week on I was always busy, and I had a lot
> of sex. I wanted to have as much sex as I could.
>   It was the best thing that ever happened to me. It was
> over, and it was time to make a new life. I had no guilt
> about it then, and I have no guilt now. I met this guy
> accidentally, but if I had it to do over again, knowing
> what I know now, I would go looking for sex imme-
> diately.
>   I used to think about Malcolm all the time, but I
> didn't want to share my grief with anybody. I guess it

was a defense mechanism, because basically I'm a very
private person. The only person I would discuss it with
was his mother, and we would sit there and cry as we
talked about him. A very painful situation. Still is.

Vincent * has always been a domestic sort of man. When he
met his first lover, *Troy*, in 1956, he wanted to shout to the
world, "I have a lover, and we have a home." Perhaps it was his
rural background or his identification with his strict Methodist
upbringing, but having a home of his own was the most important thing in his life. Vincent and Troy bought a house together
and completely remodeled it themselves. Then, after they had
lived in the house for four years, Troy began to have delusions
that people were out to get him and that his brother was con-
spiring with the U.S. marshal to take the house away. These
hallucinations continued for seven years. Troy stayed up late at
night to read law books and write long letters to governmental
agencies, telling them about the plot to take his house away.
When Vincent protested, Troy would only gaze at him coldly
and say, "There's no way I'll stop now. I mean to pursue this to
the bitter end."

> Other people were recognizing something I was loath
> to recognize myself, the capacity for madness in some-
> one you love. At that time I remember my rationalizing
> the whole situation. "Well, if he had been crippled in
> an automobile accident and were physically ill, I
> wouldn't leave him over that." I certainly had an en-
> lightened view, I felt. There were sides to his nature
> that I could live with. I was willing to put up with any-
> thing to keep the relationship going. That's what I felt
> life was all about, to have an ongoing lover relationship,
> and I was willing to pay a very high price for it.

It became unbearable after three or four years. Troy had
become a paranoid psychotic who saw hostile motivations in
neighbors and passersby in the streets. He even broke the win-
dows of a neighbor's house because the neighbor cut some of
the flowers in his flower bed; Troy claimed it was part of his
brother's plot to get rid of him. One day he turned on Vincent.

> I almost left him. I can't remember today what it was
> all about. It ended up . . . this is a hard thing to tell
> you . . . he came up behind me with both hands to-

gether, and he brought them down on my back just as
hard as he could. It really hurt, and it brought me to
my knees. And I was really filled with anger, and I went
into the bedroom and I got a gun. I released the safety,
and I walked back into the room.

I said, "Troy, I'm going to let you have it, now, right
in the stomach and guts, and I understand that it'll take
a little longer for you to die, and that's what I want to
see with my own eyes. That's what I want to see, and I
want to see you have some pain just like you've given
me." And I was ready to do it.

It's a funny thing, Doctor. When you're at that point,
you can understand why people go ahead and do it. If
I were asked to be a juror at a murder trial, I don't think
I could do it.

Vincent was confused about the plot fears; Troy's brother was,
in fact, a hostile person. Vincent did not realize that the actual
fraternal hostility was merely the seed for the psychosis that was
engulfing his lover. Finally the psychological pain became too
great for Troy, and he called the police, saying, "Come and get
me, I'm tired of trying to cope with the world. They're all out
to cheat me."

The police were very kind, very sympathetic. They
looked at me in such a strange way. It was as if to say,
"How can you live with this asshole?" It was really
weird. Then they took him off to San Francisco Psychiatric Hospital.

That night Vincent visited Troy in the psychiatric hospital.
He was told by the doctor that Troy had been diagnosed as
paranoid.

At that point I suppose I could have said that if love is
pity and pity is love, then I still loved him. He had no
one to help him. And I resolved to see it all the way
down the line.

It didn't help when the local radio station announced the
hospitalization and it was printed in a local newspaper. That
was how Vincent's parents learned of it. Then came the sanity
hearing. Troy decided that he wanted to fight being committed
to the hospital, and Vincent stood by him. The opposing attor-
ney decided to use their homosexuality against Troy.

He tried to make something dirty out of our relation-

> ship in front of the jury. He was trying to show the bias
> in my testimony. He said, "Isn't it true that you're
> roommates?" And I said, "No, we're not roommates.
> We share a house." He said, "Well, it is true, isn't
> it, that you feel a great and deep affection for Mr.
> X?" You know, by then I was just tired of playing
> games, and I just said, "Yes, I love him with all my
> heart." And you could have heard a pin drop in the
> courtroom. It was a very dramatic moment to simply
> admit what the prosecutor was being so coy about.

Troy was found insane and taken to the violent ward at
Atascadero State Hospital in California, which was notorious for
its harsh treatment of homosexuals. Troy was very hostile and
violent, but never toward Vincent who visited him weekly. The
trip was exhausting. Atascadero is midway between Los Angeles
and San Francisco, and Vincent had to ride an overnight bus
to get there. Later, he requested they transfer Troy back to the
San Francisco hospital, but the authorities at the hospital refused, saying that Troy would be there all his life.

"Well, I'm going to fight you for him," was Vincent's response, and through some friendy political influence Troy was
released in Vincent's custody. While at Atascadero, Troy had a
heart attack that caused more serious paranoid delusions. Troy's
heart continued to give him trouble after he returned to Vincent.

> It's funny. After you take care of someone who's been
> ill, you miss the responsibility of taking care of them
> . . . know what I mean? You want to fulfill whatever
> needs have evolved out of the relationship that you
> actually wanted. Although at the time, my God, I'd
> wake up at three in the morning and he'd say, "I'm
> having another fibrillation," and we'd call the ambu-
> lance and get him to the doctor. He had to be electri-
> cally hit on the chest with those two leather things.
> He was having auricular fibrillation, and that finally
> went into ventricular fibrillation. I don't know, my
> God, eight or nine different pills . . . in the course of
> twenty-four hours . . . to keep track of all those pills
> . . . what time they should be given to him. I had it
> all written down, but it got so complicated.

Eventually Troy had to be taken back to the hospital because
of the heart condition, but not before he finished one painting.

> He did this marvelous painting. I think it was an indi-

cation of his real feelings. The picture was called "For the Birds." The foreground was that of a large cliff. To the left was a camellia bush. They were white camellias. And these two somewhat angry little birds nestled in out of the rain, and as you look across the cliffs at the painting, you see the angry scuttling clouds in the sky and the water below. Sort of Troy's idea of the world, you might say, at that time in his life. But yet beautifully done. I was very proud of that.

Then one day I got home about eight o'clock, and the phone rang. It was Troy's sister-in-law. She said, as kindly as she could, "I have something to tell you." And you know, I knew. I knew he was going to die, of course. He already had his third heart attack in a year and a half. Still, you're never as prepared for it as you think.

I took it very hard. It was as if he died twice, Doctor. He died the first time when they took him off to that mental hospital. Then he died a second time, you see.

The next year, Vincent became an alcoholic. He moved and had a series of tragic affairs, until he joined AA, stopped drinking, and sought good therapeutic help. Through the gay church in his town he met his current lover, with whom he has been living for the past eight years. But just a year ago something very important happened.

I had this dream about Troy. That I was walking through several streets and buildings and up and down stairs and alleys. There were all sorts of open and closed areas. And then I saw Troy. He was off to one side, and I turned and went over to him. He looked at me and smiled. He said, "I'm dead, you know." And I said, "Yes, I know you're dead." And he said, "Well, you have other interests now, and I'm not going to be in your life any longer." And I said, "But I'll always love you. There's always a place for you." He said, "I know. But I know you have other things and someone else." And I looked up, and I had this tremendous feeling of relief.

And in a way it was a very therapeutic dream.

Carlos was barely twenty years old in 1968 when he and his lover, *Skip*, were "married" by a minister of the Metropolitan Community Church on the West Coast. Neither was particularly interested in having the ceremony, but Carlos' mother insisted.

Since it meant so much to her, they agreed. It must have been quite an affair; the guest list exceeded two hundred. Many of them were cops, both straight and gay, all of them members of a large city police force on the West Coast. Skip was a cop, and perhaps some of his fellow officers came out of curiosity or amusement, waiting for the moment when the minister would say, "And I now pronounce you husband and . . . and what?" Whatever the reason, the cops were to find the love between Carlos and Skip lasting. The two established a fully monogamous relationship for the next nine and a half years that outlasted many of the heterosexual marriages represented at the wedding. Skip's fellow cops became very useful to Carlos in the tragedy that occurred almost ten years after the ceremony.

Cops like to frequent certain bars, and in this large city all the gay cops went to the same gay bar when they were off duty. One Saturday night Skip and Carlos were in the bar, together with two other gay cops. It was a crowded night, and the cops were playing pool with Carlos watching. One of them noticed a man walk into the bar, pull out a gun, and demand money from the bartender. Skip instantly headed for the robber.

> When I saw Skip running up to the robber, I realized that I had Skip's gun. Skip usually wears his gun on his leg, but that night he was wearing very tight jeans so he couldn't put it on. So he asked me to put his gun in my purse, and that's where it was when he went running after this robber with the gun. And then Skip came running back, yelling, "Where's my gun? Give me my gun!" I opened the handbag, and I was so nervous I couldn't find it. It was right there in front of my eyes, but I didn't see it. Skip grabbed it, and he ran away. Everyone started looking at me. They said, "You're in love with a cop?" They arrested the guy, and there was no trouble.

Skip's gun was always a source of trouble between them. Carlos never liked having a gun around the house, and he was encouraged in this by superstitious nonsense from his mother, who repeatedly warned him that Skip might have a nightmare and shoot Carlos. For quite a while Carlos would hide Skip's revolver before they went to bed, only to forget the next day exactly where he had hidden it. For years, their mornings were spent looking for the gun, arguing back and forth about the merits of tucking it away so safely. They argued about nothing else in their relationship.

But one spring night in 1976, Carlos and Skip were leaving their favorite bar at 10 P.M. because Carlos had to get to work early the next morning.

> We said good-bye to another cop who was at the door, and we didn't see the car that was double-parked in front of the bar. The engine and lights were on. Three guys get out of the car, and they start shooting. When Skip heard the first shot, he pushed me with his elbow so I went down to the floor, and I looked up right away, and I see him get shot in the head. And then another one hit his chest, another one his neck. There were five shots. He fell to the ground, and I took him in my arms, and he looked at me. He was bleeding from his mouth. And he said, "I love you . . . this hurts . . . call the police . . . take me to a doctor . . . this hurts a lot . . . I love you." And all these fucking queens around there, they didn't help me at all.
>
> He was dying on my hands. I was wearing a white shirt, and there was blood all over it. This man in my arms, dying. Nobody helped me. Nobody did a goddamned thing. Then someone in the bar called an ambulance, but he was already dead. Died in my arms. One of the other cops . . . one who was in the bar . . . took Skip's badge and gun and put them in his pocket, so the other cops wouldn't know that a gay cop was killed outside a gay bar. They would find out later, but he wanted to protect Skip right now.
>
> A lot of police cars showed up—the first car that came, two cops came out, both straight, but they knew that Skip and I were lovers. They said, "Oh, no!" One of them pushed me away. He was rough with me, but he was trying to protect me. He didn't want me to stay there with my dead lover in my arms. He knows me. I was destroyed. I was screaming. I was hysterical. He took me down the street, and he put me in another police car, and he tried to console me. He took me down to the hospital. I was crying and crying and crying in the police car—and then I fainted. He was a straight cop, married, with two children, but he used to visit Skip and I a lot, and he was trying to console me, but he couldn't console me. He was screaming to the other cop driving, "Hurry up, hurry up," but then I passed out.

After Carlos was released from the hospital, he began getting death threats from whoever had murdered Skip. The reasons for the murder were obscure, but the letters and phone calls were plain enough. The police provided protection for Carlos on their off-duty hours. They accompanied him wherever he went.

> They would take me out to dinner and visit me, beside the protection. My straight friends and the gay cops knew we were lovers and would sometimes let me spend weekends in their houses. They helped me a lot. Some would take me shopping on my day off, even the straight cops who knew Skip and I were lovers. None of the cops, straight or gay cops, were nasty to me. They all helped. Skip's partner was straight, and they got along good.
>
> It was the worst time possible. I wanted to get a gun and shoot them back. I hate Puerto Ricans. I hate blacks. They were two Puerto Ricans who shot him. A lot of things came to my mind, why it happened, why him, why me, why God, a lot of whys. I thought of all the good moments we had together. I kept dreaming that he was only wounded so I could quit my job and take care of him, but all these thoughts were driving me crazy.

Carlos' anger toward blacks and Puerto Ricans is ironic, given the fact that he comes from one of the Third World countries himself. Almost precisely a year after Skip was murdered, Carlos was raped by three black men in Central Park. The rape was particularly brutal, and Carlos was taken to the emergency room of a local hospital where he remained for a month, so extensive was the physical damage to the anal sphincters and rectum.

The experience left Carlos with more than just bitterness and anger. He became frightened of sex. Even in the hospital while recovering from his injuries, he would tense up when a friend took his hand to comfort him. He avoided blacks in the street whenever he could and shook violently whenever he had to walk past them. He never allowed anyone to kiss him from then on, not even his closest friends. "I didn't even jerk off."

The bitterness has not yet abated. As Carlos tells the stories, the listener feels his anger and desire for revenge against these unknown enemies. In the past year he has relaxed some, enough to try to establish a new relationship, but it is difficult to manage the internal conflict between loving and fearing men at the same time. At the moment, Skip's murder and the subsequent rape are roadblocks in the way of future happiness.

Ben was born in 1934. His birth was a disappointment to his parents, who had already decided to name their second child Martha. Other disappointments followed, such as Ben's intense intellectual curiosity and his superior performance at school, while his older brother and father played ball together. Much to the horror of his family, Ben developed an overwhelming love of opera, to which he listened whenever his father was out of the house. His parents called him "the skinny runt with a brain," even his mother, with whom he was on unusually good terms. For instance, there was the time thirty years before when she wanted Ben to swallow a pill, and he "went through one of my gagging routines" and kept spitting it on the floor. His mother hit him with a leg of lamb, called him a "skinny runt with a brain," and sent him to his room. But most of the time Ben waited until the family went shopping in the afternoon so he could turn on the living room radio.

> I would fantasize that way. I had marbles, and I would set them up as an audience and pretend that I was on the stage, performing. I would do that until I heard the garage door, and then I'd turn it off and run upstairs.

When Ben was seventeen years old, he tricked one night with a man he met at a local bar. The sex was pleasant but not remarkable. The next evening, the fellow, *Buddy*, arrived at Ben's apartment.

> And he stood on the other side of the bedroom by the door, and he took a pair of socks out of one pocket and a pair of undershorts out of the other pocket and said, "I'm moving in."

Ben didn't take it very seriously. One pair of socks and one set of underwear wouldn't last that long, but he was pleased that someone wanted him so badly, and he was lonely. "Why not?" was Ben's thought. That evening started a ten-year love affair that was as fulfilling to Ben as he had ever dreamed.

The couple had been together for eight years when Buddy's illness began. It was on the fifteenth of January, 1959. Buddy had missed two days of work because of a slight temperature and general physical exhaustion when Ben finally convinced him to see a doctor. That day Buddy was admitted to the hospital. After some tests, Ben was told that Buddy had Hodgkin's disease. The main lymph gland in the middle of his chest was gigantic, as large as his heart, and all of his other glands were swollen and infected. First the doctors tried a new treatment, using nitrogen mustard, but it proved almost fatal, and cobalt treatments were initiated. Buddy had ninety of them in all. Neither the doctors nor Ben told Buddy that he had cancer, and he didn't figure it out for himself. Buddy could block out things that he didn't want to know. But one day he found out.

> It was my birthday, June 3, 1959. I came home, and we had our first major fight in his illness. He had gone for a cobalt treatment. He only had three or four more to go, and the stupid radiologist left the chart in the room. Buddy was always nosy, so he picked up the chart and he read the words, "Hodgkin's disease." And I was confronted when I walked in from work that day with, "You knew, you hid it from me." And I was physically attacked. He was pretty violent. I let him go. I didn't run. I let him beat me up.
>
> I'm not a physical masochist, but if that was his way of letting out his anger, let it out. You see, he was given three months to live. He lived twenty-three months, and those twenty-three months were a nightmare. This is where it gets very confusing to me, because looking on it now I can honestly say they were a nightmare to him, and with me it was self-pity. At the time it was self-pity, all right, but it was a nightmare. Why me? I had never had a fling in my life. I was in my twenties. I had everything. He was only forty years old when he got sick. Why would they take him?
>
> I don't know how I would react if I were either told or read something like that. He was a man who wanted to live, and he should have lived. I know at the time that I wanted to die when I was told. Why him? Me? I was the little bastard who always wanted things in life and finally finagled to get them, and he was so good, and his brothers and sisters were such bastards, and he did everything for his parents. And yet here he was going to die.
>
> His adjustment to the disease was poor. He rejected people. He looked horrible as time went on. He never

used the word cancer in the two years he was sick. Toward the end he was getting transfusions every couple of days because the cobalt was killing his bone marrow, and he could not manufacture any blood. His family would call every night when I came back from the hospital to find out how things were going, but not once did they ever come to see him. They said Buddy was being taken care of, and they didn't want to see pain. They didn't believe it was going to happen either.

It was taking so long. I reached the point where I didn't think it was going to happen either. Friends at work would say, "We don't want to hear about it. He's going to outlive you." Those last two years changed a lot with us. I decided that I had had everything. Now it was his turn. I knew he wanted two things, an apartment with a terrace and a dog. I convinced Buddy we could afford it, and I got a penthouse in Murray Hill which he loved; he literally lived on that terrace. And we got a miniature schnauzer which we had for a year and a half, until about six months before he died. And that dog received probably all his love. We lost most of our friends except for the straight friends. Gay friends said they couldn't take looking at Buddy.

Sexually he did not go down. He was given a lot of hormones towards the end that almost turned him into a woman. I was given the go-ahead; it was fine. But then the drinking got worse. My drinking was impossible, but his was worse because one drink would completely destroy him. He became violent. If we had Bell Tel up once, we had them ten times. He would rip the phones out of the walls.

That April the dog started to shy away from him. He was a beautiful dog. I loved that animal. Buddy would reach down, and the dog would not come near him. But the dog was his whole life, and he tried to grab the dog, and it bit him. And he was bleeding, and I had to get Buddy to the hospital, and the dog had to go the next day. We gave the dog to Buddy's niece.

He was very hurt that the dog shied away from him and bit him. But he understood why we had to give it away. I'm not sure what was in his mind. I'm sure he knew why the dog responded the way he did. And that hurt him. Dogs shy away from sickness.

Neither Ben nor Buddy knew how often they would have to go for blood transfusions, but in the twenty-three months of his illness, Buddy received over four hundred pints of blood. Sometimes Buddy would refuse to go, yelling, "I will not die!" These were particularly difficult moments for Ben, who had to be strong and get Buddy to the hospital for whatever help the doctors could offer. He yearned for a chance to express his own weakness and longed for the times when Buddy had taken care of him. During the final six months, Ben could no longer sleep in the same room with Buddy. He moved into the living room.

One Friday Ben got a call from the hospital, telling him to bring Buddy's clothes and a suitcase. They were discharging him, and in another week he could go back to work. Ben decided to pick up Buddy the next morning, but early Saturday morning the phone rang. It was Buddy, crying. He said, "Don't come, leave me alone." Ben rushed to the hospital.

> People were running in and out behind screens. I sat there for four hours. I wasn't allowed into the room. Then finally a nurse asked me to come in and help her. They couldn't get the bed down. I took one look and said, "Why?"
>
> I remember them rushing the bed out of the room and the plasma hitting the doorjamb and smashing all over, and I called my friend, and her husband came and sat with me because I wouldn't leave. I wanted to make sure he was alive. I told the charge nurse to get the priest for last rites, and she said she would. The doctors were very nice. They listed me as a cousin.
>
> This is important. The first time I talked about this, I did what they call a fifth step in AA. I broke up at this point. I don't break up anymore. The crying is over.
>
> I went back the next night. Meanwhile, the family still would not come to see their dying brother. The mother had died the year before. The father had not been told his son was dying. He was now seventy-eight years old.
>
> The priest arrived. He was standing there with the wafer, and Buddy came to, and Buddy threw the priest out of the room. That was Buddy's conception of religion. I laugh at it now, but I know he did not want to admit to last rites.

For the next few days and nights Buddy remained unconscious, with occasional interludes of lucidity. Then one night Ben decided that he needed some company for himself.

For the first time in twenty-three months I said to him,

'I will not be here tomorrow night." Toward the end
he told me every time I came to the hospital not to
come. He said, "Go out. Enjoy your life. Don't come
to me. It's over." But I guess he wanted me to come.
He would have been very hurt.

That night I met someone who I had a date with
Thursday night for cocktails. So I told Buddy. He just
sort of nodded and went back off. He was all wired to
those machines. I left. I felt good I had told him and
he knew I was going out. That night I met the man at
Rockefeller Center, and we went to my apartment for
cocktails. Then the phone rang, and it was the doctor.
He said Buddy was critical. I said, "I'm coming." He
said, "Don't." I said, "I'm coming!" He said, "OK,
I'll wait for you."

The doctor took me into the room, and I didn't
notice anything. I left the hospital room, and I told
the nurse again to get the priest, and she nodded, and
I left because he looked no different than he did the
night before. I went home. We (the date and I) had
dinner. Nothing ever happened. We became friends for
a short time after that, but we never went to bed. I
went to work the next morning, and as I walked in the
secretary just looked at me and said, "Dr. X called.
Will you please call him at the hospital?" I just walked
into my office and closed the door because I knew. And
I called, and he had died at three-thirty-four in the
morning.

And at that point I knew. I remembered what I had
seen the night before. They had taken all life-support-
ing equipment out of him. There was no intravenous.
There was nothing. They were letting him go, which
was good at that point. But I didn't notice it then.

I started to think that Buddy was free. He had told
me to go out and live, and I finally had a date, so I was
secure. I was with someone. And that was what he had
done for me in ten years, to be there, and that night
he knew someone was going to be there for me, and
he died.

Buddy wanted a military funeral, and I got it for
him. That funeral was something. It was my funeral,
not his. The family was decent enough to allow me
into the room first, and I came walking out, ranting
and raving like a madman. They put too much powder
in his hair. He was not gray. Then as the family arrived
each day, one by one they would stand at the door,
and they would scream my name, not his, and they

would come over and cry and kiss me. Even the monsignor blessed me. How ludicrous! He was given a High Requiem Mass. At the funeral, Buddy's sister was handed the flag. She handed it to me, which caused many raised eyebrows in the family, I'm sure.

The next few months were a continuation of Ben's nightmare. He became an alcoholic. Even before the funeral, for a five-day period Ben "wasn't sober for a minute." He absorbed himself in opera and music and was about to begin a very destructive five-year affair. He changed things around in the apartment, hoping it would help him forget, but it didn't work. Neighbors and shop owners constantly reminded him of the tragedy of Buddy's death. They would ask, "How are you? How are you feeling?" They were trying to be kind, but it was rubbing salt in the wound.

> At that point I not only moved—I decided that the only way I was going to break the relationship was to accept the fact that it was over. It was not like a broken love affair. I couldn't have the person back. He was dead. He was six feet under. I knew I had to get away from this constant reminder of what we had and live for today. I was twenty-five years old. Why not? So I moved—and proceeded to drink myself into oblivion.
>
> I lost everything—self-destructive—most alcoholics are. We don't destroy other people; we destroy ourselves. My drinking had nothing to do with Buddy. Absolutely nothing! In no way do I relate his death to my drinking. I drank heavily before I met him. The eight years before he got sick, that was social drinking, if there is such a thing.
>
> But I had no reason to drink. I drank heavily in the hospital before he died. And when he died, I found it a perfect excuse to drink. I liked to drink. It was getting me away from the one thing I had in my life for ten years of being needed—of being wanted. In sharing my life. I had nothing to share anymore.

It was then that all the "old tapes" were played back, the memories of being the skinny runt with a brain and getting hit with a leg of lamb. He felt like that same child, isolated in his room, listening to music, a child whose communication with his parents was nonexistent, a child who could not please his parents bv being Martha. The alcohol helped to assuage those memories of childhood, and his alcoholism lasted until a year ago, when with the help of AA Ben stopped drinking and began to work again. His memories are still of Buddy—the good times, the conflicts, and the final months—though now he can start to think about the future.

> Buddy was everything to me. I didn't want a mother or father, but I had those things in him. I had a lover, and he was certainly capable there. I guess like Sam, the dog, was to Buddy toward the end, Buddy was to me. It was just being wanted and being held.
>
> I would buy Buddy anything. He gave me all the things my parents never did, and no man has ever done that. I don't look for other men. If it happens again, it happens. I don't care if it doesn't happen again. I did have it for ten years.

Most of us don't really know how much we love the man we claim to love. Those who have spent many years with one man, or a series of other men, can appreciate the confusing array of motivations that impel us to live with and love another man— the pleasures of intimate friendships, the need to give or to get compassion, the excitement of frequent sex, loneliness, whatever. Serious illness is a test of our love. Even the fantasy of illness is a test; we wonder how we would feel if our lover were dead or diagnosed as terminally ill and how we'd plan our last few months together. This fantasy usually uncovers the center of feelings about a lover—indeed, whether it is love at all. The memories of ancient arguments and the battles over control and power fade away. Only the feelings remain. These fantasies can uncover poignant perceptions and feelings usually obscured by the humdrum of day-to-day life.

There are some general characteristics shared by those who have experienced the death of a lover. Some of the emotions and reactions are universal, though individual differences must always be allowed. For instance, the couple's relationship is almost always described as tranquil. In just about every interview with a survivor, the dead lover was depicted as so perfect a character, the relationship so free from conflict, that the experience of death seemed to have dissolved completely whatever difficulty the couple might have had in creating and maintaining the relationship. Most of these relationships sounded too good to be true. Often, perhaps, the past had been changed, the old tapes erased, and only the good feelings survived as memories. The single exception to this was the interview with Ben, whose memory of the history and problems of his ten-year love affair with Buddy was extraordinary.

Anger is another emotion felt by survivors—but it is a confusing emotion. Toward whom or what can they direct their anger? The unknown murderer? The cancer or heart attacks? The neurotic survivors blame themselves, but the emotion isn't anger, it is self-absorption; chances are, they've always blamed themselves. Often survivors blame the dead lover. We are sometimes furious when our lovers die, because we feel abandoned and left alone in the world. One interview expressed this perfectly.

> I was at the funeral and everyone was crying, but I wasn't. I just looked at the box, and I thought, "You son of a bitch." I felt like I wanted to open the box and hit him on the face. And I'll be damned if I let anyone make me feel guilty about that.

Anger at a lover's death may be the result of feeling that we have lost the shield that protects us from the painful memories and the old ghosts of childhood and young adulthood. Other separations—the death of a parent, the loss of a childhood friend or an old love—return to haunt us. With the death of a lover, each death or past loss is experienced again. The survivors are caught in a web of memories. Although such memories take many forms, two predominate.

Sometimes we remember the fun and activities shared with lovers. We remember the times of collaboration, the joyful events of the relationship, the special occasions, the saving for a house or a car. These were the times of support and confidence. It was as if we would always be together. With a lover's death, a part of us dies as well. The good memories, like good ghosts, bring a mixture of happiness and sadness.

Other survivors play a different tape. In the foreground of their memories are the moments of conflict—the errors they made with a lover, the lack of trust, the accusations, the "tit-for-tat" games played endlessly by lover/competitors—all part of a strategy to change him, to make him more like oneself. These survivors feel guilty. "If only I . . ." Fill in the blank. Endlessly, they think of how they hurt the dead one, and other dead ones from the past. Willingly they burden themselves with all the failings and inadequacies of the dead, as if death absolved the dead of all their shortcomings. "He was good," is equivalent to, "I am bad," and some survivors wear the "bad" label like a badge of honor.

Most people are sympathetic toward these lovers. They seem to be in such pain, so involved in the self-destructive process of blame that they invoke consolation, words of absolution. I react differently. I view their actions not as the supreme sacrifice, but rather as supreme selfishness. They upstage the dead lover by diverting attention from him. They make everyone feel sorry for them, the survivors. Their guilt is invariably a trait designed to call attention to themselves and thereby gain sympathy—which invariably doesn't help. There is a special reason for this.

"Trait guilt" is designed to punish other people. It has nothing to do with legitimate feelings of guilt that occur in every life. Trait guilt is a hostile act of the survivor toward other people; it is meant to demonstrate that, no matter how hard anyone tries, no matter what techniques are used, no matter what sacrifices are made, the survivor cannot be aided. Those who try are —or must eventually become—impotent in their efforts, proving to the survivor what he thought he knew all the time—that no one really cares or understands. Such a person grieves for himself. This form of guilt is frequently manifested in the conflicts that arise in any relationship, gay or straight; but in all the interviews during this study there was no gay person who grieved more for himself than for his lover. The voluntary nature of the sample may be the reason, or perhaps gay couples have less resentment and use guilt less than heterosexual couples.

Another common reaction to the death or imminent death of a lover is the survivor's desire for outside sex. It is remarkable how often this occurs; descriptions of the process are reliably reported. Survivors aren't seeking a sexy experience; they aren't looking for a substitute for the sex they've done without for months during a lover's prolonged illness. They are lonely. These men have maintained a facade of strength and fortitude for months or years. They have been strong for a lover who is losing his own strength. The survivor longs for a moment of weakness, for the compassion of another man, for the opportunity to be passive, in the true sense of the word, and to absorb the strength of another. This need was powerful in many of the men interviewed, and it rarely made any of them feel guilty, nor should it.

Friends are almost always responsive. Most of the men interviewed found themselves surrounded by helpful friends, giving sympathy at first and then aiding them in starting life anew. It is strange how few gays know just how supportive their friends can be. In many ways, both old and new friends take on the role of a family and make whatever sacrifices are necessary.

If all experiences in life can lead to personal growth, then the death of a lover is a crisis that can either help or harm the survivor's growth. The choice is his own. Psychologically, the process is complicated by the task of accepting the lover's death while keeping his memory alive. If the lover is not allowed to die in the psychological sense, if he is kept alive to haunt the survivor like a dybbuk or a ghost, then the survivor will be unable to reach out into the world and find companionship. At the same time, the survivor must realize that a new lover cannot replace the old, cannot substitute for what was lost. That would be unfair to both the dead lover and the new one. The old relationship will have been an important part of his life, but any new relationship must stand on its own, without dependence on the past. It is not an easy task. If he can love more during life, he will have less to grieve for after death.

CHAPTER TWELVE

Josh and Andy:
Fifty Years Plus One

Grow old along with me!
The best is yet to be,
The last of life, for which the first was made.

ROBERT BROWNING

Josh Goodman at age twenty-one had just opened a wallpaper-
and-paint store in a small town in Pennsylvania. He considered
himself fortunate that he was in business for himself; he had
spent his entire adolescence working for others. Josh didn't
know very much about wallpaper or paint, but that didn't discourage him; he would learn about it soon enough. A hard
worker, Josh made his store one of the most successful busi-
nesses in town. The year was 1924.

Josh was born in 1903, the second of six children, in a rural
area of Pennsylvania. For the most part his childhood was unremarkable: he went through the usual bickering with brothers
and sisters, the scraps, the illnesses, and the drudgery of home-
work. Unlike his older brother, he had no interest in sports and
rarely went to the playground. But in one way he stood out.
Josh was called the "kissing bug." He loved to kiss everyone—
family, strangers, and friends—if they allowed it. He particularly
liked kissing men and boys, especially his uncle Eddie. As Josh
says, "I got a real thrill out of it."

Josh's sexual interests began early. Even today he vividly re-
members getting an erection while sitting on his father's lap. At
the time he was just seven years old. He had no consciousness
of it as a homosexual reaction, and he wasn't embarrassed by it.
In fact, it was his favorite place to sit. Of course, all this kissing
stuff had to lead to further activities. He and his older brother
went from kissing to mutual sucking. One day his mother walked

into the bedroom and found the two of them stark naked on the bed in a sixty-nine position—with their mouths full. Josh was only nine at the time, and, though he was afraid of being punished, neither parent ever mentioned it again, and no punishment was forthcoming. The brothers continued to do it until the excitement waned and Josh's brother became interested in girls. Josh was never very close to his brothers, and the sex was nothing more than childhood experimentation.

At age ten, Josh outraged his family. Like many towns in that part of Pennsylvania, one outlying street was filled with houses of prostitution, and that was where Josh found his best friends. Josh speaks for himself.

> When I was ten years old I used to go with the whores. I lived on a street where all the whorehouses were. And these girls used to work in a high-class place where all the politicians and the mayor used to come. I used to sit with the whores on the steps and laugh and tell jokes. But when the mayor was coming, they made me hide so he would think no one knew.
>
> The girls were very good to me. I used to buy them things and do their errands, and they would tip me for doing this. I went to the drugstore to buy their heroin and needles. You know, years ago you could buy heroin in the drugstore. I didn't care what they did. I just liked the way they treated me, and we had a lot of fun together, gossiping and laughing on the steps of that house.

Josh's lover still teases him about those days, saying, "You were just one of the girls." Josh continued sitting on the steps with the prostitutes for four years, watching the local politicians, religious leaders, and starchy husbands (who had sworn fidelity to their wives) go in and out of the establishment. Josh was probably the best-informed kid around. His Hebrew teacher was appalled at Josh's association with whores, and he gave Josh an ultimatum. "Leave the whores or leave the Hebrew school." And so ended Josh's religious life!

These childhood pastimes came to an end, and at fourteen Josh had to go out and earn a living. It may seem an early age to us, but there was nothing unusual about a fourteen-year-old boy earning "his keep" in those days. He went to work at his uncle's secondhand clothes store, earning three dollars a week.

The hours were seven A.M. to eight P.M. seven days a week. Josh preferred waiting on attractive men. For some reason, no matter how certain they were of their size, he always found it necessary to take their measurements.

> I used to measure the attractive men by putting my
> finger by their *schmeckle* to see if it was too tight.*
> Some men liked it, and some didn't.

Inevitably this resulted in kind words and an occasional pat on the head, at least from men who thought Josh quite nice. When no one was watching, a man might put his arms around Josh, but it rarely went any further. Once, when Josh was still fourteen, he had sex with a man in the dressing room. It was the first and last time anything like that ever happened in the store. By that time he knew he was a homosexual but didn't believe there was anything wrong with it (though he was well aware that very few people in town would agree).

At seventeen, Josh got a job managing a shoe store in another town by convincing the owner that he was twenty-one. Then, at twenty-one, his father lent him enough money to buy the wallpaper-and-paint business, and Josh settled back into his hometown.

It was then that he met *Andy*. Andy was the paperboy, and, the moment he walked into Josh's store with the daily paper, Josh fell in love. "He had the cutest little face and a beautiful head of hair. I fell in love with him the first day I saw him." But Andy was only eleven years old and Josh twenty-one. Josh was a businessman and Andy a paperboy, one sexually mature and the other preadolescent. Josh hid his feelings and decided to wait.

Things don't change very quickly in small towns. Three years later, Josh was a successful businessman, and Andy was still his paperboy. But on November 15, 1927, Andy was fourteen and Josh twenty-four. That day, when Andy came to deliver the paper, Josh proposed, "Let's go downstairs to the basement, and I'll show you my etchings." Andy was delighted by his invitation, knowing full well that aesthetics would soon turn to *schmeckles*. How could Josh have known that Andy, the paper-

---

* *Schmeckle* is a slang Yiddish word for penis, but more jocular in tone and more affectionate than *schmuck*.

boy, had also been waiting for the past three years to "see Josh's etchings"? They mark that day, Andy's first experience with sex (Josh was none too experienced, either) as their anniversary. Andy liked older men.

> You see, I never got any love from my father. I did from my mother and aunts, but my father would never hug or kiss me. So I always wanted to be close to an older man. I wished they would hug me or kiss me or cuddle me or anything . . . something.

Andy never thought of these feelings as homosexual. He had never even heard of a homosexual. He only knew that he had missed something in his relationships with men and saw a chance to find it with the owner of the wallpaper-and-paint store.

> Every time I saw this man something would happen to me. I liked the way he looked. I admired men with gray hair, and when he took me downstairs and started kissing me, and he showed love toward me . . . I wanted it. And right away you know what happens [sex]. I got an erection right away. And I loved it. And I had sex for the first time that day. So then I wanted to have more.

Still, Andy didn't know that Josh was gay. The sense of a personal sexual identity would not develop for quite a while yet. All he knew was that Josh had a large head of bushy hair and a warm smile, and he loved him. "His hair was beautiful (it was sort of frosted then). I admired his hair, and I admired him."

Josh uses fewer words to tell the story of that first day in the basement. He says, "We fell in love with each other."

It couldn't have been easy—a fourteen-year-old boy with a twenty-four-year-old lover in "redneck" territory. Living together was out of the question; Andy lived at home with his parents, and the community would hardly have tolerated a pair of homosexual lovers (much less a couple in which one was a teenager). They would meet two or three times a week, after school and on weekends, spending a lot of time examining "etchings." Josh was also a frequent visitor to Andy's house, and Andy's mother liked him very much. If anyone in Andy's family suspected, they never let on, though Andy was always leery of two nosy relatives.

> I had two aunts who were maiden schoolteachers. I
> didn't want them to find out what was going on. You
> know how schoolteachers talk.

Sometimes Josh and Andy would drive out of town and have
sex in the car, or go to the movies at places where neither of
them was known. For years they never met anyone else who
was homosexual. They heard a story about some other man in
town who was reputed to be gay, but they never checked it out.
That would have been too venturesome for them, at least at that
time.

Incredibly, they spent the first twenty-four years of their relationship living in separate apartments in the town. During
those twenty-four years, no one knew they were lovers. They
ate breakfast and lunch together as often as possible. They
continued to have sex in the store basement after hours, since
both were afraid of gossip if they brought someone home.
Though isolated from other gay men, they would sometimes
hear stories. Andy's mother provided them with some uninten-
tional information.

> I didn't know from gay people. But I did hear some
> stories. My mother was working in a department store,
> and she told me some stories about some gays in an-
> other town and the good times they had in Greenwich
> Village when they went to New York. Of course, she
> wouldn't elaborate to me, but I knew what she meant.
> I heard about the Village in New York City. I heard
> about the homosexuals . . . that two men have sex
> together, and so forth and so on. That was the place
> where all the gay people went. I was always curious
> what it was all about, but when we went to Ne York
> we never went to the Village. Not until later on.

In fact, their first few trips to New York City (they took their
vacations together) were devoted to seeing Broadway shows. In
one day, they saw Patti Page at the Paramount in the morning,
then Josephine Baker at the Roxy, the first matinee Judy Gar-
land gave at the Palace, and, in the evening, *Guys and Dolls*!
Year after year they went to New York on their vacation and
never once sought the company of other gay men. They can
hardly say why. Perhaps it was the years of isolation and dependence on each other, fear of the unknown, or perhaps just
the shyness experienced by small-town boys in the hubbub of

the fast city. It was not until their first trip to Europe that Josh and Andy looked for and found other gay men. That was 1958, when Josh was fifty-five and Andy forty-five. In 1958 they had been lovers for thirty-one years! But I'm getting ahead of the story.

Andy worked in a beauty salon. He got into it quite naturally.

> I used to like to do my sister's hair. She couldn't curl her hair too well in the back, and she asked me to help. We used a curling iron in those days. Then when my mother went to the beauty shop, I would go along with her and watch Mrs. Johnson work. The finger wave was starting to come out at that time, and she showed me how to do it with this heavy, gooey finger-waving lotion. So then I tried it on my sister's hair. Then some of my sister's girl friends wanted me to do their hair. And I charged everyone a quarter.
>
> Pretty soon I was going to people's homes with all my solutions and hair nets. I set their hair for them. Later I went to beauty school and worked for another shop for a while—maybe a year—and then I opened my own.

Andy opened his place in 1937 when he was twenty-four. He and Josh had already been lovers for ten years. The beauty shop was just across the street from the wallpaper store (it, too, had a basement). The shop measured nine by twelve feet, and at the height of the rush nine people worked there. When Andy advertised a permanent wave for a dollar (a very reasonable price), women flocked to his shop from miles around. On weekends the women had to sit on the steps to wait their turn for the one-dollar permanent wave. Josh loved to watch from across the street.

But World War II interrupted everything. At thirty-eight, Josh was too old to be drafted, but Andy was eligible and was called up. His experience in the army was a combination of fear and hilarity.

> It was a riot. From being a hairdresser, they stuck me in a tank. They did that because I passed some fool test. I said I knew which way the wheels turn.

For the next five years Andy, the hairdresser, the man who loved cuddling and affection, drove around North Africa in a tank. To complete the irony, he served under General Patton.

> That son of a bitch. He was a real bastard. The first
> time he was introduced to us in a stadium in England
> . . . there were these nurses there, and young people
> . . . and the language he used . . . I was shocked to
> hear an intelligent man use that foul language.

It was very difficult for both Josh and Andy. Neither could
express his sorrow at separation with anyone else. Josh wrote
every day for five years, and even today, remembering those
lonely times, tears come to his eyes. The letters were so important to him. "It was the only way we could be together,"
Josh says.

Josh didn't know whether Andy would return trom the war,
and the thought of Andy's death terrified him. Each day people
would come into his store and talk about their husbands or sons
fighting overseas, but Josh couldn't say anything to them about
his worries for his man.

Andy was severely homesick after he was drafted. In the first
month, he lost thirty pounds.

> Here I am, and I don't know what's going to be. It was
> a terrible thing because I was in the first group drafted
> from our town. Leaving Josh was like the whole world
> was taken from me. I always had this idea that maybe I
> wouldn't come back. Maybe I would never see Josh
> again.

But the army experience provided Andy with an opportunity
to meet other men, some of whom had to be gay. While in train-
ing in Georgia, he and an army buddy went out drinking one
Saturday night. This friend kissed Andy on the cheek, and
Andy thought, "Oh! He must be gay," but Andy didn't respond.
Shortly after:

> Then one day we had to clean the tanks. This one kid
> was built very big, and I see he's leaning against the
> tank . . . and he had a hard-on. Well, you couldn't
> miss seeing it; this guy was standing by the tank with
> this bulge in his pants, and he said, "Come on, let's
> play." But I was afraid to, so I said, "Hey, what are
> you here for?" And I told him to wash the tank. Later
> on I was teamed up with this guy again, and we had to
> sleep in the same bed, and he wanted to have sex, but I
> wouldn't do it.

In the army, the gays were least uptight in the special services unit, the group assigned to entertainment. They had their own parties, and, from Andy's descriptions, they were wonderful. Three gay men in the unit always arrived dressed as the Andrews Sisters, one of them an officer, but then, most of the officers were gay. The refreshment served at these parties was called the "buzz bomb," a five-gallon water can filled with wine, cognac, and whiskey.

During one party a soldier tried to get Andy drunk. He succeeded, though Andy knew what was going on. The man propositioned Andy, and they went to bed. This was Andy's first outside sex. It was the only time in his five-year army career that Andy had sex. The soldier who propositioned Andy wanted to repeat the experience and at one point gave Andy a bracelet as a gift. But Andy rejected further advances, feeling it wasn't fair to Josh who was waiting at home. Andy wrote to Josh and reported what had happened, and Josh replied that he shouldn't worry, it was OK. They were never jealous or competitive with one another, either before or after the army experience, and Josh did nothing to upset Andy.

Andy returned from the war in 1946. It was then he learned that Josh had had a stroke, as chance would have it, one month after Andy had entered the service. Throughout the war, Josh was silent about the illness, saying afterwards, "Why should I make him worry? He was troubled enough." While Andy had been feeling homesick and losing thirty pounds, Josh had been lying in the hospital for six weeks.

In 1946, Andy opened up his beauty shop again, just across the street from Josh's wallpaper-and-paint store. The next year, in 1947, Josh had his first heart attack. It was at this time in their lives that they became painfully aware of the difference in their ages. Josh, then forty-four, had already had a stroke and a heart attack; Andy was thirty-four and in the best of health. They decided to change their vacation plans and look for a warm place to retire. Rather than travel to New York each year, they trekked to Miami and the Florida sun. After just one vacation in the sun, they decided to leave Pennsylvania and make Miami their home. Now they would live together.

Josh was particularly anxious about leaving. He was tired of the store, Pennsylvania, and living apart. For years he had watched heterosexuals marry and divorce, while his love for

Andy never wavered. He wanted to retire and spend his last years with the man he loved. "When are we going to get away?" he kept saying. But Andy was in a quandary. His mother was all alone, and he felt responsible for her.

But Josh wouldn't be put off any longer, and he gave Andy an ultimatum: "We have to set a date when we're leaving for Florida, and we have to keep it—no matter what." Summer 1951 was the target.

In 1951 they were forty-eight and thirty-eight respectively; they were both successful businessmen, and their relationship had already lasted for twenty-four years. And to them it seemed as if they were *running away*, like two teenagers escaping home. They still call it running away. It was to be a complete break of all past ties. Andy says:

> So we decided that he would leave his business, and I would leave my business. In the meantime we were collecting things, blankets, a radio, different little things we were going to bring down to Florida. Josh bought a new car, and we were storing all the stuff in the beauty shop. I was also taking some of the things from my home and bringing them to the shop, like my records. My clothes, too. I would take only one suit at a time to the cleaners . . . I didn't want him to suspect . . . and bring them to the shop, never back home.
>
> So this year, 1951, we made up our minds we were running away to Miami and we were never coming back. But I couldn't tell my mother we weren't coming back. I knew she would get hysterical. And Josh couldn't tell his family he wasn't coming back. So that's why we were running away.

Andy decided to give his business to his mother, the income serving to support her until her death (which came in 1954). After that he didn't care about it. He felt he could find enough work for himself in Miami. Josh had a small disability payment each month and couldn't have cared less what happened to his business. He told no one he was leaving, neither employees nor relatives. As far as he was concerned, when he left for his vacation to Miami, he was finished with Pennsylvania, and anyone who wanted could take the business. To this day he hasn't the faintest idea what happened to it and doesn't care.

Everyone was used to seeing Andy and Josh go off on vacation together. The big day finally arrived, and the new car was loaded with all the supplies for Miami. Andy tells about the last-minute hitch:

> It was really a funny story. I'm Catholic. My mother was a very good Catholic, and she used to go to church every Sunday, faithfully . . . faithfully. Well, this Sunday when I was getting ready to leave, suddenly she says, "You have to have something to eat before you leave. I'll go to Mass later." I said, "No, don't bother. Josh will be over at any moment." You see, he couldn't come over with the new car because it was filled with the trousseau. It was loaded to the top, and we didn't want anyone to see that. So he was coming with the old car, and then we were going to switch cars and leave.
>
> But a few minutes before nine I get a telephone call. It was Josh. "Guess what," Josh said. "The old car has a flat tire, and I can't bring it. I have to bring the new one to pick you up." I said, "My God, how is this going to be? My mother's making me breakfast, and she's going to see the new car and the trousseau."

Andy took the frying pan out of his mother's hands, insisted she go off to church instantly—and it worked. She left. "Finally Josh arrived, I got in the car, and we ran."

> There was a small bridge at the end of town, and as we approached it Josh said to me, "Once we go over this bridge there's no turning back." So we went over the bridge . . . and we never came back.

Intentionally or not, they rented an apartment in the cruisy gay section of Miami in the downtown beach area. For the first time they saw a gay bar and men dancing together. It was the Circus Bar. What a wonder to behold—after twenty-five years of a relationship, they were discovering other gay men and the fun of recreational sex. Andy reports:

> There was a men's room on Sixth Street. I think they called it a tearoom. It was just a couple of blocks from where we lived . . . and we never never knew it. It was notorious. So one day Josh says to me, "Let's go over here to this beach," and so we went. Then I had to take a pee, and you know . . . everybody was cruising in there. I didn't know what was going on in the booths . . . I didn't know there were holes between them. Then someone told us about it, so I took a look.

> I never knew these things went on. You could sit in one booth and see someone sitting and playing with their things, or maybe putting their finger through the hole waiting for you to put your thing through Not me! I was afraid to.
>
> I was shocked to see those things going on that open. I never saw it before. I was afraid to participate. I couldn't have sex with anyone I didn't know, and I was afraid of getting some disease. But anyway, I went back to tell Josh what I saw.

Josh already knew about the tearoom, but, like Andy, he wasn't interested. They spent much of their time on the gay beach, gossiping with other gays and with the drag queens who worked in the bars. The drag queens sat on their blankets sewing costumes, surrounded by wigs, sequins, and stuff of all sorts. Many of the men swam nude, and Andy enjoyed swimming with them but never took off his bathing suit. Josh couldn't go into the water because of his heart condition (his second heart attack occurred the year they went to Florida).

> There was also the jetty. You almost had to be a goat to get out there. You could see things going on . . . browning [fucking] and sucking. Right there in the open. We never went out there because one of our friends did, and he broke his leg jumping. But we loved all the sex going on. It was paradise compared to where we came from.

Josh had retired, so Andy left all the financial duties to him. Andy gave Josh his weekly earnings, and Josh began saving for a vacation. They had never been to Europe, and they decided to take at least one trip a year (they have averaged two!). Josh did most of the cooking, since Andy worked all day. Josh claims he specialized in hamburgers and meat loaf. They had their first vacation in 1954; they went to Niagara Falls for their silver anniversary (even though it was their twenty-seventh year together).

The first European trip took place in 1958, when Josh was fifty-five and Andy forty-five. They have taken a trip every year since then. Before the first trip, Josh said to Andy, "When we go to Europe, we don't have to stay together. If you meet someone you want to go to bed with, it's OK. But we're still lovers."

Andy: P.S. He went to bed all the time. I never went to

bed with anyone.

Josh: Everybody thought I was gorgeous!

Andy: They thought he was the rich one! He used to give me his wallet and all his money before he would go with someone. But that wasn't all. I didn't know who these people were. Maybe someone would hurt Josh. So I would follow them, but sometimes they would lose me. I thought to myself, if I at least know where they are going . . . if he doesn't come back, I'll know where to look.

Josh never suspected that Andy was following him. Even though they had been perfectly monogamous throughout their years together, neither felt at all jealous. "He was on vacation, so let him have a good time," was the way Andy reacted. One day a rich Italian began squeezing Andy ("squeezing me to death") and importuning him. Andy refused.

Josh visited tearooms occasionally; the first visit was the most interesting.

I met a couple of monks in Genoa. I met one of them in a toilet. He asked me to come in, and then he started blessing me with the cross . . . and carrying on [sucking] with me at the same time. Then in Palermo there was a monk who was crazy about me. So Andy took my wallet, and the monk took me to the monastery. He had this big key and opened the door. He took me upstairs, and, with all the saints watching, he "carried on" with me. Wasn't that something?

Andy continues:

Then on a holiday, when they were carrying the saints in the street, we met another fellow, and he did Josh right on the church steps. I was watching. He wanted to do me, too, but I wouldn't. How would that be? Here I am a Catholic and being done on the church steps.

Somebody told us about a bathhouse in Holland, so we went there. First we took a shower and went into the steam room. Nothing was happening there, so while Josh stayed, I started to wander about. And I'm wandering around, so I discovered there was an upstairs. So I go upstairs, and here is this great big room, and across the room is a big curtain like a theatrical curtain across the whole room. And I see people going in and coming out. So naturally I was curious, so I went behind the curtain, onto a stage, and there was everybody on this stage . . . doing things. It was a whole kind of party going on. They were fucking and sucking, and they were playing with one another. It was an orgy. So I take a look . . . I never saw anything like that before in my life. It was like a movie or something you read about . . . a Roman orgy.

So I ran downstairs to look for Josh. I said, "Josh, you must come upstairs. You won't believe what I found." So Josh came up, and we both walked behind the curtain. And pretty soon someone came over and started to do Josh while I watched. Then someone started to do me. It was very nice; you just stand there, and someone does whatever you want!

One good thing naturally leads to another, and someone suggested the baths in Paris as a "hot place." So the next year tnev were Paris-bound.

They gave us sheets which we hung up and then went into the steam bath. Lo and behold, someone turns out the lights. It's all black. All of a sudden I feel like a million hands all over my body, like an octopus. Then, when the door would open, you could see what was going on. All of a sudden someone takes me by the hand and starts kissing me and carrying on. Then the door opened, and I could see this attractive American boy, and someone was kissing him . . . and someone was fucking him at the same time, and a third person was pushing his cock into the boy's mouth. And someone else was sucking him off. I aidn't know so many things could happen at the same time!

By mutual agreement, they decided to maintain strict fidelity while in the United States but "be on vacation" while in Europe. Outside sex was frequent in Europe, and only much later did they import it to the United States. Josh was more aggressive sexually, always looking for new adventures, while Andy was timid about making contacts or accepting sexual advances from strangers. He had difficulty with recreational sex and preferred some social context and affection before the sport. But Andy never objected to Josh's adventures, nor did he feel jealous of Josh's popularity or possessive about his body. Andy rather admired Josh's ability to find gay men so easily.

For instance, one year when they were returning from Europe on the S. S. *Rotterdam* Josh said that he thought the waiter was gay. Andy didn't think so Not two hours later Josh was in bed with the waiter, their mini-affair continuing till their arrival in New York City. When Andy asked Josh how he knew, Josh replied, "Royalty recognizes royalty."

Andy had his chance in London. They had just seen a show and were having a warm beer in a pub when a man began talking to Andy. It was obvious that he was interested in sex.

> I was standing toward the bar, and he was standing with his back toward the bar, and before I knew it he had my zipper down. Well, it was a lit bar, and I didn't know what to do. He said, "Do you have a place to stay?" And I said, "I'm staying at the Regent Palace. I'm staying with my uncle." I said, "I'll have to talk to my uncle first about this." So Uncle Josh said he looked nice, so I said yes. So the two of us had a party, and Uncle just watched us.

In Tangiers (where everything was outrageous), they met a sixty-year-old Englishman who was interested in young boys. Generous to a fault, the Englishman offered his "houseboy" to Josh and Andy for the evening but cautioned them not to give the boy more than one dollar. "Mustn't spoil them chaps, you know." In Casablanca, Josh wanted to see the local synagogue, and the man who showed it to him ended up in his bed an hour later.

Some of their time in Europe was spent buying art objects. They never came home without quite a bit of baggage, for in those days they were allowed $500 (wholesale) duty-free per person. In recent years, with money tighter, they have sold these objects to finance their current trips. The walls are a bit emptier now, but Andy and Josh are ready to go on a trip any day. They prefer travel to paintings.

In 1969, their forty-second year together, Josh's health took a serious turn for the worse. A combination of a stroke, a stone in his bladder, and poor medical treatment made their lives very difficult. Their own words express it best. Andy reports:

> Josh had a slight stroke, and then he fell out of bed. They X-rayed him and found that he had a stone in his bladder. They told him they would give him a cystoscope to crush the stone, and that it would be nothing. Well, they gave him the cystoscope, and they poked around, and they pushed the stone under his prostate, and it really loused him up. So they had to operate on

him. They had to take out the gland and the stone. They couldn't crush the stone because it was so hard.

It was a terrible ordeal. I got down on my knees and prayed every night because the doctor said he had only one chance in a hundred to live because of his condition, because of his previous heart attacks and stroke. I was working at the time, too. I would come home from work and stay with him in the hospital until seven P.M., come home and try to eat . . . but I couldn't eat. Josh would say, "If you don't stop worrying like that you're going to the hospital, too." He would say, "Why don't you go home and rest? You look terrible."

The hospital was having trouble at the time. Nurses were asking for a raise. They had a real mean nun on the floor. I mean really mean. I would let her have it, too. I told her she should go to confession more often. She always tried to stop me from seeing Josh, but I told them he was my uncle.

And Josh would tell me these awful stories. "You know," he said, "I don't think I'll ever come home." Josh was down to eighty-five pounds, and he wasn't eating. And the nurses refused to feed him. The nurses used to put the food tray on a table where Josh couldn't reach it, and they refused to bring it to him. Those bastards. Only I fed him.

I could see that he was losing weight. I was worried . . . praying. After the operation they didn't know if he was going to live, and he said to me that he couldn't urinate yet. I said to drink a lot of water, drink as much as you can.

Josh: So I drank fifteen glasses of water a day.

When he awoke he was all wet. He felt better, but then he got the hiccups so bad while he was in the hospital, and they sent him home that way. They said they couldn't do anything more for him.

When Josh came home from the hospital, I had to take care of him, all eighty-five pounds of him. I can't believe how skinny he was, laying in the bed like a refugee from a concentration camp. And I got him back together. It's like they say . . . lots of love and care.

Josh was all right for a few years. Then in 1973, when Josh was seventy, he entered the hospital again, first for twelve days, then for seven weeks.

They didn't know what he had. At first they thought it was some contagious disease, and I had to wear a

mask and a gown. Then he begged his doctor to send
him home. He came home, and you wouldn't believe
what I had for four days. I couldn't handle it. He was
perspiring, he wouldn't eat or sleep, so I had to get him
back to the hospital. They were feeding him intra-
venously in one arm, and they were giving him antibiotics in the other arm. And there he was, strapped
more or less. I mean he couldn't even move. And they
still didn't come in to feed him. They don't do that unless you have a private nurse, and we couldn't afford
that.

He was there for seven weeks. It was a siege. And I
prayed again. I would think what would happen . . .
what would happen if he should die. I didn't know what
to do with myself. What would I do without him . . .
it was a terrible thing.

All those weeks his back was bothering him, and the
doctor said it was because he was lying down all the
time. So I would take him out for walks each day.
Every day I'd walk him back and forth in the hallway,
with these two things hanging . . . those two gadgets,
you know [the IV and antibiotics]. Oh! And they also
had a bag because he couldn't hold his water. I carried
the bag, and he held on to the gadgets attached to his
arms. It was pitiful, really.

They finally decided to let him come home. But he
couldn't walk. Josh couldn't walk, and the doctor said
it was nothing. Nothing! He had arthritis of the spine
. . . some nothing! You shouldn't have this "nothing."
The doctor didn't even want to take care of him. He suggested I take Josh to an osteopath. So a friend came
down in his car, and we carried Josh to the car and
took him to the osteopath. He got two shots of whatever
it was. He used a big, long needle. Then Josh started to
walk. He would lay in bed every day, and I would take
him for little walks. He was still suffering from the first
operation because he still had a drip problem. I had to
keep changing him.* I would take him for a walk, and
he would get wet. Good thing I have patience. It was a
good thing I loved him.

Some of Josh's friends said, why don't you send
him to a nursing home? I said if I sent him to a nursing
home he would die. Really he would. Josh is that kind of
guy . . . he's very sentimental . . . he would just die
away from me.

* Even with the wetness, Andy slept in the same bed with Josh. He
changed the sheets twice a night.

We had some friends who helped. One of them came over in the morning when I went to work, and he stayed until noon. Then another friend who was eighty came over to watch Josh in the afternoon, and he stayed until I came home from work. At that time I was only working three days a week.

In 1975 trouble struck again. But this time it was Andy who got sick. At the time Andy was sixty-two (Josh was seventy-two), and they had been together for forty-eight years. They were seeing some shows in New York City when Andy began to have severe chest and left-arm pains. They returned to Miami where Andy entered a VA hospital and had a heart attack just as they were giving him an EKG. Josh got hysterical. They both thought Andy was going to die that day

> They put me in a room with all the gadgets on me. They had seven doctors look at me. They gave me the test where they put dye in your veins and see how the dye is going through the veins. The next day they had a consultation with me and told me I had three arteries blocked, and I needed a bypass operation. They wanted to take a vein out of my leg and use that. I said I don't know, I'll have to wait until my uncle gets here. Josh was my uncle. He was always my uncle to other people. So when Uncle Josh came, the doctors had a consultation with him and told him what they wanted to do.
> They told me you can have the operation or die, so I took a chance.
> *Josh*: I knew he was very, very sick.

They operated the next morning, and Andy came through it well. Medical care in the VA hospital was excellent. Andy remained in the hospital for a month.

> It was awful for Josh. Visiting hours didn't begin until noon. Josh was there at nine A.M. I could hear him coming down the hall. "Why does he come so early?" I said to myself. "Why doesn't he rest?" One morning he came in, and he was all banged up. He fell at home. I felt terrible.
> Josh would stay until seven P.M. He would have lunch in the cafeteria and then buy ice cream for both of us. Sometimes he would sit in my room and close his eyes for a while and take a nap, and I would watch him. I was worried about him   . just like he was worried about me. He never skipped a day.

Listening to the story brings tears to Josh's eyes. Now seventy-five years old, a veteran of three heart attacks and two strokes, he cries, remembering the past good times and some of the bad ones. "I call him Sarah Bernhardt," says Andy. And Josh says, "I hate the nights to come." "Oh!" responds Andy. "Everybody hates the nights to come. We don't know what to expect. Especially at our ages and in our condition. You have to forgive and forget . . . and you have to love a lot."

> *Josh*: When you're young, the years pass very slowly.
> But when you're old, the years go very quickly.

It is impossible for two men to forget the spectre of illness that has entered their lives so often. But even with the possibility of death, their sense of humor keeps their spirits up. For instance, they made out their wills in 1961. Josh decided to be cremated, but not Andy.

> If there's another world, I don't want to come back as
> a shadow.

Josh and Andy still live in Miami in the apartment they first rented twenty-seven years ago Recently they celebrated their golden anniversary—fifty years of love and friendship since the day the man in the wallpaper-and-paint store said to his paper-boy, "Let's go downstairs to the basement, and I'll show you my etchings." An old friend gave them an anniversary party; he flew them out to the Midwest, and gay friends visited and shared memories. For the first time in their lives, Josh and Andy were celebrities—an example for all those who believe that gay relationships can last.

At the party everyone wanted to know how they had stayed together so long, and after dinner a friend showed porno movies. The next day they were the center of attention at a local gay bar, everyone kissing them, with a stage show performed in their honor. They spent a week in the Midwest.

They stay at home now more than they did before, but they still have sex. They have friends who occasionally come over for recreational sex, and they love it.* It has cooled off a bit, espe-

---

* Josh still prefers sucking and "sixty-nine"—or "seventy." "That's 'sixty-nine' with someone watching."

cially since Andy's operation, but they still look at men a lot. Their block has always had its share of gay people, and the neighbors say hello each day and invite them to dinner. The young couples especially value the presence of Josh and Andy as models for their own relationships.

Fifty-one years have passed since the etchings, and Josh and Andy are called senior citizens now. Money is tight (not that it has stopped them from visiting Europe this year), they no longer have a car, and they would like to live among people their own age. They have been watching a new building going up in Florida, a senior citizens' home with government subsidy. They have written for an application. They want to live their last years together there. It would be so much easier than where they live now.

But they are a little worried about whether the authorities will allow two men to live together. Maybe they won't like the idea. Maybe there will be some silly rule that only married people can live together in the same room. After fifty-one years they are not about to live in separate rooms. But Andy figures that the authorities can't object to relatives being together, and, after all, Josh is still ten years older than Andy.

"I'll just tell them this is my Uncle Josh."

Josh and Andy—Chronology

1903   Josh is born
1912   Andy is born
——   Josh sits with the whores (age ten)
1917   Josh works for his uncle (age fourteen)
1920   Josh manages a shoe store (age seventeen)
1924   Josh opens his wallpaper-and-paint store
            (age twenty-one)
——   Josh and Andy meet (ages twenty-one and eleven)
1927   First sex (ages twenty-four and fourteen)
1937   Andy opens his beauty shop (age twenty-four)
1941   Andy enters the army and is assigned
            to a tank (age twenty-eight)
1942   Josh has his first stroke (age thirty-nine)
1946   Andy leaves the army (age thirty-two)
1947   Josh has first heart attack (age forty-four)
1951   Josh and Andy run away to Florida
            (ages forty-eight and thirty-eight)

Variations

——— Josh has his second heart attack
1954 Josh and Andy celebrate their twenty-fifth
    anniversary at Niagara Falls
    (ages fifty-one and forty-one)
1958 Their first trip to Europe and first outside
    sex (ages fifty-five and forty-five)
1969 Josh's second stroke and stone
    (age sixty-six)
1973 Josh's twelve-day hospitalization
    (age seventy)
1975 Andy's cardiac bypass operation
    (age sixty-two)
——— Andy retires as a hairdresser
1977 Their fiftieth anniversary party given
    by friends (ages seventy-four and sixty-four)

Postscript

The interviews with Josh and Andy were conducted early in 1978. In July, 1980, I traveled to Miami on family business, and while there I decided to visit Josh and Andy to learn what had transpired in their lives during the intervening two years.

Early in February, 1979, Josh began to lose weight. Andy insisted that Josh go for his check-up earlier than scheduled. Josh resisted because he feared the doctor would first hospitalize him and then put him into a nursing home. But Andy said, "Don't you know that as long as I'm alive I'll take care of you?" Josh went for the examination and the tests showed he had cancer in his liver. Given Josh's age and physical condition, no treatment was recommended.

> Josh always wanted to say something to me. You could see him sitting there with his head forward, like he wanted you to know something. Well, one night he looked like he wanted to say something—and then he just said, "I love you." We both had a good cry.

On the evening of March 17, 1979, Josh died quietly in his sleep. During the three weeks he was back from the hospital, Josh never complained of pain, and he remained in good spirits. He even joked about wanting Andy to spread the ashes from his cremation on the Sixth Street beach [the formerly gay beach].

The ashes from Josh's cremation remain in the house, contained in a small box covered with wrapping paper. Every day

Andy talks to Josh, and cries. Even as Andy was telling me the story of Josh's death and his own current life, tears flooded his eyes, and I could easily see that a part of Andy had died as well. But not the love; that was still there.

Just a few weeks before, Andy visited New York City where he and Josh had spent so many vacations together. Andy stayed at the same hotel and walked the same streets that he and Josh had walked so many times together; Fifth Avenue, the park near The Plaza Hotel, and the streets of Greenwich Village.

> But I kept thinking about Josh and that he should be here. It wasn't good for me walking alone.

Friends still help. Andy can visit friends in cities across the country. But travel can't remove the feeling of profound loss after the death of his lover of fifty-one years.

> I have a relative who has been married four times. She doesn't know what love is. People like that—they don't know what love is about. Josh and I knew.

CHAPTER THIRTEEN

Conclusions
and Speculations

This study of gay love relationships began with five goals: to examine the major themes in gay male relationships; to examine the father/son relationship and how it may affect later life; to hypothesize how the coming-out experience may shed light on the origin of homosexuality; what the effects of early sexual and emotional experiences may be on the choice of lovers; and, finally, to examine the geographical diversity of gay life in the United States.

The following chapter represents the results of this study. Some of the conclusions are based firmly on the data collected, while others are drawn from observation and my own thoughts—looser statements as a result of the limited information gathered, problems of sampling, and the techniques used in gathering the information. Some of the speculations are based on interpretation, and certain readers may disagree with them. Some researchers believe that a study of this nature should stay close to the data, should be atheoretical and maintain a fierce objectivity in the presentation and collection of data. That style of investigation and reporting has not been chosen here. My purpose has been to highlight the fluidity of love relationships, not to freeze the moment as tightly controlled research does so well. In an area of investigation like homosexuality in which knowledge is limited, an important contribution is made by raising new questions, or by looking at old ones in a different way, and thus generating a set of testable hypotheses for future research.

Whenever a study illuminates an area of interest, the results will suggest a number of hypotheses that can be confirmed or rejected in future research. In no area of research can one person or team have the last word. We all stand on the shoulders of those who went before us and perhaps see a bit higher than our teachers.

There are sure to be faults found in this work. Some of them might as well be mentioned here. In the matter of family relationships, the mothers of gay men have been ignored completely. Whether they conform to the overprotective label claimed so often by psychoanalytic literature could not be ascertained on the basis of this sample of 190 men. No reasonable researcher could possibly claim that mothers are unimportant in teaching their male children, gay or straight, about the meaning and demonstration of love. But there was neither the time nor the resources needed to complete a study of the mother's influence on her children and how her relationship to her husband creates a model for gays to emulate or reject in their own search for love.

There will surely be questions about the sample chosen for study. By and large, the men interviewed for this book were all well-educated white men, almost all professionals or businessmen. The few blacks interviewed belonged in the same class. Nor was there a good sample of other ethnic minorities. These criticisms are obvious. There were also other kinds of gay men I tried unsuccessfully to interview. Since some anthropologists have claimed that American Indians are accepting of homosexuality, I tried to interview native Americans and their lovers. But even the few who agreed to be interviewed either canceled their appointments or just didn't appear. I had hoped to interview blind and deaf gays and their lovers, but problems of time and other responsibilities made it impossible to meet with them. There is little written here about the love relationships of previously and currently married gay men or the effects on their children if they live with their gay fathers and their lovers. These are certainly legitimate areas of discussion. The lives of transvestites and transsexuals in love relationships have been ignored, so, too, those in S and M relationships.

There is no end to the permutations of gay life. My greatest problem of the past two years in collecting and analyzing the material has been to prevent this work from becoming encyclopedic and taking a decade to finish. Of necessity, one person with a tape recorder and a part-time secretary can do only a portion of the work. Fortunately, others may continue the research halted here.

It is in spite of these qualifications that the following conclusions and speculations are offered.

Gay Sons and Their Fathers

The frequency with which sexual fantasies of the father appeared in the men interviewed was surprising since this is not a subject discussed in the gay press or in previous studies of family relationships of gay men. One wonders why. The following theory is proposed as significant for the development of gay men.

One can conceptualize the sexual fantasies of a gay son toward his father as a mirror image of Freud's Oedipus complex, in which the son desires sexual union with his mother. This psychoanalytic notion (still unproven) is based on the Greek myth of Oedipus, who unknowingly killed his own father and married a woman who turned out to be his mother. For violating the taboo of incest, Oedipus blinded himself. Most people know this much. More interesting for gay men is the account in Greek mythology of Laius, Oedipus' father, who was the "inventor" of homosexuality, the first mortal homosexual (in contrast to the Greek gods whose pansexualism defies categories).* In keeping with the tradition of Greek mythological analogies for family constellations, I suggest the notion of a Laius complex to typify the relationship between a father and his homosexual to-be son. The concept of a Laius complex is a metaphor that provides us with a convenient label for a complex relationship.

This complex represents the unconsummated love between a father and his gay son. It is comprised of the experience of feeling rejected by a father and seeing the father love another (usually the mother and/or a sibling). It also includes the father's denial of physical contact, both rough and sensuous, with the son. And finally it is, at least for some gay boys, a rejection of the son as a sexual suitor. The boy wants his father to love him,

* In fact, Euripides wrote a play based on the myth of Chrysippus, in which Laius, king of Thebes, was so overcome by the beauty of Chrysippus, son of Pelops, that he carried him off. In other words, while Laius had no sexual attachment to his own son (Oedipus, prince of Thebes), he carried off the son of another king. The parallel is interesting. Laius first appears in *Oedipus Rex* by Sophocles (430 B.C.), and later in a Roman version by Seneca called *Oedipus*.

care for him, and teach him about the world. Since the father is usually the first sexually mature man the son perceives, the boy is likely to develop a variety of fantasies about him that may be described on a continuum from tender and touching to pornographic. I view this initial attraction to the father as a stage or way station on the path to adult love. Up to now this idea has been obscured and blocked by the unthinkable combination of incest and homosexuality.

Both love and sex are legitimate needs of the young boy, and these needs first develop within the family. It is only later that tney are directed outward. In the past we have allowed ourselves to consider only love as a genuine need, having feared our sexual strivings. Parents have been overburdened by the fear of sexuality toward their children, and fathers particularly have had to learn new ways to touch their maturing daughters, lest they cross the boundary between affection and desire. The desire to touch their sons sexually has been suppressed even more rigorously. This suppression of sexual feelings in the family constantly replenishes the army of boys seeking physical and emotional love from other older men instead. We are accustomed to accept that most fathers, after their sons reach puberty, avoid touching the boys because this contact violates masculine behavior: men shake hands, rather than kiss. While this is likely, there may be a second reason. Physical contact between father and son may be diminished because of the possibility that tenderness may lead to sex. And there is no reason to assume that it will always be the father who terminates the physical tenderness; it is just as likely to be the son.

Recognizing the sexual needs of a gay son does not mean turning the family into an orgy with generational lines dissolved and sons competing with mothers in bed. But today it is impossible to define clearly the parameters of sexual/sensual contact between father and son because the very subject strikes terror. We imagine a family going awry, gay sons sleeping with fathers and straight ones with mothers—husband and wife finding each other only from time to time. Such a nightmare is just an indication of our discomfort with sexual ideas. One can only speculate why the subject of father/son sex is so anxiety provoking. It immediately suggests the possibility of a host of dirty jokes— such as a father yelling at his teenage son, "If you don't turn

down that mindless disco music, you don't get a blow job to-
night!" But such a satirical joke may be just the point. Sexual
and emotional contact between the father and the son breaks
down the power of one generation to control the other; sex
between these two generations may lead to egalitarianism in the
family which violates the historical role of family structure.

It is likely that much of the sexual interest of gay sons toward
their fathers is a fantasy of caring, and once that is satisfied,
the gay boy can move on with the job of meeting other men
who are potential adult lovers. Perhaps the sexual fantasies
themselves are only a cover-up for the wish to be loved and
cared for. For many men, sexual fantasies are easier to experience than tender ones.

Few men have actually had sex with their fathers. It is not
common, as is father/daughter sex. Explaining these fantasies
of gay men presents difficulties. Sometimes they express the desire to worship the father's penis as a source of warmth and
love; at other times the fantasy appears to represent a wish to
share the power symbolized by the possession of a phallus. Or
it is simply the desire to have sex, and the father appears available. The unresolved sexual fantasies of gay men toward their
fathers frequently result in a phantom father, a sort of ghost
who haunts any potential lover, creating a distorted picture of
what a gay man expects his lover to be and to do. Some of the
breakups observed in gay love affairs can be attributed to one
lover demanding that the other play two different roles in the
relationship, lover and father. If this occurs, the lover is bound
to feel confused, frustrated, and unappreciated for whatever
assets he brings to the relationship.

Regarding the outcome of an incestuous relationship between
a father and a son, only two examples were found in this study:
Walter had a clearly psychotic father who had a disastrous effect
on the son; the other man, Philip, had a sexual relationship with
his father that has continued for many years, and, according to
the gay man, it was the only real emotional contact between
him and his father. My impression is that if the sexual exploration were acted out with the father in a teaching role (if limited
in time and free from possessiveness), it could be helpful to both
father and son.

But the question arises as to whether this proposed Laius complex is universal in all gay men. As youngsters, did all gay men want to have sex with their fathers but repress the feelings in adulthood? At the moment there is no reliable answer to the question. One might postulate that the relationship between the father and the gay son is very special, indeed, but such a statement could not justify the conclusion that father/son sexual desire is universal among gay men. It is one thing to claim that the father is an important role model for all gay men, but quite another to propose that part of the thesis of emulation is the desire for a sexual relationship. I simply do not know.

This discussion brings to mind some subsidiary questions not studied but necessary to mention. Is the relationship between a straight son and his father as idyllic as had previously been believed? We have always assumed that, since they agree on the definition of masculine behavior and because the son models his behavior on guidelines from the father, they enjoy a comrade-like relationship. The theory is fine, but the facts may turn out otherwise. The similarity of their goals may create tension due to competition. We might find that fathers and straight sons end up with more strife and conflict than do gay sons and their fathers. It would be a worthwhile topic for research.

It may be recalled that some gay boys fantasize about sex with their fathers as a symbol of love and compassion, while others do so exclusively as a sexual thrill. In this area one may speculate whether there is a developmental relationship between these two types of sons and the categories of boys (i.e., "comrades" and "romantics") proposed in Chapter Two. It may be that the son who just wants sex with his father becomes a "school yard comrade," while the one who wants compassion becomes a "romantic." And still later in life, it may be that the excitement-seeking man is an adult version of the "school yard comrade," whereas the home builder develops from the "romantic." Although no perfect correlations could be expected because of intervening life experiences, it is possible that enduring life patterns exist. Only a longitudinal study conducted over years of a subject's life could provide the answer.

There is also some indication from a few sparse anecdotes that fathers of gay sons understand the feelings of their sons, at least the emotional ones. These stories have been told to me in my therapeutic practice, not by the people reported here, but they are pertinent. As adults, some gay men have attempted to establish new relationships with their fathers, and, when successful, the fathers have divulged the knowledge that their gay sons were more attached to them, more reliable in their feelings of love and caring, than were the straight ones. This implies that at least some fathers of gay sons understand that there is something special in their relationship to the gay son. This may not be universal, but it, too, is a part of what needs to be researched further.

Obviously, potential father/son sexual contact is not the only reason for faulty family communication. Sibling rivalry, alcoholism, workaholism, neurotic interaction between parents—all contribute to a wealth of potential problems within the family. These have been excluded here because they are not specifically gay issues.

The Origin of Homosexuality

When asked of their first awareness of homosexuality, gay men responded with a wide range of ages from preschool (even the sandbox) to the mid-twenties. It is easy to demonstrate that the awareness that came late in life was the result of sexual repression. The early memories, however, are more interesting. Quite a few men claimed that they always knew they were gay, were always interested in men: many of them recounted convincing stories of energy expended seeking out and playing with other boys and men. Most of them also remember not being fully aware of exactly what physical acts were possible; hence, the experiences are vague and unfocused. Desire was present but planned action impossible.

These reports suggest that homosexuality may have its origin outside of family communication patterns and be impervious to learning or modeling. Whether inheritance or some combination of hormonal variables during gestation is a factor is impossible to ascertain or even to suggest, given the data of this study. But neither should be discounted completely. It is possible that a complicated set of interactions is required between physiological processes and perceptual experiences to produce a predisposition toward same-sex stimuli.* Some kind of "trigger mechanism" would then be necessary so that the perceptual experience (seeing an attractive man) in the environment gets transmitted to the brain as sexual. The brain then creates the physiological responses that we identify as sexual interest.

Hypothesizing that an important human trait like sexual orientation may be present at birth or shortly thereafter is uncomfortable to many people. It is fashionable in the twentieth century to believe that free will and opportunity are available to all. Fashion may be misleading; there may be limitations to the empirical view that we can change our behavior on the basis of various kinds of learning. Certain behavior may not be amenable to change, or only in limited ways.

The reader should note, however, that the suggestion that homosexuality may be present at birth or shortly thereafter is a statement about the direction of sexual orientation. This direction leads to a sexual and emotional interest in people of the same sex. It implies nothing about how one deals with one's sexual interest, how one chooses a lover, or what kinds of sexual experiences will be preferred. All these would certainly depend upon other factors such as family relationships and social norms. It should also be noted that there are many profound variables influencing the infant, including inheritance, hormonal forces before and after birth, and the maturation of the nervous system. It is not a simple process.

If homosexuality is an early characteristic, then the relationship between father and son is extremely crucial, and our notion of family interaction must be changed accordingly. We have always assumed, for instance, that all sons and all daughters need the same kind of caring and love from both their parents. This may not be true. A predisposed homosexual son will perceive and have physical and emotional needs toward his father qualitatively different from those of the straight son. Under these circumstances, the father becomes special for the gay son in a way neither the father nor any of his straight sons can understand.

At the moment, there is no way to substantiate or refute this hypothesis. We simply do not have the research skills to identify

* Suggesting that some process is a predisposition is not an explanation. Whenever we use "predisposition," we are suggesting that we need to learn more about how something happens.

the origin of homosexuality. While various forms of learning theories have been heavily advertised in the twentieth century, they, too, have been resistant to proof. We have only theories that can not be documented. The current liberal view that homosexuality is a "choice" seems to this writer to be politically motivated, but without substantiation. People experience sexuality as an unfolding process, not as an equally divided set of alternatives.

The Effects of Early Experience on Gay Love

Early experiences in sex and love can influence later success in love. The perception of the self as either wholesome or sinful has also been discussed in relationship to religion. Boyhood exploits with peers are certainly a significant indicator of later love relationships. Those who had the opportunity to develop love affairs with other boys appear to continue these relationships in adult life, and most often with great success. Others have had introductions to gay life through kindly adults who acted as sexual guides.

There is one aspect of early experience that should be mentioned here. It is the self-hatred of some gay men, what has been fashionable these days to call "homophobia." It most often begins during the childhood years and continues into adulthood. One of the most consistent statements made by some of the men interviewed for this book is their powerful belief that homosexuality is sinful and wrong. But if we examine their testimony closely, we find that their self-hatred as homosexuals is the surface expression of a more comprehensive problem—profound personal guilt as a sexual being. That is what makes them suffer. These men, upset by their sexual desires for other men, are not at all comfortable with the idea of heterosexuality. It is obvious that if these men had been heterosexual, they would be just as mangled in their heterosexuality, just as chained to and frightened of women as they are of men. This is one of the reasons why the current treatments (cures) for homosexuality fail so consistently. These men are being taught to respond sexually to women, when fear makes them incapable of responding sexually at all. Inhibition of sexual feelings is taught in childhood. In consequence, all future sexual behavior is curtailed. It is impossible for parents to inhibit one form of sexual expression without inhibiting all feelings of sexual pleasure. Childhood inhibitions can show up in related ways. One is the repression of sexual feelings. Another is the allowance of sexual feelings, but only toward one class of men, usually those who maintain a proper masculine appearance. This depiction of men as either "butch" or "femme" may be fading, but it is still used as a criterion for choosing a lover. It is not just an aspect of old-time role playing but fear of being seen in public with the wrong kind of person, and hence, being identified as homosexual.

Man/Teenager Love

No rational reason could be found in this study for the frequent condemnation of man/teenager love. Adults most often condemn man/teenager sexuality on the basis of exploitation, but exactly what is meant by exploitation is unclear. Certainly there are some exploitative people, adults and teenagers, and both physical and psychological damage caused by exploitation can be documented. But nonexploitative relationships between adults and teenagers also occur in which both parties benefit from the arrangement. One argument used by many adults, including gay men, is that the difference in ages creates a power differential, with the adult man controlling all aspects of the relationship. The adult has more money, more experience in the world, and a reasonably stable life—all of which can be used to force or manipulate the youngster to the adult's wishes. But this ignores the fact that the teenager has some assets of his own, such as his youth, his looks, and the freedom of his body. Since the youth was chosen by the adult man for these assets, they may carry as much power in a relationship as a big bank account.

There is certainly a variety of relationships possible between adults and teenagers. Some are only sexual contracts in which neither party feigns love. In other relationships, love is an important feature. Some are transient affairs that end quickly, and others last a lifetime. What is most apparent from this study is that age-disparate love affairs are as diverse as age-comparable affairs. By no means can we assume that age differences give us any reliable information about the quality of the relationship.

A number of the men interviewed had been runaways during

their teen years. They lived in the homes of gay men (sometimes with, sometimes without sex). Though behaving like gangsters in their own homes, they were almost always reasonable and compliant in the presence of an adult gay man. Many accounts have been given of the adult man persuading the boy back into school and helping him to plan for his future. If this were a more reasonable society, we would rehabilitate gay runaways in the homes of adult gay men who are willing to spend the time and energy (and money) caring for them. Some gay teenagers fare better this way than by "working the streets" or allowing chance meetings to determine a benefactor. Such a program could be administered by the same social agencies that currently take runaway gay teenagers and place them in poorly run youth shelters. Those who object to such an arrangement might wonder whether their objection is based on concern for the welfare of the youngsters or upon imposing a rigid value system. Many gay couples desire to raise a child, so appropriate homes could be found.

Geographical Differences

Geographical differences influence the lives of gay men. The differences in life-styles are most apparent when examining the lives of gay men in America's largest cities and comparing them with life-styles in rural areas and small- to medium-sized cities. By and large, men who live in large cities with visible gay communities come out earlier than men from smaller communities. Adolescent and preadolescent boys from rural communities and small towns have just as many sexual experiences as sophisticated city boys (in some cases, they have far more male-to-male sexual contact), but often in the guise of sexual playfulness and childhood games, and often with the knowledge of parents who interpret such behavior as part of the growing process. It is all expected to end after adolescence and to be replaced with sexual interest in women, and this seems to be exactly what happens. This sexual playfulness is not interpreted as homosexual by at least some of the boys who will become adult homosexuals, nor by their heterosexual playmates.

Repression of the homosexual identity appears more successful in the boondocks of America and in many of the small- to medium-sized cities of the South, the Southwest, and Midwest. Especially in the heartland of America, it's possible for men to reach age twenty or more before becoming aware of their homosexual needs; this is quite different from the case in larger cities in which some men make a *decision* to suppress and refuse their homosexuality. Men who have married without knowing they were gay live everywhere, but are probably less prevalent in the largest cities than elsewhere.

It is not possible to conclude with any degree of certainty how the lives of married gays differ in various parts of the country. Those who volunteered to participate in this study were already a part of the gay community, and they always referred to the number of married gay men in their local area, but since such men dread exposure I had no chance to interview them. In some cases, particularly in the sparsely populated states in the northern Midwest, volunteers reported that most of the married gay men they knew lived without gay sex at all. It remains somewhat mysterious as to how the respondents knew these men were gay. Secrecy for married gay men in large cities is as stressed as it is in the heartland, but with one difference: larger cities allow the married men the opportunity to come out into the gay community with discretion. An additional advantage for married gay men in the city over those in the country is the rise of married men's networks, an urban system that has become more available in the past few years. Such networks—in which one married gay man knows and meets another married gay man—have always been an informal element of life in cities such as New York and Los Angeles, but now we find them springing up not only in smaller cities on both coasts but in a couple of midwestern cities as well. These groups serve a variety of needs: social, emotional, and sexual experiences are provided. No doubt the spread of married men's networks will bring many changes to the gay movement and the perception of marriage in the gay community. Those married men who continue to live in out-of-the-way rural communities have little chance to participate in these groups; hence, we have every reason to believe that these men are not able to see any of the advantages of being gay.

Hustlers in one midwestern city reported that their clientele was comprised exclusively of married men who were uptight.

commanding in their requests, and not at all at ease in the situation; they also reported a fear of disclosure and the necessity to conceal identity. However, we should view all of these comments about married gay men in the boondocks as gross speculation, since only hearsay is reported. Pending direct investigation, we won't know how married gay men perceive themselves or what kind of lives they live.

Religion is a different phenomenon in the heartland than in the coastal cities; once again the differences are glaring. Without considerable time spent in religiously oriented communities, it is impossible to appreciate how effectively religion can blanket the lives of a population. Gays in the large coastal cities are accustomed to heterogeneity, the spectrum of ethnic, national, and religious groups. In a place like New York City, comparative religion could be learned by walking the streets of a few neighborhoods; a three-day weekend of attending services could take the student to Moslem mosques on Friday, Jewish synagogues on Saturday, and Catholic churches on Sunday, let alone Protestant, Russian Orthodox, and Greek Orthodox churches, and even a bevy of fundamentalist groups. Cathedrals, churches, storefronts—every possible physical structure would be encountered, as well as differences in cultural pursuits and social participation.

Not so in the heartland of America, where a particular church, frequently Baptist (of some variety) or Gospel, can approach the power of a state church. Though diversity is growing, it has been a slower process in the heartland, and the unified, unquestioned power of a local church has wielded a pernicious influence over the lives of gay men.

Walking through the streets of one midwestern city, I was impressed with the advertisements of many churches, all rivals in claiming which was the most fundamentalist. Midwesterners do not take their religion lightly, nor do these fundamentalist groups take homosexuality lightly; it is condemned with great vigor at all times. But the attack of fundamentalist groups goes much further than just condemning sexual contact between people of the same sex. The more primitive religions still so powerful in the heartland of America are after bigger game than homosexuality. They assault all forms of premarital and non-reproductive sex, as well as homosexuality. Sex is not yet an idea

whose time has come in the heartland, as it is in the freewheeling
East and West. The churches teach generalized guilt concerning
all feelings of sexuality; the body is so holy that touching it becomes a sin. The force of religion and the lack of alternatives
in the heartland have unquestionably prevented many gay men
from experiencing their homosexuality and in some cases prevented them from awareness of it until later years. Obviously,
guilt about homosexuality runs very deep in these areas, and a
new social service provided by the church is the cure of homosexuality in Christians, with many claims to successful "con-
version." *

Yet even the condemnation of sex is not the basis of the conflict between primitive religious groups and homosexuality. The
fundamentalists insist that all members of the religious community subordinate their personal feelings and goals to those of the
group—individuals share the love of Jesus, and the rules for loving are laid down by the church elders. Homosexuality respects
individual rights and identifies with personal goals. Therefore, being gay is not only a violation of theology (as fundamentalists see it), but an attack on the power of social control
in the community. Those who fail to recognize this group-versus-

* In 1977 I was doing a national publicity tour for my book, *A Family Matter: A Parent's Guide to Homosexuality* (McGraw-Hill).
During my stay in Houston, I found myself in the offices of a Baptist
radio station, about to be interviewed (without warning from my
publisher) by a friend of Anita Bryant. She refused to tape the interview without asking me a few questions beforehand. I consented,
believing it would be the shortest interview in the station's history.
Her first question was, "Do you believe in the family?" That was an
easy one to answer, especially so because of its ambiguity. "Yes," I
said. The second question was more pointed. "Do you think children
should come out?" As she said that, a commercial came on the air,
an advertisement for Jesus, and I decided to say it straight, so to
speak. "Yes," I said, "I believe that children should come out." She
smiled with great relief, relaxed her previously suspicious attitude,
and invited me, in all my confusion at her response, into the studio
to tape the interview. It was only after we were in the studio discussing "coming out" for a while that I realized that our readings of
"coming out" were totally different. She meant "coming out for
Jesus," while "coming out" for easterners could only mean coming
out of the closet. No midwestern fundamentalist would have made
my mistake. No, I didn't inform her of the confusion in terminology.

individual conflict will miss seeing the fear of homosexuality in fundamentalist churches for what it is and accordingly have less compassion for gays raised in those communities.

Homosexuality among the clergy appears to be no more or less prevalent in the heartland than in the big cities. There are as many reports of gay men seduced by clergymen in small communities as in the big cities, so the hypocrisy of the church appears evenly distributed throughout the country. The preacher from groups such as the Pentecostal Church, the Church of Christ, or the Church of God might have sex with a member of the congregation and then preach against sexual sins on Sunday and be the most homophobic force in town. Naturally enough, some gay men are angry at being seduced by a clergyman one day and preached against the next. But there are other gay men who seem unaware of the contradiction, or at least don't appear bothered by it. They would be worthy of further study.

Gays in large cities generally believe that leading gay lives in the hinterland is impossible, that only the freedom of the large city can bring peace and happiness. This turns out to be a myth. Even in the rural "Bible Belt" one finds large numbers of gay couples who have lived there voluntarily all their lives and prefer it to the frenetic pace and impersonality of cities. They do not view their lives as limited, although this is primarily true of couples rather than single gays who feel lonelier in sparsely populated regions than do couples. "Shake the trees and they'll come dropping out," is the way one man expressed how many gay couples live comfortably in the Southwest and Midwest. He was absolutely right. Gay couples live in every imaginable area of the country, have always lived there, and are drawing others to join them.

As a rule, these couples are made up of partners who have been born and raised in small towns or rural areas and who prefer the slowness of local life to the confusion of large cities, put off by coldness, demands of professional competition, and urban excitement. They do not want to live in places like New York, Chicago, or San Francisco. The very idea frightens them. They hear about city activities ("Is there really such a thing called 'fist fucking' in New York?" asked one college student in the Midwest. "And do gays wear leather?") and wonder why people dance all night at discos and use drugs. They have very little interest in such activities; many have never been to a disco, nor do they want to go. Younger couples will be more adventurous, seeking some of the opportunities of the exciting city. But most prefer to return home afterwards and relax.

On the whole, gays in a community tend to be very similar to straights in the community. While many coastal and large city gays are indeed dancing all night, rural gays are cooking supper and going to sleep early; while city gays visit back rooms seeking variety in sex, rural couples seem interested in only one man —the lover. While some city gays claim never to be able to find another man to love, others in the heartland are celebrating silver anniversaries. Of course, this can be attributed in part to the difference between being single and being part of a couple. Generally, having a lover gives the rural and small-town gay man greater status than in the large cities, and rural gays put a high premium on long-lasting relationships. Couples outside of large city life don't view their lives as oppressive, nor do they spend much energy fighting the established community order. What discrimination may exist against these gays, they find manageable and tolerable.

Many eastern gays have a picture of midwestern and farm family life as tight-knit and loving, while perceiving their own families as cold, with noticeably high divorce rates. This turned out to be false. For instance, there is a staggering amount of alcoholism in the heartland, and alcoholics do not make loving parents. Of course, large-city gays are not immune to alcoholism in the family, but nowhere in large cities have I observed it as commonly as in some midwestern areas. In one northern midwestern town I visited, every single gay man interviewed had at least one alcoholic in his immediate family, and frequently both parents were alcoholics. Violence, or the potential for violence, was always a fear haunting their childhood.

Coming out to parents appears to be more difficult in the heartland. Parents tend to be conservative, like their neighbors. The smaller and more homogeneous the community, the more difficult it is for a gay person to establish his identity personally and publicly. The heterogeneity of the large coastal cities makes coming out considerably easier. A lack of gay support groups also makes the coming-out process difficult, although in recent years more gay organizations have appeared in the heartland.

Then there is the question of sexual opportunity. Much depends on where the gay person lives, especially the young gay who is not ready to settle down yet. There are areas of the country where gay visibility is so limited that even the most sexually motivated man or youth has few opportunities to meet other gay men. City gays can't possibly appreciate what it means to have to drive two or three hundred miles to a gay bar. It was not at all uncommon to find men driving such distances to spend a weekend in some city where there were a couple of gay bars and a bath. In one town I visited, it was the custom to drive six hundred miles to have sex. How different this is from a place like New York City, where people can cruise in their building elevators! Since a certain amount of anonymity is required for many men to lead a comfortable sex life, too few sexual choices in a town may motivate gays to drive to faraway large cities because of fear of gossip in their hometowns. By and large, it is difficult to be single, but often delightful to be a couple, in the hinterland. Therefore, most couples remain together, but many singles migrate to the large cities.

Sexuality in Gay Men

Gay men have a reputation for sexual virtuosity. This belongs in the category of a stereotyped and feared group. During the Nazi period in Germany, for instance, Jewish men were described as sexually powerful and the Aryan women in danger of being seduced by them. Here in America, black men still are similarly described. The attribution of sexual prowess appears frequently in stereotypes. While the attribution of unusual sexual abilities is obviously false, there is no doubt that the sex lives of some gay men are, to the heterosexual world, a wonder to behold. There are some gay men who can justly claim to have had sex with thousands of partners in their lifetimes. To the straight world, to many lesbians, and to some gay men, this is a perfect example of the "promiscuity" of the homosexual male—the stereotype of insatiable lust among gay men.

The respondents who volunteered for this study spent a high proportion of their time discussing their experiences and feelings about sexuality to the exclusion of other interests; this was no less true of men who were together for many years than of those still in the romantic period of a relationship.

There is no question in my mind (although others may disagree) that male homosexuality is predominantly a phenomenon of masculinity, that lesbianism is predominantly a phenomenon of femininity. Male gays are first and foremost men; they act like men and feel like men, and this is particularly true with regard to their sexual inclinations. In a sense, I am suggesting that straight men and gay men are far more similar than they are dissimilar when it comes to sexual behavior and attitudes toward sex. Similarly, lesbians are first and foremost women and only secondarily gay. The male's attitude toward sexual feelings and his behavior toward his sexual partner are very much expressions of both the male psyche and the historical role of masculinity in society.

One style of masculine behavior prominent on the gay scene in certain cities I have called cult masculinity. This refers to the traditional symbols of male aggression institutionalized throughout history, symbols that represent power and competition expressed through sexual deeds. I have described the "cock ring" as a fetish, worshiped by some gay men as dutifully as by some of our masculine ancestors who built large statues of the phallus as part of their religious rites. Many of the "butch" accoutrements, the ultra-masculine attire fashionable in the coastal cities, and the almost hysterical use of drugs seem to me to be part of the image of cult masculinity that represents power and sex as a ritual, rather than physical pleasure.*

I view cult masculinity as an antisexual movement, even though outwardly it praises and glories in sexual abandon. It is not the frequency with which cult masculinity adherents change partners that is the issue, but whether the needs being satisfied are physical or symbolic. My interpretation is that they are symbolic and therefore neither pleasurable nor sexual. Cult masculinity does not appear possible without building an environment, a fantasy world where the symbols of masculinity hide real sexual needs, where power, coldness, and competition replace physical sensuousness. I see this symbolization as antithetical to sexual pleasure and certainly to the acceptance of a love relationship, except of the briefest variety. Men who identify with cult masculinity could hardly establish a relationship with a competitor.

* Men who dress this way have been labeled "clones" by the gay press—an apt description.

The excessive use of drugs appears to be the price that cult masculinity men must pay to maintain a personality facade that denies them the option of expressing a broad range of emotions. It is in the nature of some mind-altering drugs to narrow the focus of experience to internal feelings to the exclusion of the other person—sometimes to the point that the other man is almost superfluous. The overuse of drugs anesthetizes the feelings of discomfort and depression that would surface without drug-taking. But ultimately habitual drug-taking over time inhibits the ability to respond sexually in many men so that both social communication and sexual pleasure are minimized. The late hours in which these dramas take place guarantee that fatigue will inhibit genuine emotional contact.

Two qualifications should be noted. In the first place, the term cult masculinity is not used here synonymously with S and M. While S and M is certainly a role-playing phenomenon that employs symbols, it is not necessarily an expression of cult masculinity. There are enough examples of S and M couples who display the full range of emotions toward each other to suggest that it is a different phenomenon from cult masculinity. Secondly, many find that some drug taking, mostly use of pot, is a sexual aid. Where drugs play the role of tuning a person to his feelings and to his partner's, the drugs serve a positive purpose. When I suggest that followers of cult masculinity use drugs excessively, I mean that drugs are used for the purpose of interfering with communication with a partner in order to maintain a fantasy of himself, and/or the other man.

But cult masculinity should not be confused with the observation that men are highly motivated sexually. They think about sex and fantasize about it constantly; they dream it and want as many experiences as possible, and they never seem to lose hope. One important characteristic of male sexuality is the speed with which men can become excited and how soon afterward, especially when presented with a new source of aesthetic wonder, they dream of more. Men seem to like variety and change, enjoy the opportunity for moments of tenderness as well as rough sexual play with an unknown person without the desire to continue into an emotional relationship. Experienced men are exceptionally competent in distinguishing between the act of sex and the commitment of love. This is apparent in the institution of "fuck buddies," very much a part of the big city scene, in which two men get together occasionally to use each other as sex objects (though such "objectification" is deplored by many gay liberationists and feminists).

There has been much written about people using each other as sexual objects. Most men adore being sex objects; they like the idea of using each other's bodies as objects of physical pleasure on a temporary basis and have no difficulty separating this from their needs for love. Sometimes it is the purest kind of lustful sex, even reaching some degree of "kinkiness," still thought weird and foreign in many areas of the country. At other times, nurturance and comfort are part of the sex play, sometimes with little sex but much warmth and human generosity—but not love. These actions seem to be legitimate ways for men to express their physical sexual needs, ways not symbolic of power and competition. To suggest that there is anything intrinsically bad about free and frequent expression with only the goal of the utmost physical pleasure seems to be once again a historic fear of and anger at human sexuality.

On the basis of the interviews and my experience as a clinical psychologist, I am constantly impressed with the degree to which men are motivated sexually. The quality of many of their sexual experiences suggests that physical sexuality in its usual and mundane forms holds only limited interest for them, at most only temporary. A brief list of what arouses a significant number of men—both gay and straight—in order from the merely "kinky" to the frankly esoteric—might include the following:

Dirty phone callers—Here two men who do not and never will see each other masturbate while trading outrageous stories over the telephone.

Fist fucking—Included here is not only the currently chic hand-to-elbow insertion, but also the plethora of other objects inserted into the rectum, such as light bulbs, candles, dildoes of heroic proportions, coke bottles, and, in one medical article I read, an empty cold cream jar with a lemon inside!

Tearoom sex—Sex in public toilets is subject to interruption by men who merely wish to use the room for its intended purposes, and entrapment by police or blackmail, or both, have occurred.

Danger freaks—These are men who seek sexual exploits with

men who appear to be and frequently are dangerous. Beatings, rapes, and murders have occurred.

Eroticized hanging—In this peculiar and fortunately atypical form of self-stimulation, the person literally hangs himself to orgasm and then releases the rope so that he doesn't actually suffocate—he hopes!

The list could continue with descriptions of jerk-off buddies, the use of fetishes, bondage and humiliation, the varieties of S and M, exhibitionism and voyeurism, sexual orgies, obsession with hair or the lack of it (or any other physical characteristic), "size queens," use of enemas, fantasized violence during sex, "dirty talk," use of hustlers, "water sports," scatology, and on and on.*

My impression, based on this sample of 190 men and my experience as a therapist for both gay and straight men, is that men experience sexuality as the combination of two (perhaps) independent drives. The first is physical genital satisfaction—the enjoyment a man receives by the stimulation of his genitals and skin. Sexual arousal and orgasm are descriptive of sexual pleasure. The second drive is a need, possibly physiological, for *excitement* that is qualitatively different from sexual arousal. It is the desire to burn, as Walter Pater, the English critic, said, with a hard, gemlike flame. The need for excitement shows up quite early and continues far into adult maturity. It is observed in the thrill of competition, the challenge against adversity, and the energy-releasing effect of danger. It is also a desired component previous to and during sex. The four situations all contain the same element of excitement, but each is attached to a different activity.

There is something very pleasurable about the production of excitement in a man; it may have something to do with the physiological changes that occur in the body: quickening of the heart rate, changes in breathing patterns, and the flow of hormones into the system. I also speculate that men vary in

* I am aware that many gay men, particularly those from small and isolated towns in the Midwest, will claim uninterest in these activities, commenting that only weird city gays in places like New York and San Francisco participate in these sexual practices. The fact is, most gay men from rural areas look forward to coming to the big cities "just to look" and end up by bringing back home some new ideas and the latest diseases.

physical excitement, some men want it often, while others are more frugal in their demands. This variation in excitement motivation suggests that there is an optimum level of excitement for different men and that any production of physiological excitement above the optimal level is experienced as painful, while any below it as tedious. The combination of these two drives—genital release and excitement motivation—will determine whether a man views any particular sexual experience as "hot sex" or "cold comfort." *

A number of hypotheses immediately come to mind. The first is a comparison between sexuality in men and sexuality in women. From the speculation that sexuality is a combination of physiological excitement and genitality, I might hypothesize that men emphasize excitement over sexuality, while women do the opposite. This proposition would go a long way to explain the inability of men and women to understand each other's sexual desires. I might also hypothesize that the typology of excitement seekers and home builders in my sample of gay men is an example of the diversity of the need for excitement in men, and that therefore one would expect a statistical curve for excitement within both sexes, perhaps with overlaps between the groups.†

Postulating a need for physiological excitement in men that is significantly greater than it is in women also suggests why men, in couples or alone, are so demanding about the opportunity for outside sexual experiences. I would suggest that a major

---

* There is no reason to believe that straight men are uninterested in these activities and much evidence that they are jealous of the sexual freedom of gay men. All of the sexual activities and speculations about the need for excitement should be as applicable to straight as well as gay men.

† Critics may suggest that what I call physiological excitement may be merely an example of social conditioning. Gagnon and Simon (*Sexual Conduct: The Social Sources of Human Sexuality*) suggest that children learn "sexual scripts" that are enduring through life and that these scripts include concepts of gender identity and all aspects of sexual behavior. This position is totally devoted toward a social learning approach. I differ with them only insofar as I believe that sexual scripts take over only after certain physiological demands are made on the individual. The impulse toward behavior seems to me *partly* a physical process, after which scripting directs the person toward appropriate (to him) action.

ingredient of the sexual affair is the excitement of the search, the chase and the catch, as apart from the actual physical satisfaction from two men lying together. While some men may seek outside sexual contacts because of problems in their relationships, others may have good sexual relationships but lack the optimum excitement necessary for complete fulfillment.

A reasonable critic may wonder how this hypothesis of excitement motivation relates to the idea of cult masculinity. I have described cult masculinity as an antisexual attitude emphasizing power and competition. But excitement, as described above, sounds as if it leads ultimately to cult masculinity. Is there a genuine difference between the two, or is the idea of cult masculinity merely my prejudice?

I think that cult masculinity is excitement motivation gone awry. The need for excitement overcomes the need for sensual and genital pleasure. I suggest that some balance is required between excitement and sexuality for the maintenance of a love affair and perhaps even for transient sexual enjoyment. While most men have a strong need for excitement, they are able to maintain a secondary, though not necessarily equivalent, need for sexual stimulation. Clearly, the greater the demand for excitement in a person, the less love is valued, since love implies intimacy and commitment toward only one person. The independence cherished so much by men may explain why gay men appear to have more difficulties establishing love relationships than lesbians.

One can only wonder about the mechanism that might explain the concept excitement. The differences in physiological sexual response between men and women might be an appropriate place to begin this search. According to the research of Masters and Johnson, men reach a state of physiological arousal rather quickly; this is diminished just as fast after orgasm. Women appear to need more physical stimulation and time to reach a high state of arousal, then remain on a plateau (with the capacity for multiple orgasms), and diminish comparatively slowly after orgasm. In a sense, male sexuality is characterized by peaks and valleys, while female sexuality is a plateau of arousal. The steepness of the peaks and valleys of male sexuality may be related to the physiological measurement of excitement.

If these speculations about excitement motivation in men and women are correct, then our distinction between homosexual and heterosexual may be artificial. As far as sex and love are concerned, there may be no difference between homosexual and heterosexual. The real differentiation may be between male and female, regardless of sexual orientation. Research designed to test these hypotheses would be helpful in determining whether these are quaint ideas or useful categories.

The degree of excitement required by men during sex may help to explain the antagonism between some gay men and some women, both lesbian and straight, who perceive gay male sexuality as cold and loveless. The women's movement sometimes casts itself as a Victorian matron grimacing at the sexual ferocity of the male gay world. The antisexual turn of some forces in the women's movement appears to me as an inability to separate sexual expression in gay men from that of straight men. Frequent, quick, and impersonal sex has always been seen by women as ignorance of women's sexual needs and as a way to subjugate women. Without question, women have been subjected to sexual inferiority. Feminists see pornography as a way for men to express their hatred toward women, and no doubt some straight men do just that. Feminists are also horrified at the idea of adult men sleeping with adolescents, because so many young women have been forced into incestuous scenes with fathers and because of the frequency of rape and the leniency with which our society treats rapists. Some women, including some leading lesbian feminists, condemn gay male sexuality because of its "objectification" and its insistence on the distinction between sex and love. These feminists maintain that sex and love must always be integrated. I would view such a position as antisexual and in this sense similar to the antisexualism of cult masculinity. While cult masculinity adherents replace sexual feelings and responses with the fetish and the symbol, matronly feminists replace it with love and intimacy. Such women would deny us physical pleasure without commitment.

There is a genuine conflict of interest here. While the concerns of the women's movement are understandable given the role of women in society, the meaning of sexual pleasure *be-*

tween men need not be controlled by—or interpreted in the light of—the experience of women *with men.** There is no reason to believe that men's sexual diversity is oppressive to anyone, and gay men should feel free to express themselves sexually with compatible partners. It is also historically quaint to think of male sexuality as "promiscuous," a term that has its origin in heterosexual marriage. Perhaps such moral terminology had a usefulness during previous historical periods, but its use today seems motivated by those who either fear sexuality or are jealous of another's pleasures.

The issue that needs to be reconsidered is the definition of "sexuality." We are used to thinking of sexuality as a unitary response, a thing we do that can be easily investigated and explained. In everyday life we place people in any of three sexual categories: a) they may either be sexually charged (i.e., "horny") or quiescent, b) goal oriented toward some object of our lust, and c) largely in men, stimulated generally by visual perception. But the large variety of words we use to describe the experience of sexuality (genitality, sensuousness, intimacy, affection, lust, romance, love) suggests that people experience different kinds of bodily and psychological needs at different times, perhaps with different experiences mixed together under the rubric of the sexual. There are people who experience their sexual response in the groin, others in the eyes, still others in more diffuse ways (although it probably begins between the ears). Fantasy production, while universal, is more highly developed in some people than in others, and contrary to the popular belief that we want to act out our fantasies in real life, the truth is more complicated. For instance, in the most obvious example, women frequently create pleasurable fantasies of being raped, but would never want it to happen in real life. The sexual fantasy has a life of its own quite aside from our sexual contacts with other people.

The past few pages suggest that our concept of sexuality is a

---

* These disagreements with some recent antisexual currents in the women's movement should not be interpreted as an antagonism to the women's movement as a whole. The gay and women's movements have similar platforms; both are intent on freeing us from historical restraints; the failure of one will be the failure of the other. Still, friends can disagree.

multi-variate response composed of a number of different physical, psychological, and sociological factors that have been thrown into the same brew, probably because of historical reasons. The conflicts of opinion over the definitions of "normal" and "abnormal" sexuality may be, at least in part, an indication that some people are influenced more by one component of sexuality than others who may be influenced by different ones.

There can be no sexual response to our environment (or to one's fantasies) without structures that make physiological responses possible, such as brain functions, hormonal balances, and the peripheral sexual organs. But the capacity to respond is meaningless and aimless without a social structure to shape the development of the person's sexual repertoire. The question is not whether sexuality is a biological given or the result of social conditioning, since it is not *a* response, but rather an amalgamation of a number of different responses, all of which are insufficiently understood at this time.

For instance, most men appear to desire novelty in their sexual experiences, a new face to meet or a new action to take sexually. Interviews with men show that the desire to have sex outside the primary relationship is partly based upon the desire for novelty in sex. This is as true of the most extreme home builder as it is of the gay man who seeks a new partner each day. They differ only by degree. Novelty as a sexual variable, the curiosity of "what he's like," does not seem to me amenable to explanation by either biological, psychological, or sociological forces alone. Only an interaction of these forces can explain novelty as a component of sexuality.

The Gay Male Couple

One of the most frequent myths created by both the heterosexual and gay worlds is that gay lovers don't remain together. It is shocking how many young gay men believe this to be true. It isn't true. In every part of American society there are gay male couples living together in splendid compatibility for very long periods of time. Unfortunately, these couples still maintain very low visibility in the gay world. They aren't to be found in hot discos or late-night bars; they live ordinary existences just like their neighbors, who frequently are unaware that the two nice friendly men who live next door have been lovers for twenty years or more.

The heartbreaks of love celebrated so often in the myth of homosexual love relationships appear to be phenomena of the young and inexperienced, just as in the heterosexual world. Young men more easily mistake the fires of transient passion for lasting love—only to be disappointed later. When time and experience bring clearer perceptions of themselves and other men, better partnerships are made.

There are also different kinds of men. One of the more interesting results of this present study has been the distinction between excitement seekers and home builders, the former placing primary interest on the sexual compatibility of the lovers and the opportunity for frequent outside sexual encounters, while the latter are motivated primarily by the quality of the relationship between lovers and the building of permanence and stability. There is a divergence between the two, and they build different types of relationships, excitement seekers emphasizing the need for personal autonomy and home builders lasting mutuality and intimacy. No doubt few of us are one hundred percent of either, nor do we know whether this personality trait can be modified, and if so to what degree. There may indeed be some men who are both excitement seekers and home motivated, although such a man has not been found in this study.

I have no way of knowing whether this personality typography is stable over time. The evidence from the men interviewed suggests that there is no direct age correlation with excitement seeking and home building. However, it is possible that any individual, over time, may change his goals and styles of behavior. A twenty-year-old excitement seeker, say, may become a home builder at twenty-five and perhaps alternate at various periods in his life. If, after further research, it is determined that the typology is fluid within individuals, then we would look for personal and environmental influences that contributed to the changed styles of relationships. Further research may demonstrate that this typology is reliable and useful; if not, a more reliable typology should be sought.

There is no reason to believe that home builders are more

"healthy" or mature than excitement seekers. Historically we have been a marrying society, and we tend to believe that clipping two men together "until death do us part" is the most "natural" state of bliss, but there is no reason for the gay world to subscribe to this notion. The very concepts of "monogamy" and "promiscuity" appear to be useless in the gay male world, at least as far as indicated by the sample of men interviewed in this study. To be sure, there were a few men who maintained an exclusive sexual relationship with their lovers and felt this to be the only sensible approach to a love relationship. They did so either out of moral conviction or the fear of the "domino theory," in which one outside adventure invariably leads to another until the bond between the lovers collapses. But the fact is, very few couples believed in or maintained an exclusive sexual relationship. By and large, exclusivity was demanded by young lovers still in the romantic stage of their relationship, in which the men were getting to know one another and where problems of possessiveness were most acute. It seldom (but sometimes) lasted a long time.

Differences between lovers over outside affairs are the primary reason for the breakup of a love relationship. But these conflicts often reflect other problems in a relationship, such as jealousy, envy, dependence, and intimacy.

There is no reason to believe that outside sexual encounters are necessarily indicative of trouble in a relationship. They sometimes are, but not always. Gay men need not apologize for this style of couple arrangement, nor should those who prefer exclusive arrangements be made to believe that they are in the minority and somehow strange. Normative behavior should not be viewed as a rule or ideal. Diversity in the gay world has always been one of its strengths, and making rigid new rules to replace rigid old rules is not the way to improve our lives.

Some men are probably happier without a lover. Such men were found in this study. They neither wanted one nor felt lonely without one, which should not imply any kind of inadequacy on their part. Nor was there any evidence that the longevity of a relationship is any indicator of the happiness of the couple, although I rarely found a couple together for more than twenty years who regretted continuing the relationship. By and large older couples were the happiest and most content, but there were some who really didn't like each other too much, just as we find in some heterosexual marriages.

The Future of Gay Couples

It has become customary these days for writers to predict the catastrophe to come—the holocaust of gay people in America, storm troopers descending on all known gays, throwing them into concentration camps and forcing everyone back into the closet. My study of relationships around the country led me to believe otherwise. Gay men and women show more self-esteem than ever before, are more relaxed and participate openly as gays in business, education, and even labor movements. There are more social avenues open to gay people and more support from heterosexual segments of society, including some religious groups.

There are still factions of society who would bury us if they got the chance, people who seem to need to believe that we are agents of the devil and wreckers of family life. Recent nondiscrimination laws were overturned in a variety of communities. Homosexuality is still not considered an alternative by most heterosexuals. The problem may have arisen from our choice to seek changes through legal means. This has never worked for minorities, and we have no reason to believe it will work for us. Still, even in defeat, we have progressed enormously since World War II, and there is no reason to believe this progress will not continue. Much of my optimism for the future stems from the fact that gay couples have become a viable economic force in the United States.

The stability of gay lovers, so unbelievable to the heterosexual world, has had important economic consequences, especially in cities. Two men, pooling their resources without the economic and time burden of children, make significant contributions to their communities. Part of the revival of our cities has been due to gays who have bought and restored old but useful houses, and the restoration of whole neighborhoods by gays and young heterosexual married couples has not gone unnoticed by the business and political communities. Gay couples frequently serve as community leaders, working alongside heterosexual couples. The stereotypes of gay people are losing their force as straights find out what we are really like.

Very few people interviewed for this study were unhappy. There are those who still suffer from feelings of guilt as if life threw them a curve by making them gay, but their number is quickly diminishing owing to the contribution of gay liberation groups throughout the country. Being gay and finding love in the gay world are more possible than ever before. Where there is still discrimination or social isolation of gays, there is also the option to fight it in the community or to move to less oppressive areas of the country. In today's society, our problems are largely the same as those of most other minority groups—as are the personal decisions. We each are searching for compatible lovers, meeting the problems of everyday living, and finding the means by which we can establish trust and love with another man. That is as it should be.

APPENDIX

Interview Technique

Generally speaking, there are two ways to investigate behavior. One is called objective and the other, subjective. Objective studies predominantly use a questionnaire. If well designed and administered, this questionnaire is a sophisticated instrument carefully designed to reduce some of the hazards of research. For instance, questionnaires reduce (but do not eliminate) the possibility of an investigator's influence on the results of his study by the intrusion of his own personality. Since all the questions are specified in advance, other investigators can repeat the study, reporting further proof of its reliability. Other researchers have an excellent idea of just what was done and how it was done. This is very important in social science research. Computer scoring of questionnaires helps by ruling out the possibility of errors. The objective system also deliberately treats all subjects as the same. Questionnaires are very helpful in zeroing in on a specific question. In every sense, objective studies use the questionnaire as the technique to acquire information and minimize the influence of the investigator.

Subjective research does just the opposite: it emphasizes the researcher as the technique. There are good reasons for this. In many ways, the advantages of objective questionnaires are also disadvantages. For instance, objective studies are "cold" and impersonal. While they treat every person as the same, people are not the same, nor do they like being treated that way. Most people want to be appreciated for their uniqueness, and an open-ended interview is an invitation to talk freely. Subjective studies, i.e., open-ended interviews, allow the investigator to change his interviewing techniques and goals during the research because of what he has already learned.

In a sense, objective research captures the moment, but it has a poor sense of history. What is unique about gay love relationships, or any relationship, for that matter, is the fluidity of the interaction between the lovers and the way relationships change over time. Subjective techniques are better designed to investigate these changes. Of course, the very best way to learn about changes over time is to follow up couples over a period of, say, twenty years, but few of us have the resources or energy to do that. Subjective interviews are the next best way to learn about changes over time.

Subjective research is dynamic. There is no need to spend the same amount of time on each question with each person. Interviews allow the investigator to allocate his time during each interview to topics most interesting about the subject. He can also feed auxiliary sources of information into the study, such as a person's home, the community in which he lives, and any other information that clarifies the life setting. In every way possible, subjective interviews are rich in their sources of information, especially when rapport is established between investigator and subject, which in subjective studies is crucial.

The obvious disadvantage of the subjective interview is the impossibility of any other researcher knowing exactly what the original investigator did and how he did it. It cannot be exactly replicated. It is also impossible to determine to what degree the original investigator influenced his subjects and in what direction.

While a questionnaire would have been easier and less time consuming to construct and analyze, the lengthier subjective interview was chosen for this study. There were a number of reasons. It seemed to me that tightly controlled, objective research was too limiting at this stage of investigation, given that one of my most important goals has been to look for new ways to view gay relationships. I wanted to be directed by my subjects into the areas of greatest importance in their lives and to clarify the styles of relationships that exist in the country. This is best done subjectively.

But the results of the study must ultimately rest on the need for further documentation and replication by other researchers, and until the time when objective studies are designed to test the hypotheses suggested in this study, we need to consider the theories unproven. There is no competition between objective and subjective styles of research; each is appropriate at the proper time.

Finally, something should be said about the personalities of those who volunteer to take part in a study, especially a study of gay life. Social psychologists have found that volunteers differ from those who do not volunteer to participate in research, which invariably makes it difficult to generalize findings to the population at large. By and large, all volunteers want to please the investigator who is viewed as wise, good, and objective. In this study the desire to please was quite obvious. Many men were attuned to social changes, perhaps more so than the population at large. Quite a few used the interviews as a learning experience, an opportunity to interact with their lovers in an intensely emotional way, obviously motivated by personal strength.

There is no question that this sample would have changed dramatically if I had, say, asked for volunteers for a study of men who had had only bad experiences with a lover, or just good ones. No researcher can ever completely know what motivates his subjects to volunteer, and he can know absolutely nothing about those who refuse. Worst of all, he may never know whether his results would have been different if everyone had volunteered. It's all part of the ambiguity of working with humans.

Subjects

Advertisements were placed in a number of gay newspapers, asking for volunteers to participate in a study of gay male love relationships. Letters from couples came in from a variety of places throughout the country, ranging from large cities to rural communities. The couples were enthusiastic about telling their stories. Friends heard about my work, volunteered, and helped to find other gays willing to participate. In this manner I was able to compile a list of couples available for interviews. Another large group of volunteers came from interviews conducted in the course of my travels as a speaker at gay conferences and organizations. It was my custom to remain at such gatherings for two or three days, spending the time interviewing couples and single gays in the area. A few patients in my private practice also volunteered.

At the beginning of the project, I believed naively that I could interview all the people who volunteered. I soon learned otherwise. Too large a budget would have been required, so I decided to interview as many as I could by mail, using a tape recorder. I reproduced the interview form and asked the subjects to respond to the questions in the tape recorder. Most of them agreed to the procedure, and fifteen out of the 190 men (8 percent) were interviewed in this way.*

Like any procedure, taped interviews by mail have advantages and disadvantages. Some people feel quite comfortable without the presence of another person, and these men reacted to the tape recordings quite well. Others were unable to use the tape effectively and restricted their answers to the most superficial. Whether they would have been motivated to look beyond the obvious in a personal setting, I cannot know. In general, the tapes were very helpful in learning about love affairs in suburban and rural settings.

Couples and individual gay men were scheduled to meet with me for the interview, which varied in time from thirty minutes to five hours. At the interview, I explained my purpose as a study of gay male love relationships and announced that I was going to ask a number of personal questions. I also displayed the tape recorder used to record the interview and explained that the tape allowed me to listen closely and take notes afterward. The tape would be erased after my notes were taken. Subjects then filled out a short form, recording their ages, years together, occupation, etc. At the end of the interview, all subjects were asked to read and sign a permission form, allowing me to use the information in this book. Only two men refused to sign, and their material has not been included here. On two other occasions, men asked me to turn off the tape recorder briefly so that they could tell me a story they preferred not to be published. In both cases, the tape recorder was turned on again afterward.

Personal interviews were conducted in a number of geographical settings, but I cannot name them all. City people may not understand that statement. There is no problem in revealing that I interviewed many gay couples in places like New York City and Miami. These are cities with large populations of gay people,

---

* An additional twelve men were interviewed by an assistant. The other 163 men were interviewed by me personally. A number of men wrote personal letters, but since they did not follow the form of the structured interview, they have not been included in the study.

many of whom are transient. But small towns and villages are another matter, more concentrated and more gossipy. For instance, I visited a place where those who cruise do so on just one street at night, hoping for a stranger to pass by. Everyone knows everyone else who cruises, and to indicate the actual source of my sample might cause my respondents trouble. They didn't mind telling me their innermost fantasies, but they obviously don't want them discussed by their friends. So let me just say that I concentrated my interview trips to the Midwest and Southwest on small- to medium-sized towns and rural areas precisely because they have never been studied before.

No Current Lover Group

Of the 190 men who volunteered to be studied, 62 of them (32.6 percent) did not have a lover at the time of the interview. The age of the men in this group ranged from 16 to 77, with a mean of 33 years. Seven (11.3 percent) of them had been married previously. The 62 men in this group can be further subdivided into those who have never had a lover and those who have had. Thirty-four men (54.8 percent) in this group have never had a lover, and they ranged in age from 16 to 77 years, with a mean of 29.4 years. The other 28 men (45.1 percent) had had one or more lovers (of whatever duration) previous to the interview. They ranged in age from 21 to 73 years, with a mean of 37.4 years, older than those who had never had a lover. Out of these 28 men who had had lovers, 8 (12.9 percent) had lived with a lover until his death. These 8 men ranged in age from 30 to 73 years, with a mean of 49.9 years. The duration of their relationships with the deceased lovers ranged from 3 to 40 years, with a mean of 17.9 years.

Current Lover Group

Eighteen men with lovers were interviewed alone, the lover unable (primarily because of scheduling problems) or unwilling to participate in the interview. Almost all of these interviews were conducted during daytime business hours. These 18 men ranged in age from 20 to 53 years, with a mean of 39.1 years. The length of their current love relationship ranged from 1 to

15 years, with a mean of 7.4 years.* Six of them (33.3 percent) had been married previous to their gay relationships.

One hundred ten men, consisting of 55 male couples, were also interviewed, with both lovers present at the interview. They ranged in age from 16 to 82 years, with a mean of 39.6 years. The length of their current love relationships ranged from 1 to 51 years, with a mean of 7.7 years. Thirteen men (11.8 percent) had been married previous to their gay relationships.

Since the two subgroups of men with lovers (those interviewed with their lovers present and those interviewed in the absence of their lovers) appeared to be quite similar, further analysis combined them into one group representing 73 gay male couples. Of these 73 couples, 23 (31.5 percent) of them were new to their relationships. These 23 couples had been together for 1 year or less, what would be called "newlyweds" in the heterosexual world. Thirty-four couples (46.6 percent) had been together between 2 and 9 years. Nineteen couples (14.8 percent) had been together for 10 or more years.

* All relationships of one year or less have been counted as one year.

Name Index

The following men appear in more than one place in the book. After each man's name will be found the name of his lover, in parentheses.